JUMP Math K.1

Book K Part 1 of 2

T0302624

Contents

Put your name or picture here!

jump math

MULTIPLYING POTENTIAL.

JUMP Math
One Yonge Street, Suite 1014
Toronto, Ontario M5E 1E5
Canada
www.jumpmath.org

Writers: Dr. Heather Betel, Dr. Francisco Kibedi, Julie Lorinc
Editors: Megan Burns, Liane Tsui, Julie Takasaki, Natalie Francis, Jackie Dulson, Janice Dyer, Rita Vanden Heuvel
Layout and Illustrations: Linh Lam, Fely Guinasao-Fernandes, Sawyer Paul
Cover Design: Blakeley Words+Pictures
Cover Photograph: © Photo Pegah

ISBN 978-1-927457-71-9

Fifth printing October 2024

Printed and bound in Canada

A note to educators, parents, and everyone who believes that numeracy is as important as literacy for a fully functioning society

Welcome to JUMP Math

Entering the world of JUMP Math means believing that every child has the capacity to be fully numerate and to love math. Founder and mathematician John Mighton has used this premise to develop his innovative teaching method. The resulting resources isolate and describe concepts so clearly and incrementally that everyone can understand them.

JUMP Math is comprised of Teacher Resources, Digital Lesson Slides, student Assessment & Practice Books, assessment tools, outreach programs, and professional development. All of this is presented on the JUMP Math website: **www.jumpmath.org**.

The Teacher Resource is available on the website for free use. Read the introduction to the Teacher Resource before you begin using these materials. This will ensure that you understand both the philosophy and the methodology of JUMP Math. The Assessment & Practice Books are designed for use by students, with adult guidance. Each student will have unique needs and it is important to provide the student with the appropriate support and encouragement as they work through the material.

Allow students to discover the concepts by themselves as much as possible. Mathematical discoveries can be made in small, incremental steps. The discovery of a new step is like untangling the parts of a puzzle. It is exciting and rewarding.

Students will need to answer the questions marked with a in a notebook. Grid paper notebooks should always be on hand for answering extra questions or when additional room for calculation is needed.

Contents

PART 1

Unit 1: Counting and Cardinality: Numbers 1 to 5

Unit 2: Counting and Cardinality: Comparing Numbers 1 to 5

Unit 3: Geometry: Flat Shapes

Unit 4: Counting and Cardinality: Numbers 6 to 10

Unit 5: Counting and Cardinality: Comparing within 10

Unit 6: Measurement and Data: Categories and Sorting

PART 2

Unit 7: Operations and Algebraic Thinking: Addition within 5

Unit 11: Operations and Algebraic Thinking: Subtraction within 5

Unit 12: Operations and Algebraic Thinking: Subtraction within 10

Unit 13: Operations and Algebraic Thinking: Fluency within 5

Unit 14: Measurement and Data: Measurement

CCK-1 The 1 to 10 Count Sequence

☐ Color.

1.

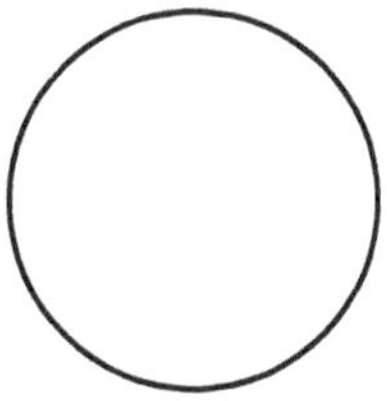

2.

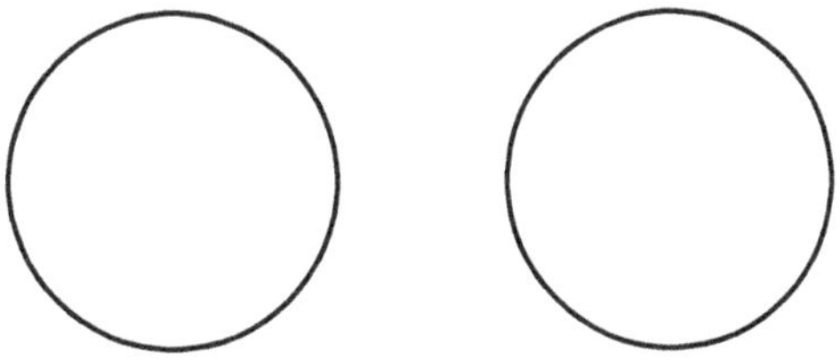

☐ Color.

3.

4.

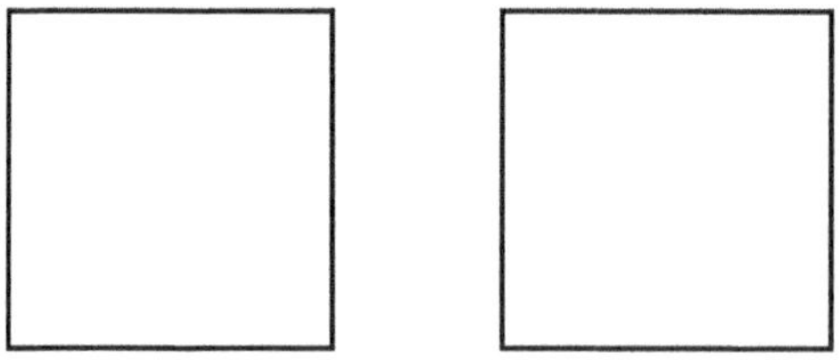

☐ Color.

5. BONUS

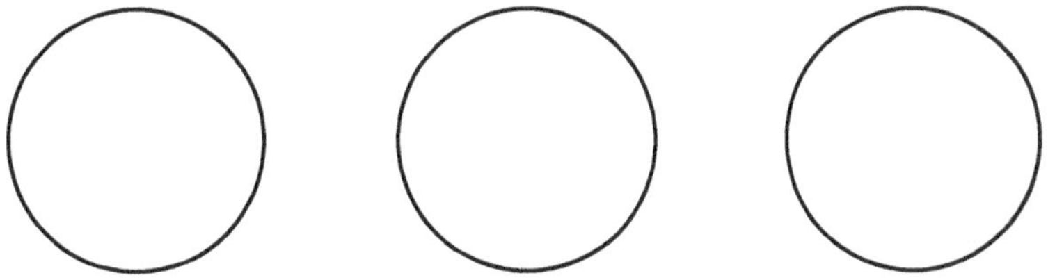

6. BONUS

CCK-2 The Numbers 1 and 2

☐ Glue the number 1 or 2.

1.

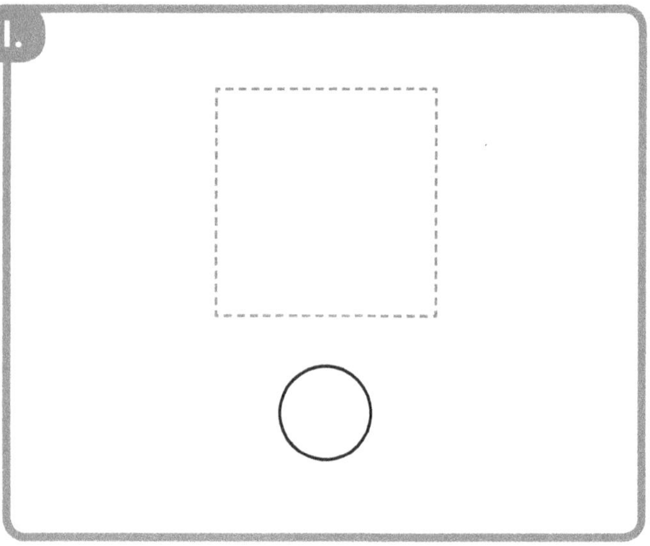

2.

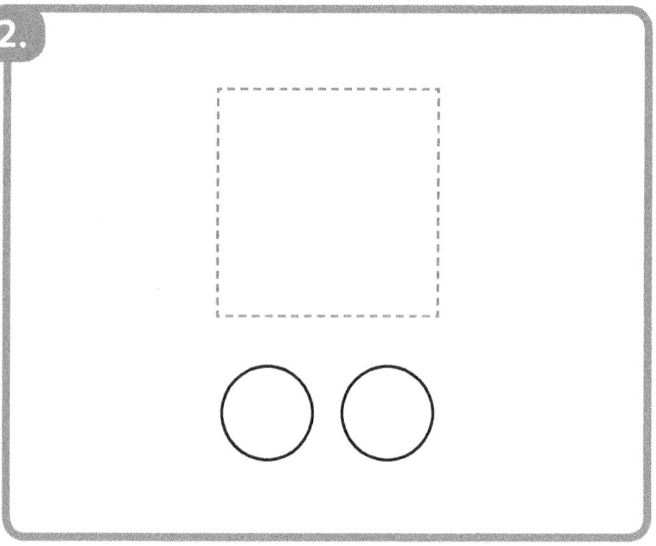

3.

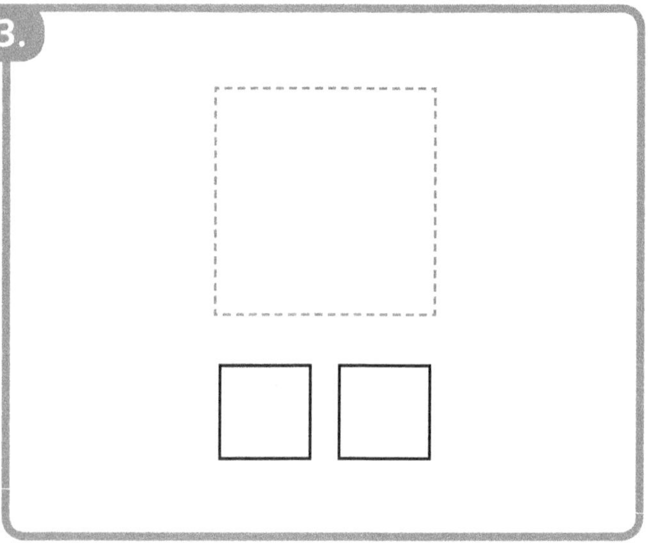

4.

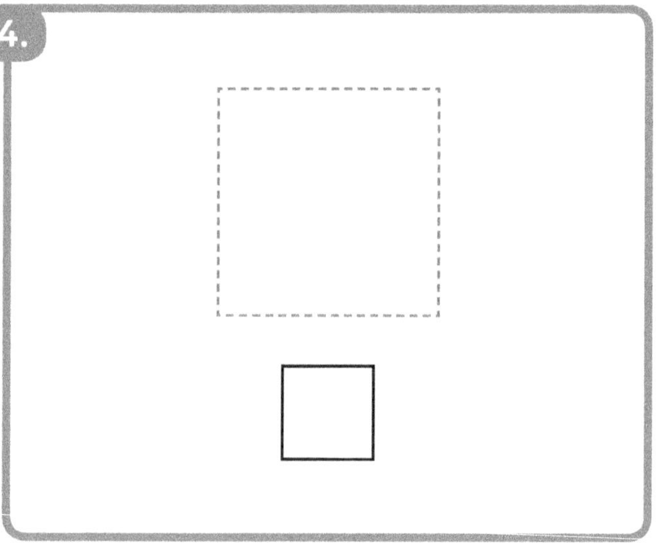

5.

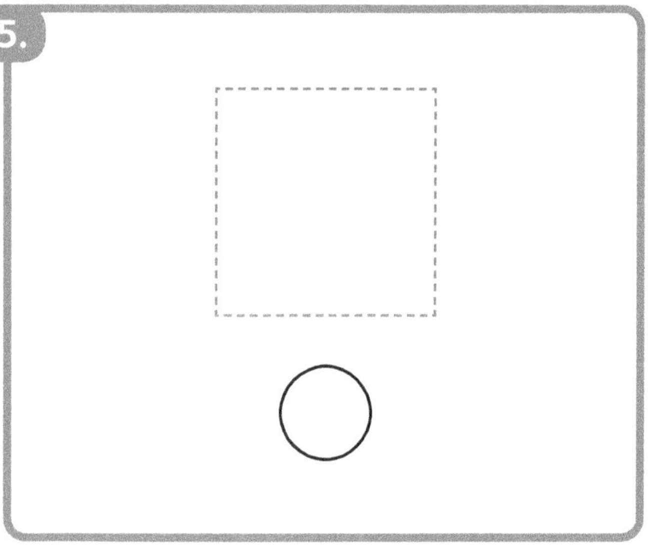

6.

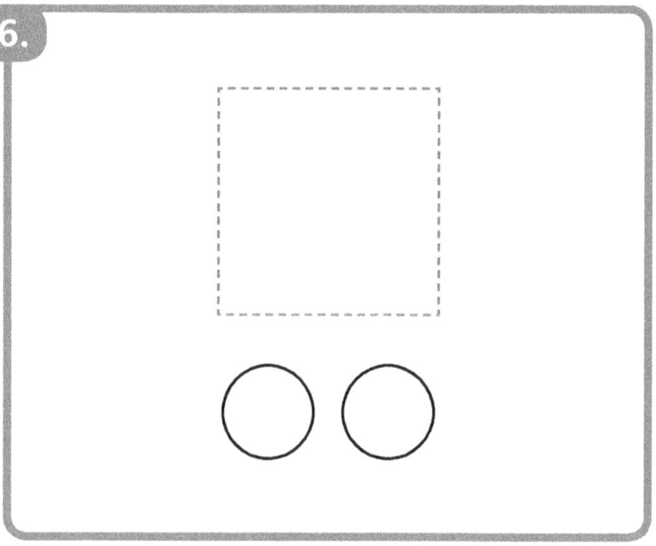

☐ Glue a picture of 1 or 2.

7.

2

8.

1

9.

1

10.

2

11.

2

12.

1

☐ **BONUS:** Color ☺ for match. Color ☹ for no match.

13.

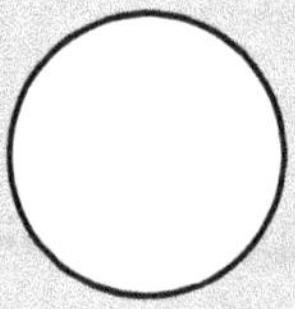

1

14.

2

15.

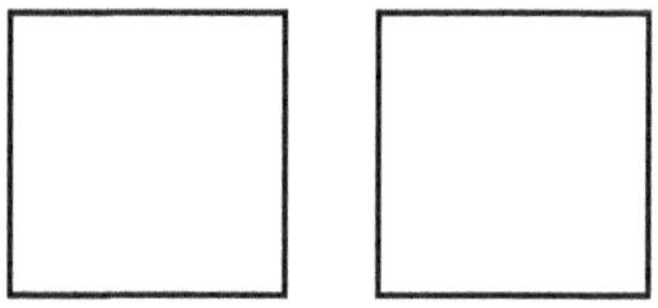

2

16.

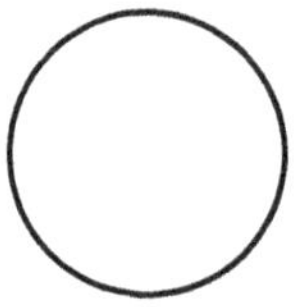

1

17.

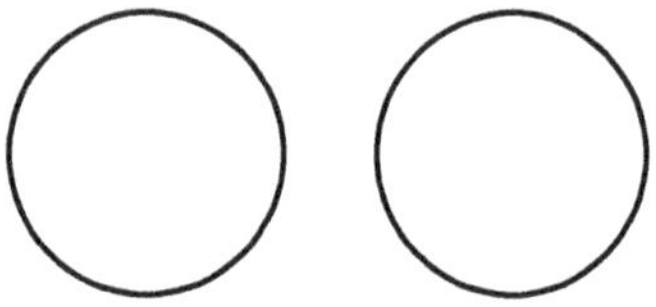

1

18.

2

CCK-3 The Number 3

☐ Glue the number 1, 2, or 3.

1.

2.

3.

4.

5.

6.

☐ Glue a picture of 1, 2, or 3.

7.

2

8.

1

9.

3

10.

2

11.

1

12.

3

☐ **BONUS:** Color 🙂 for correct. Color ☹ for not correct.

13.

2

🙂 ☹

14.

1

🙂 ☹

15.

1

🙂 ☹

16.

3

🙂 ☹

17.

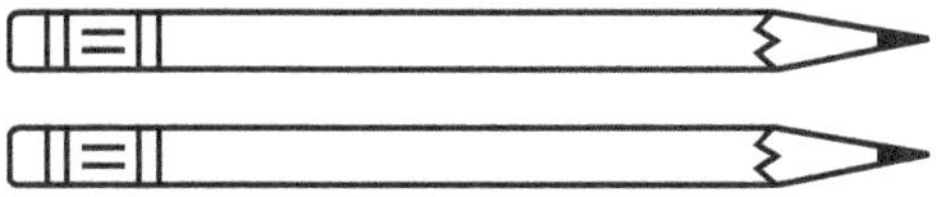

2

🙂 ☹

18.

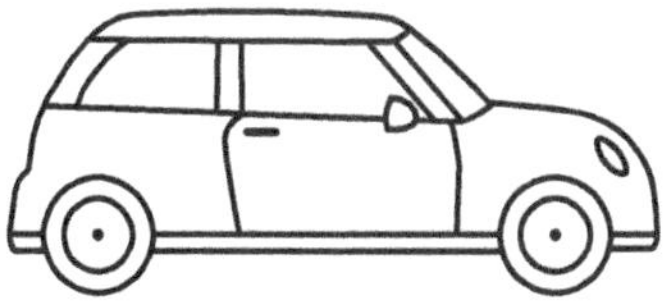

3

🙂 ☹

Counting

☐ Count.

1.

2.

3.

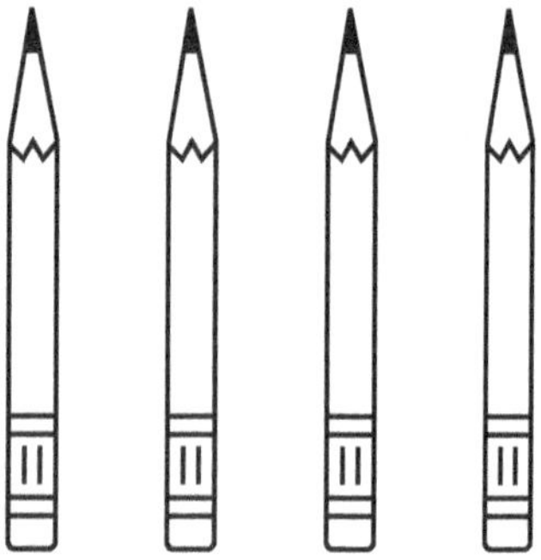

4.

5.

6.

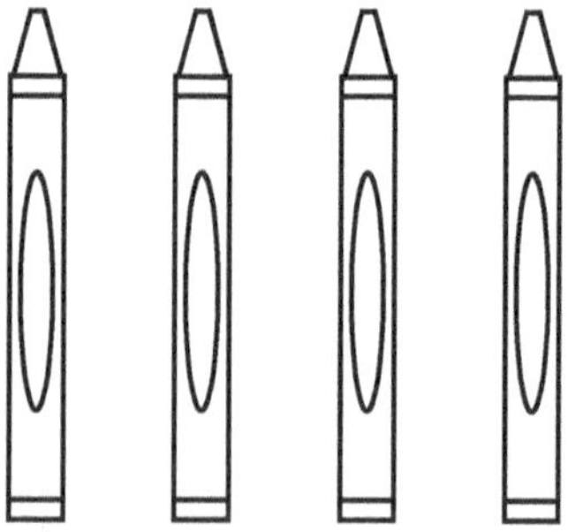

☐ Count.

7.

8.

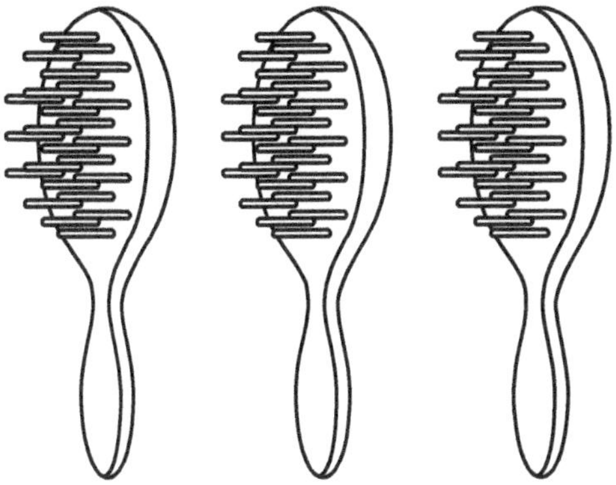

9.

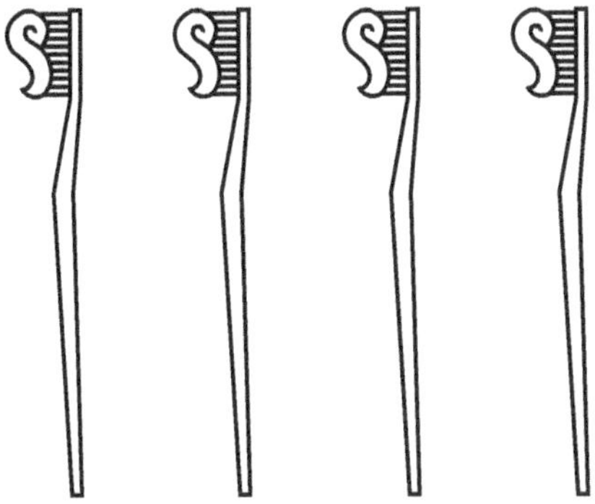

10.

11.

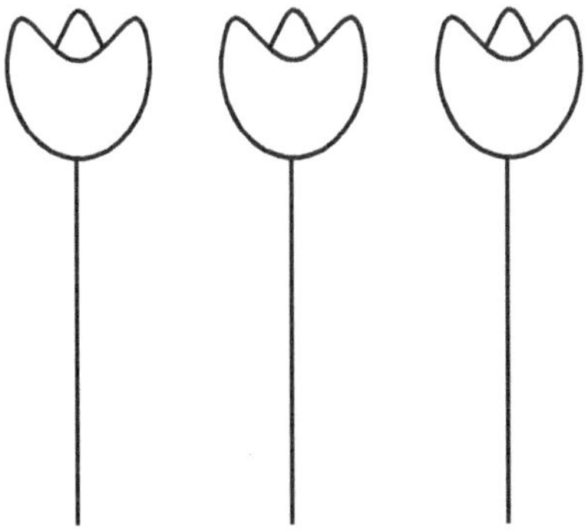

12.

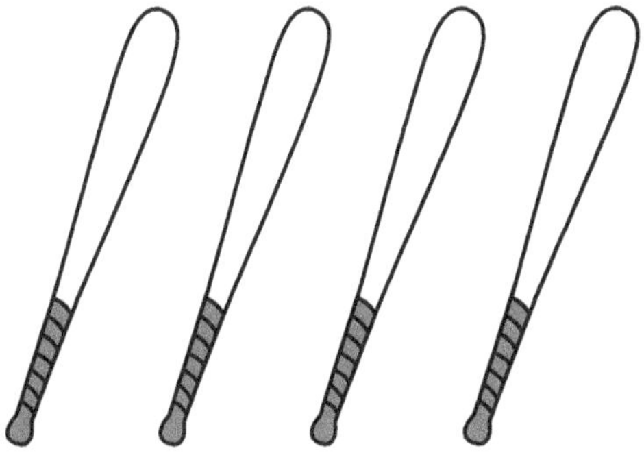

CCK-5 Counting 1, 2, and 3

☐ Use ●. Count.

1.

(1) 2 3

2.

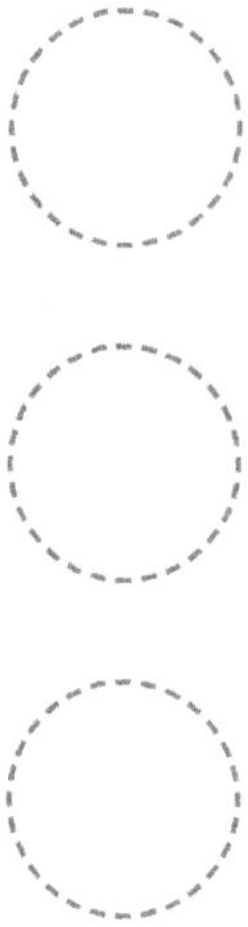

1 2 3

3.

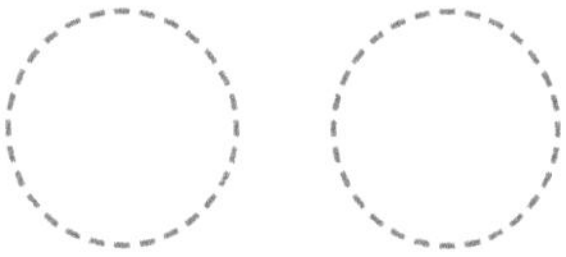

1 2 3

4.

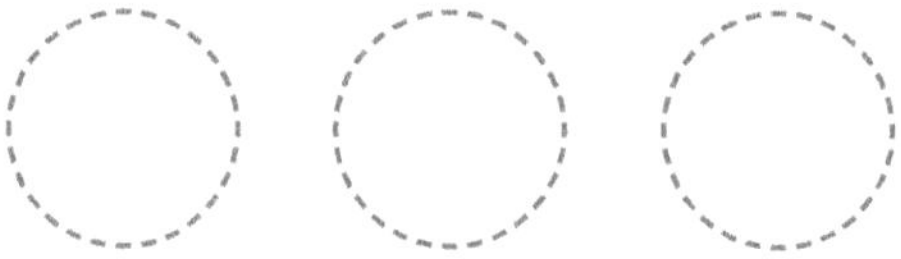

1 2 3

☐ Use ●. Count.

5.

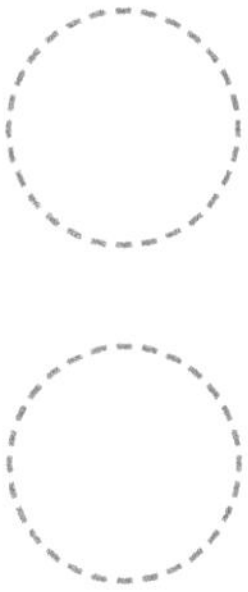

1 2 3

6.

1 2 3

7.

1 2 3

8.

1 2 3

CCK-6 Counting Out 1, 2, and 3

☐ Show counting out.

1.

3

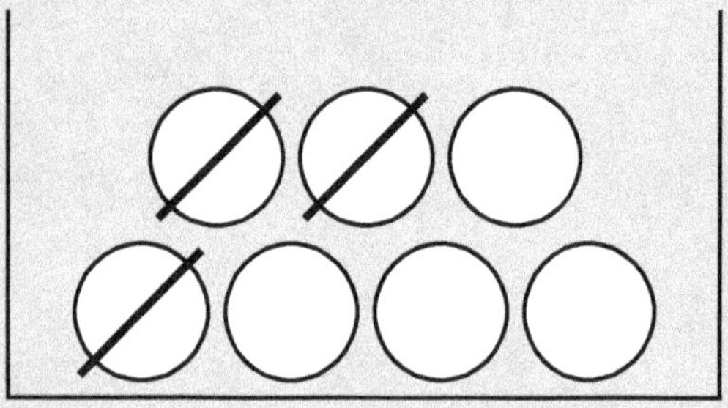

2.

1

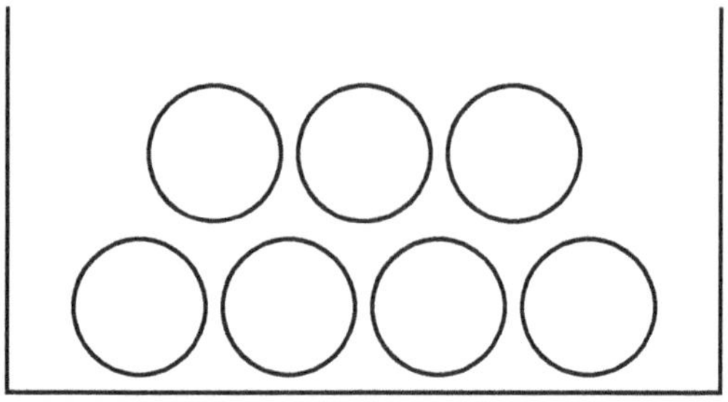

3.

2

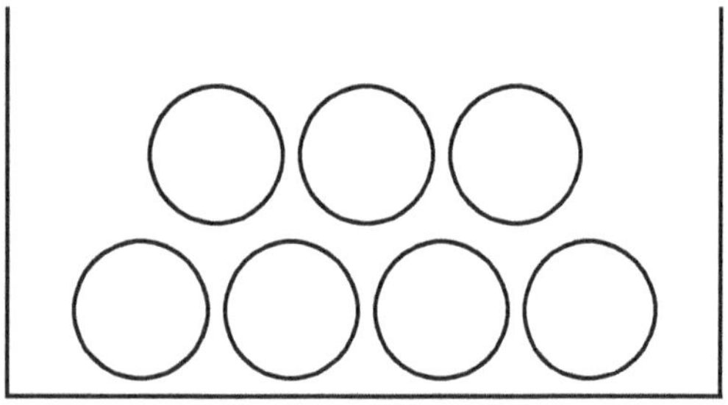

4.

3

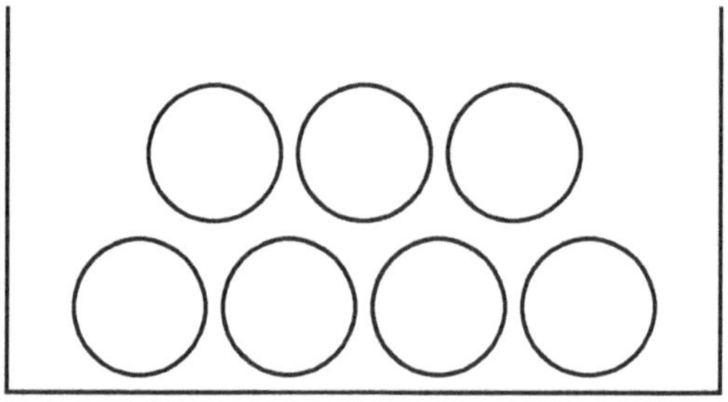

5.

1

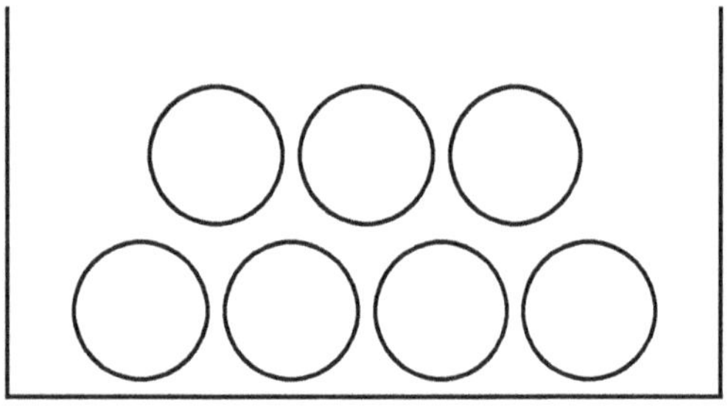

6.

2

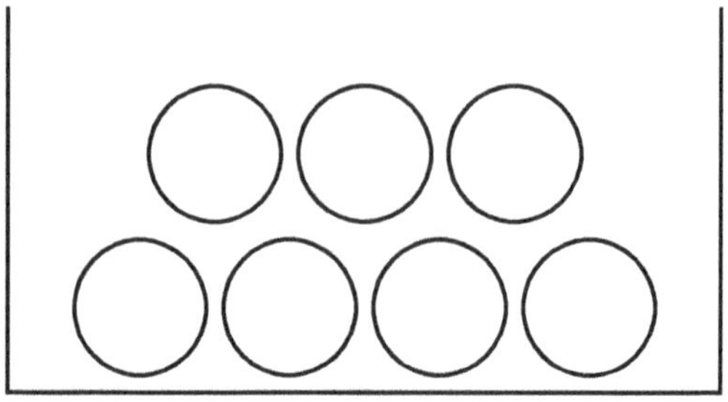

☐ **BONUS:** Show counting out.

7.

3

8.

2

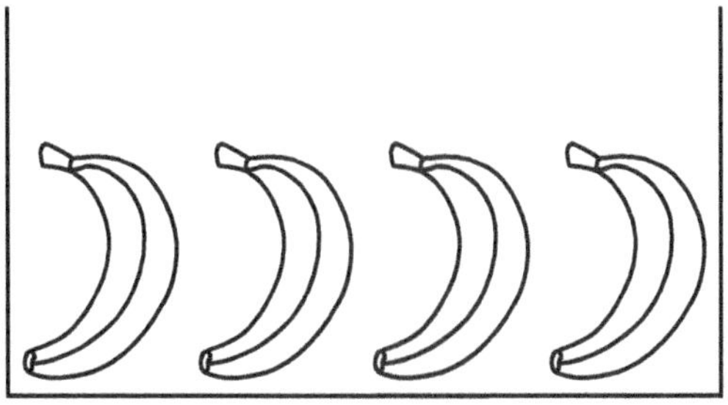

9.

1

10.

3

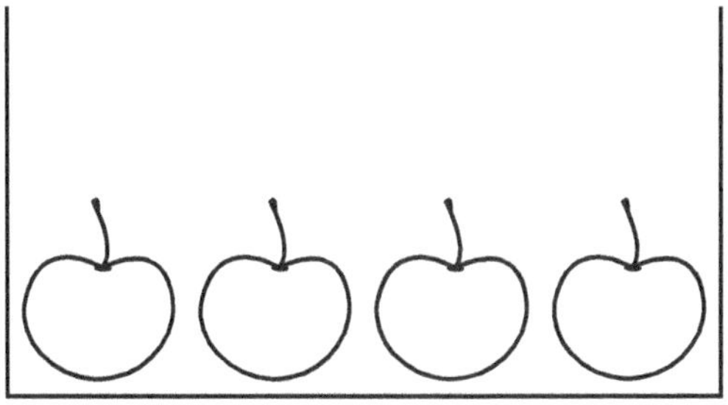

11.

2

12.

1

Writing 1, 2, and 3

☐ Trace.

1.

2.

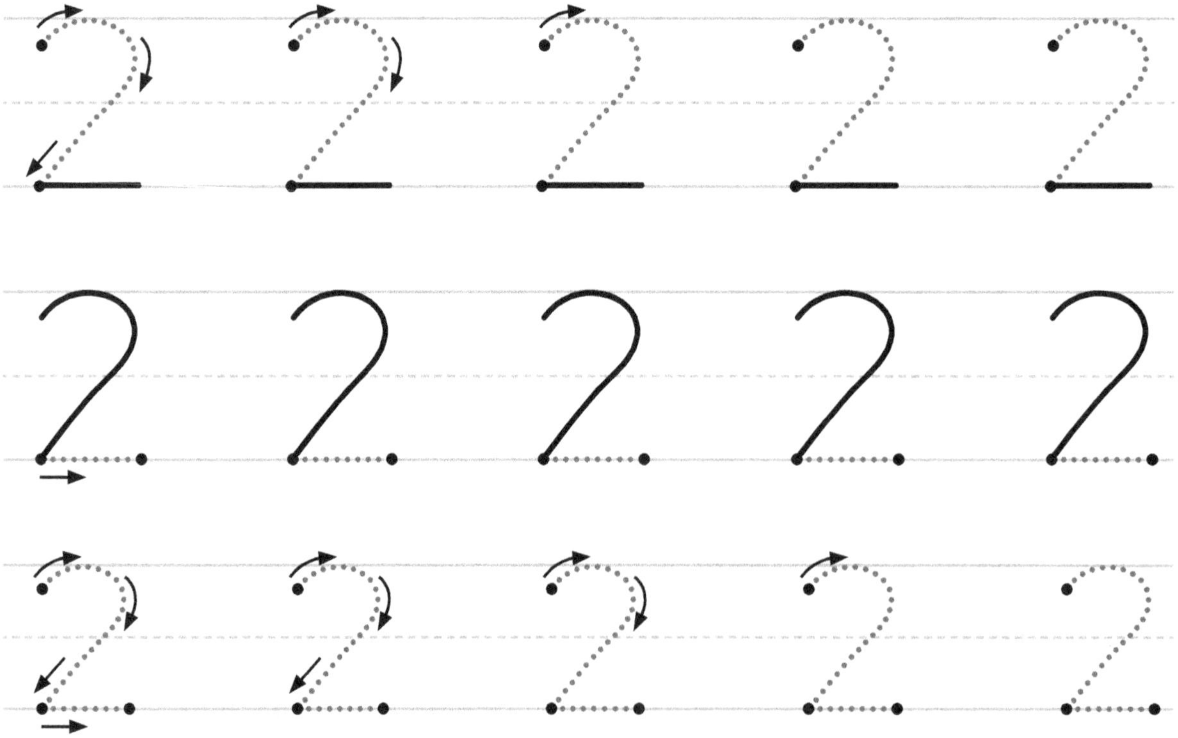

☐ Trace.

3.

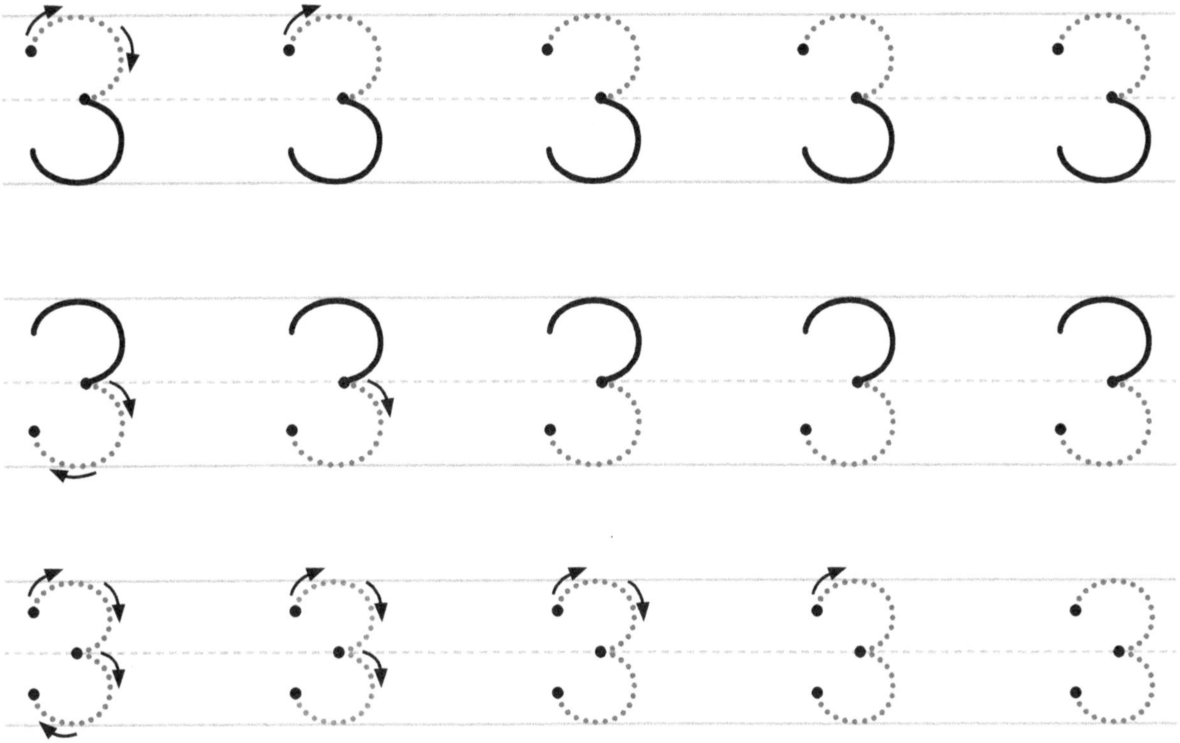

4.

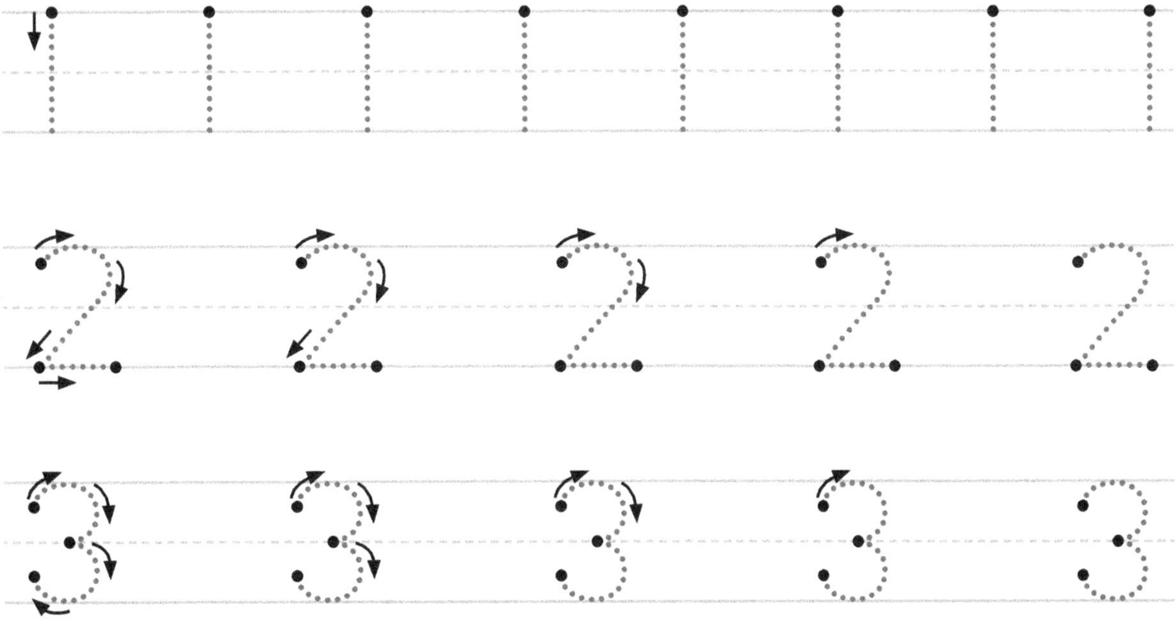

☐ Trace and color.

5.

1

6.

2

7.

3

CCK-8 Counting 4

☐ Use ●. Count.

1.

1 (2) 3 4

2.

1 2 3 4

3.

1 2 3 4

4.

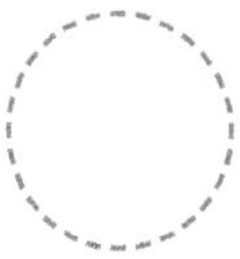

1 2 3 4

☐ Show counting out.

5.

4

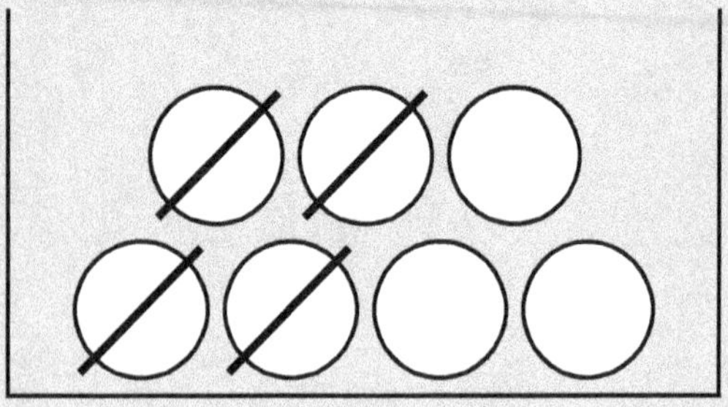

6.

2

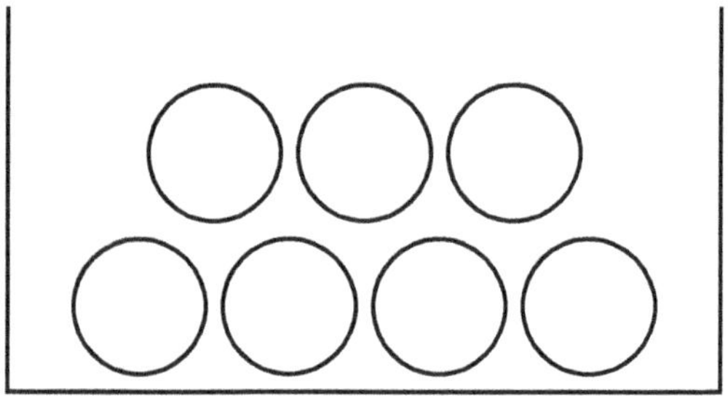

7.

1

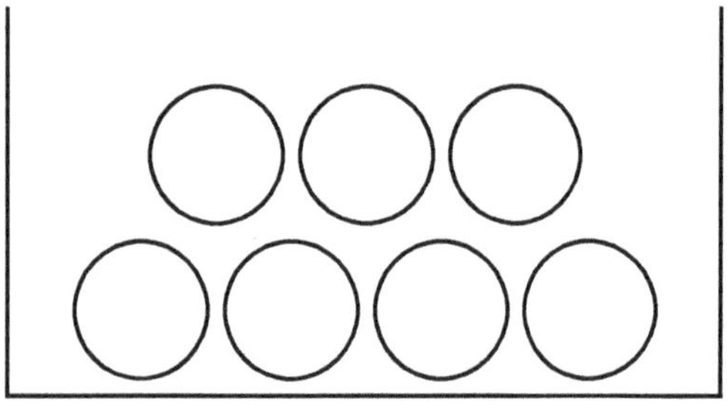

8.

3

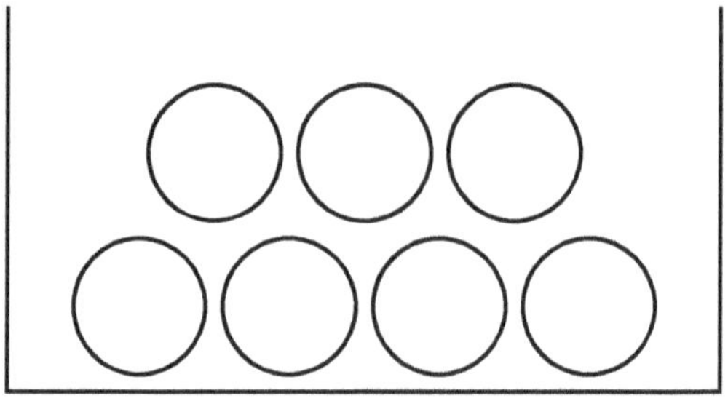

9.

3

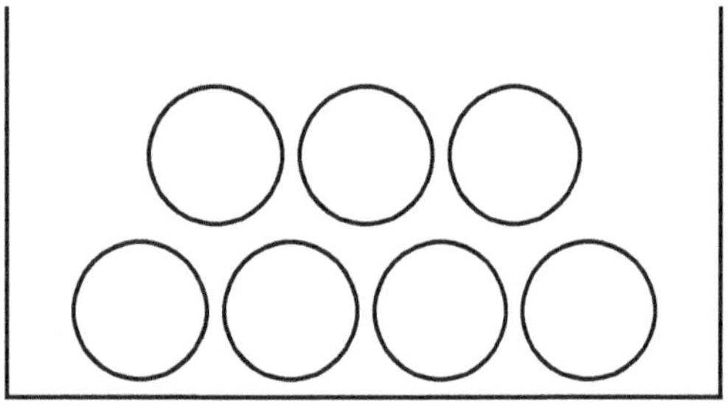

10.

4

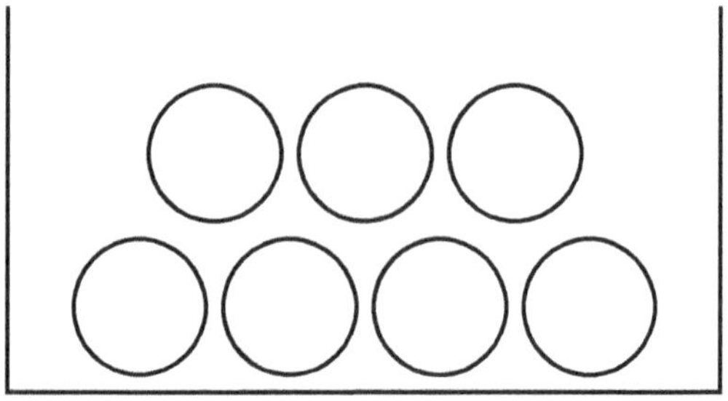

BONUS: Show counting out.

11.

3

12.

2

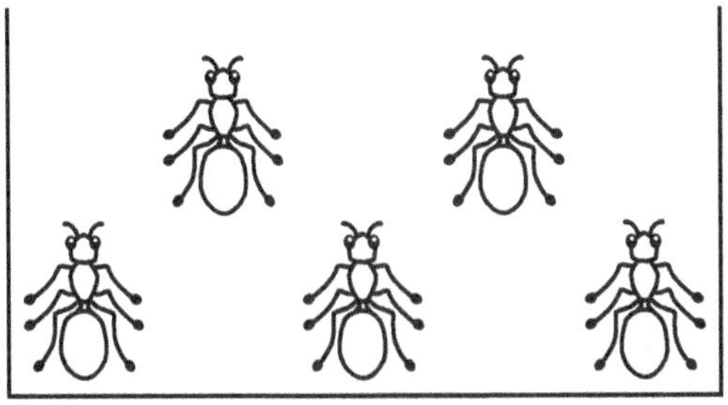

13.

4

14.

1

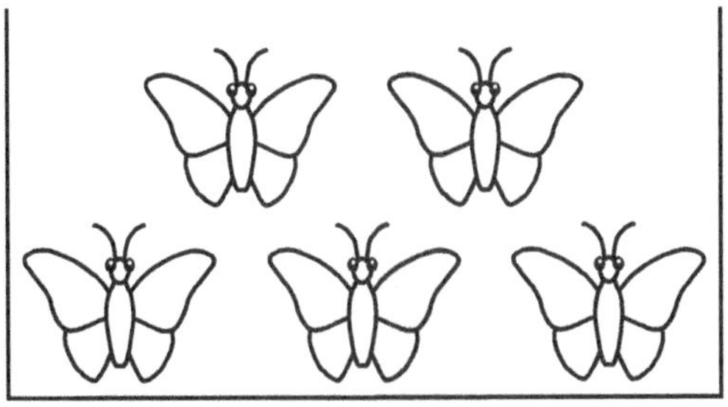

15.

3

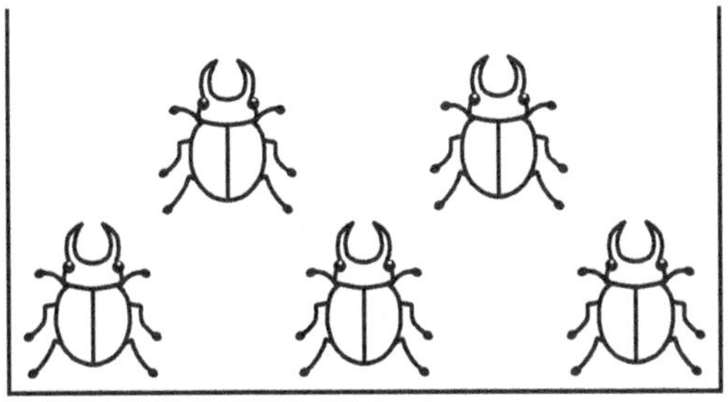

16.

4

CCK-9 The Number 4

☐ Glue the number 3 or 4.

1.

2.

3.

4.

5.

6.

Glue the number 1, 2, 3, or 4.

7.

8.

9.

10.

11.

12.

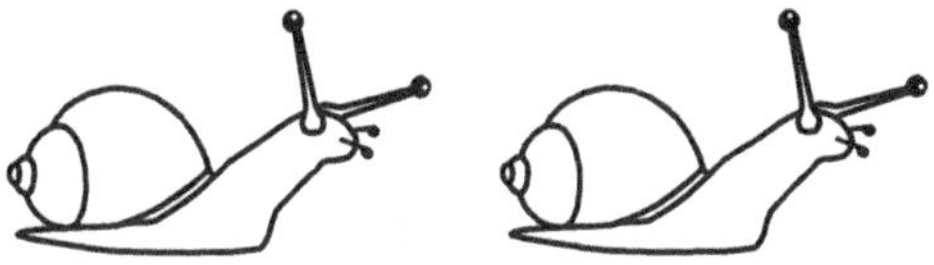

☐ Glue a picture of 1, 2, 3, or 4.

13\.

3

14\.

1

15\.

2

16\.

4

17\.

4

18\.

3

☐ **BONUS:** Color ☺ for correct. Color ☹ for not correct.

19.

4

20.

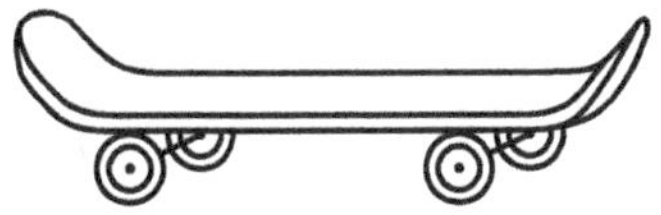

2

21.

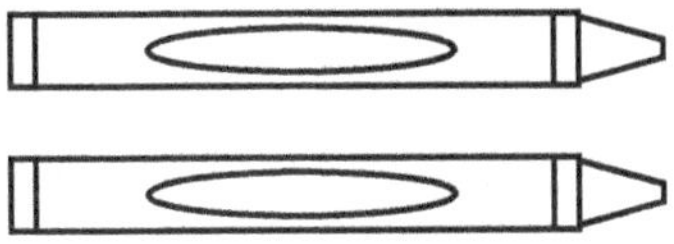

1

22.

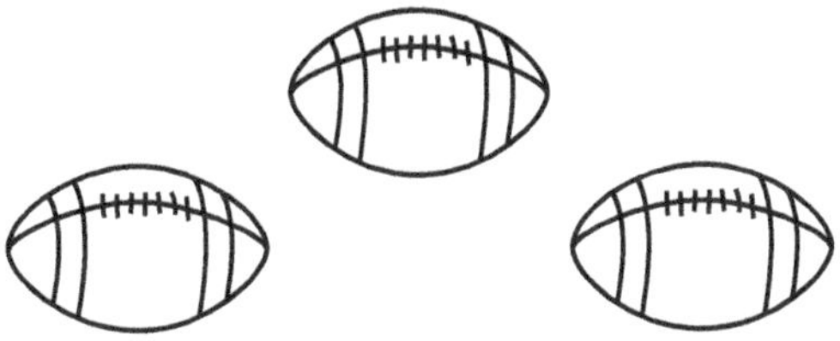

3

23.

2

24.

4

Writing 4

☐ Trace.

1.

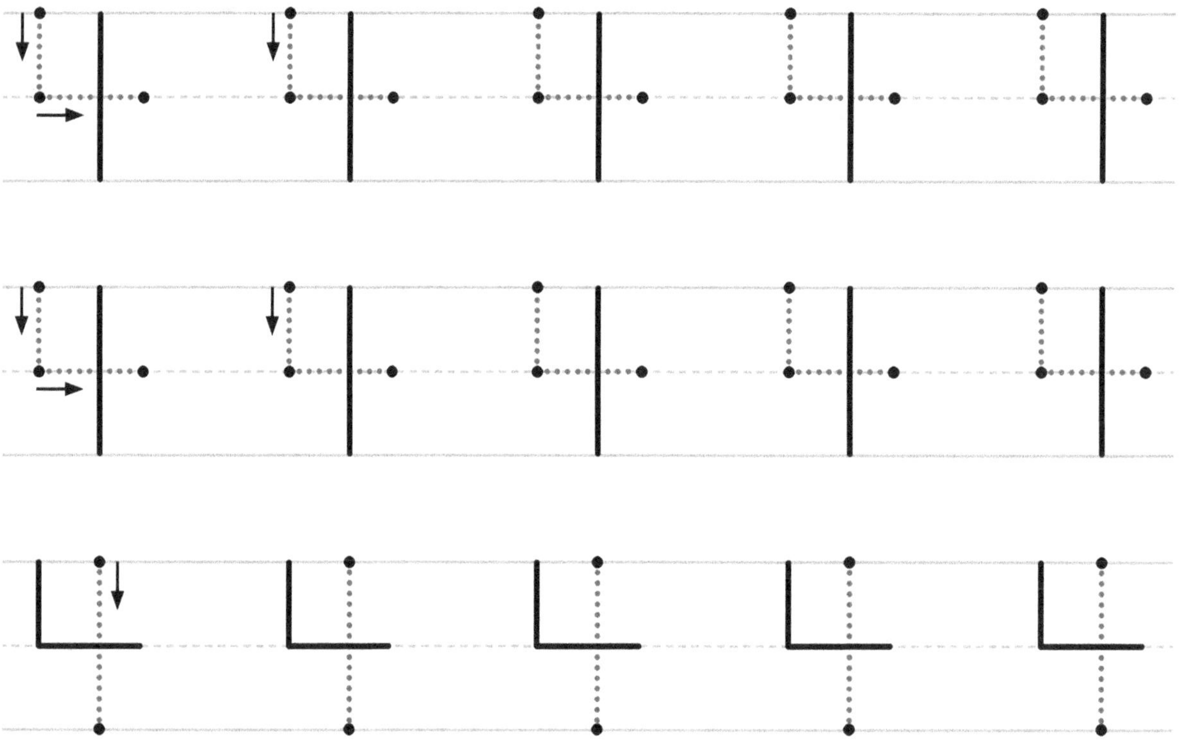

2.

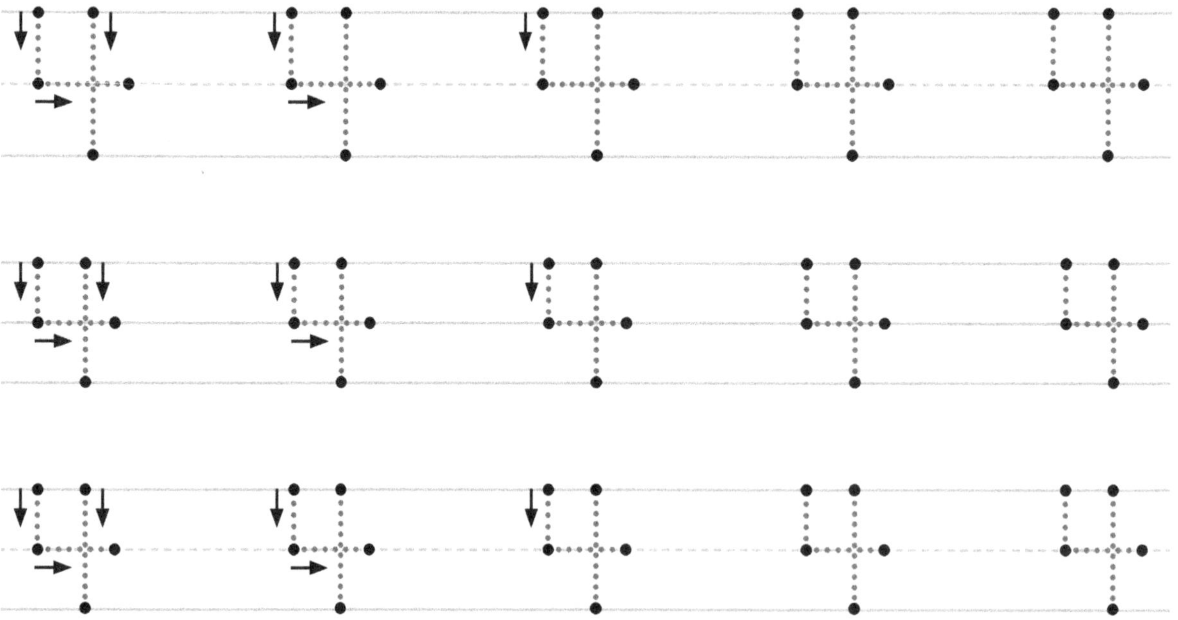

☐ Trace and color.

3.

1

4.

2

5.

3

6.

4

☐ Use ●. Count.

1.

1 (2) 3 4 5

2.

1 2 3 4 5

3.

1 2 3 4 5

4.

1 2 3 4 5

☐ Use ●. Count.

5.

1 2 3 4 5

6.

1 2 3 4 5

7.

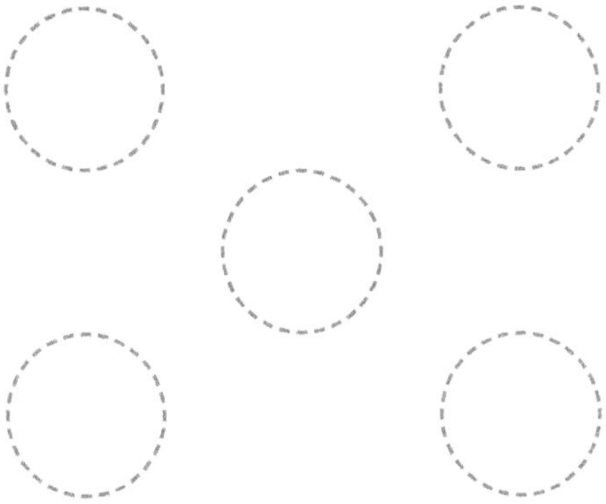

1 2 3 4 5

8.

1 2 3 4 5

☐ Show counting out.

9.

3

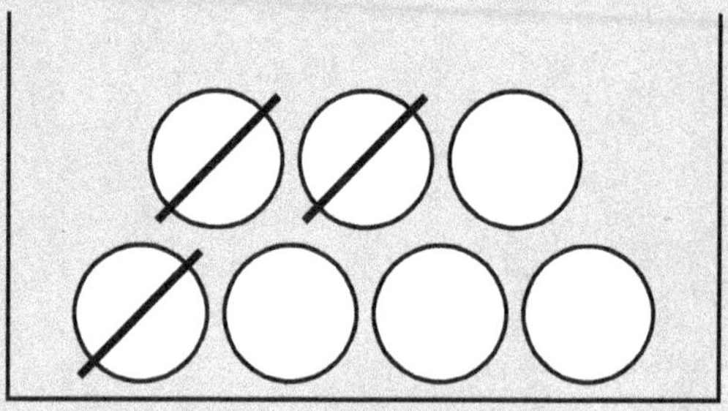

10.

5

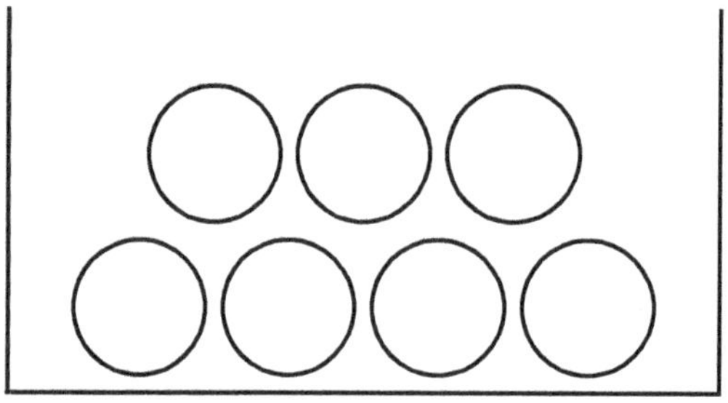

11.

2

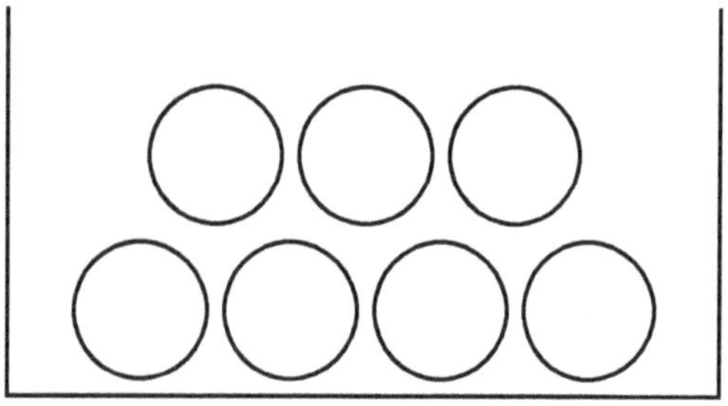

12.

4

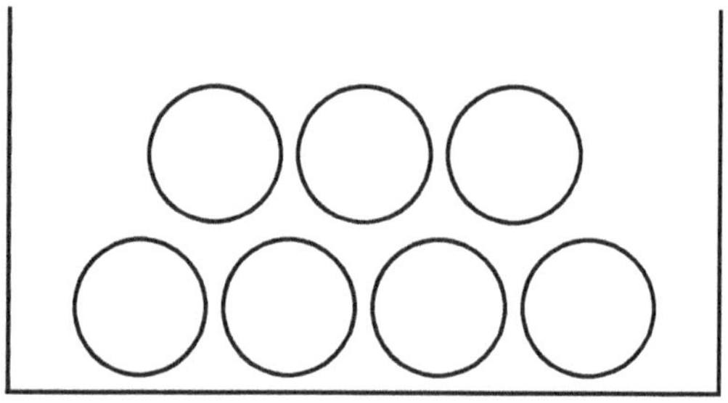

13.

5

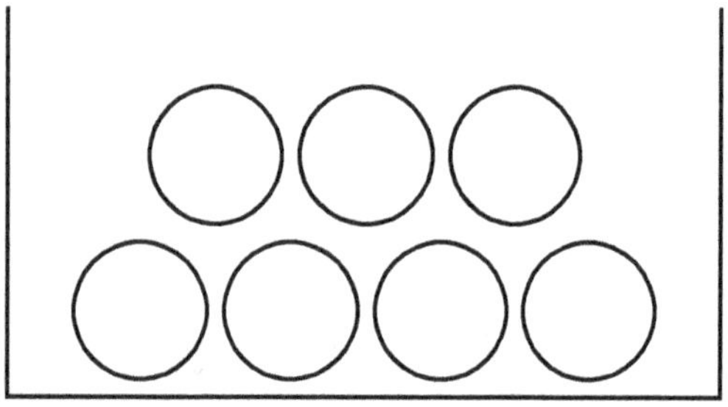

14.

1

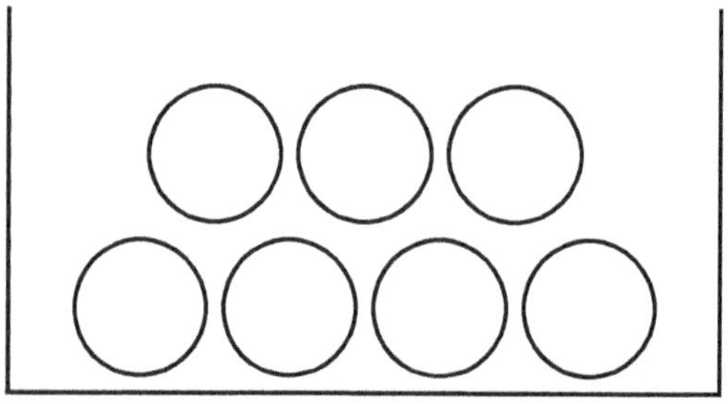

BONUS: Show counting out.

15.

4

16.

3

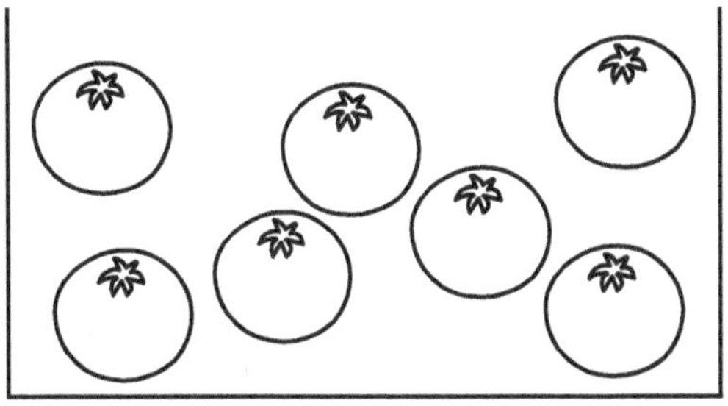

17.

5

18.

2

19.

3

20.

5

CCK-12 The Number 5

☐ Glue the number 1, 2, 3, 4, or 5.

1.

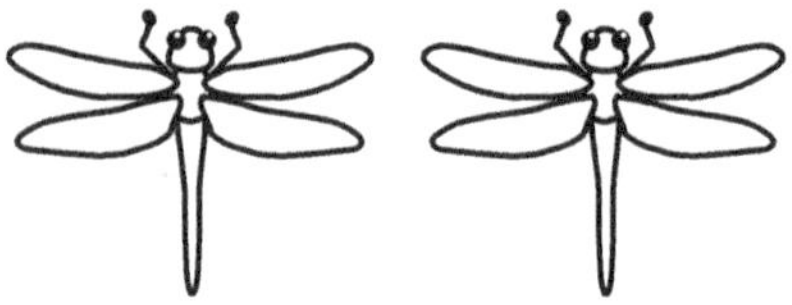

2.

3.

4.

5.

6.

☐ Glue a picture of 1, 2, 3, 4, or 5.

7.

3

8.

2

9.

5

10.

4

11.

1

12.

5

☐ **BONUS:** Color ☺ for correct. Color ☹ for not correct.

13.

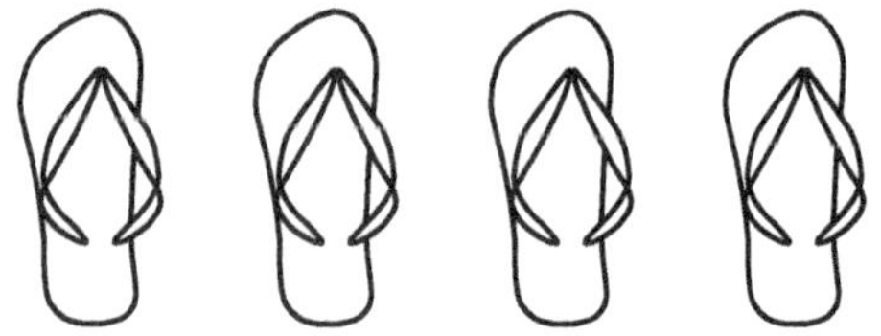

5

☺ ☹

14.

2

☺ ☹

15.

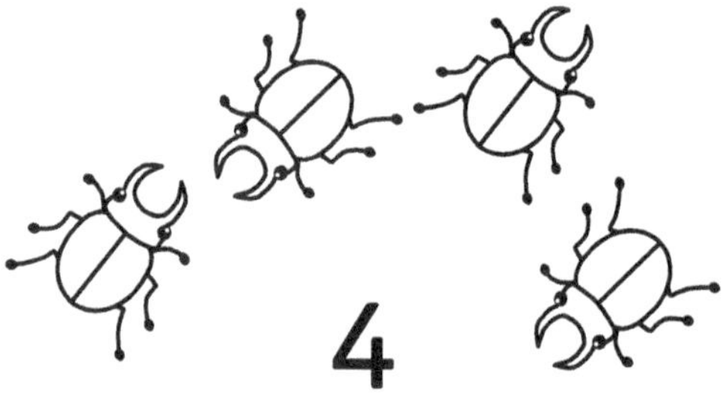

4

☺ ☹

16.

3

☺ ☹

17.

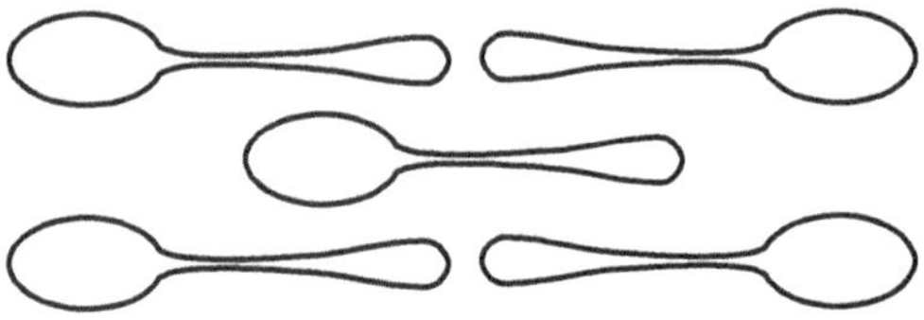

5

☺ ☹

18.

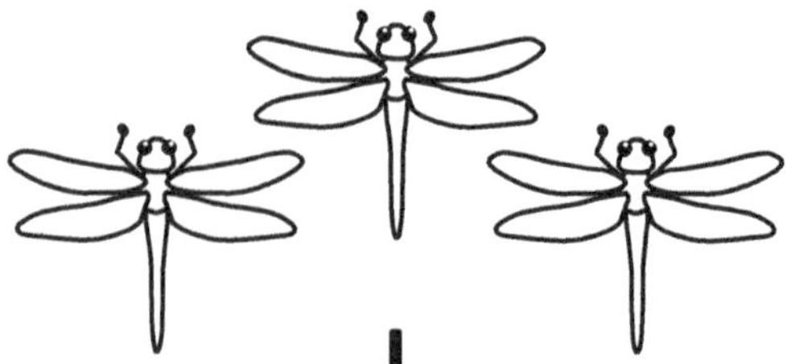

1

☺ ☹

CCK-13 Writing 5

☐ Trace.

1.

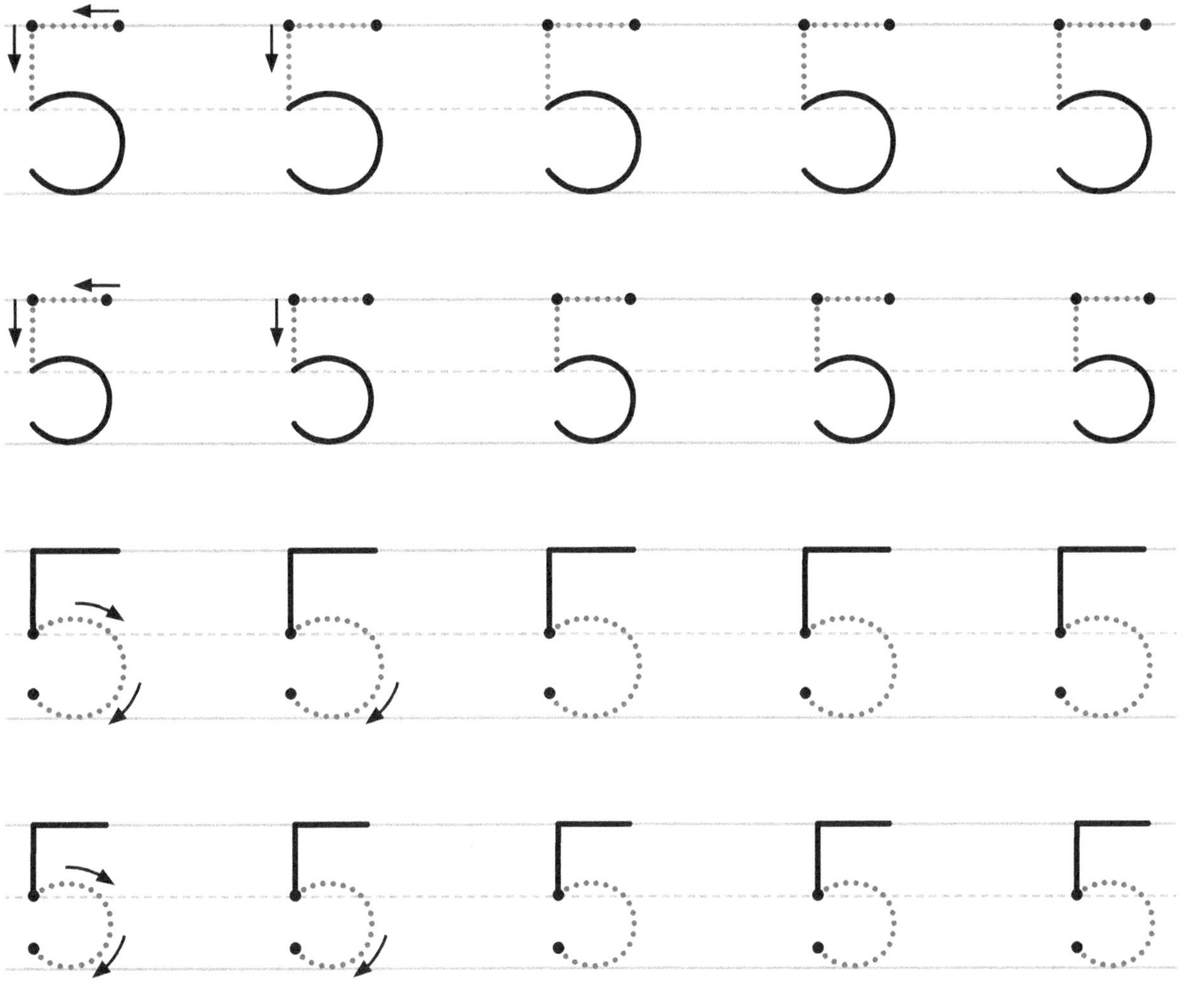

2.

☐ Trace and color.

3.

2 2 2

4.

3 3 3

5.

4 4 4

6.

5 5 5

CCK-14 Review of 1, 2, 3, 4, and 5

☐ Color.

1.

1

2.

2

3.

3

4.

4

5.

5

☐ Color.

6.

1

7.

2

8.

3

9.

4

10.

5

CCK-15 Counting to 20

☐ Trace.

1.

10 11 12

13 14 15

16 17 18

19 20

2.

3.

CCK-16 **More**

☐ Color the ☼ for the group that has **more**.

1.

2.

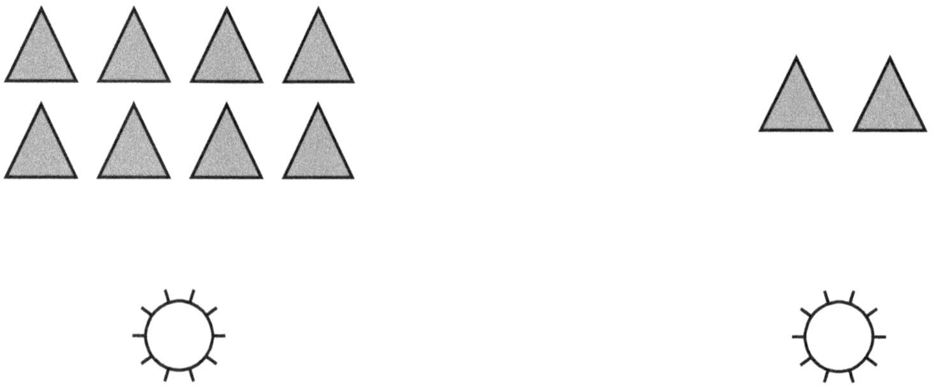

3.

☐ Color the ☼ for the group that has more.

4.

5.

6.

☐ Join the dots.

7.
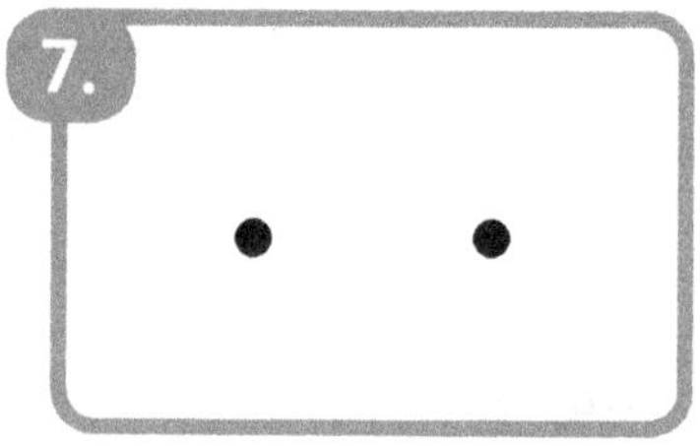

8.

9.

10.
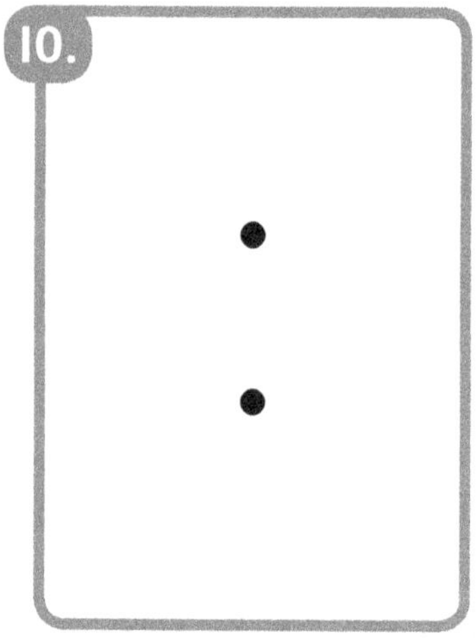

11.
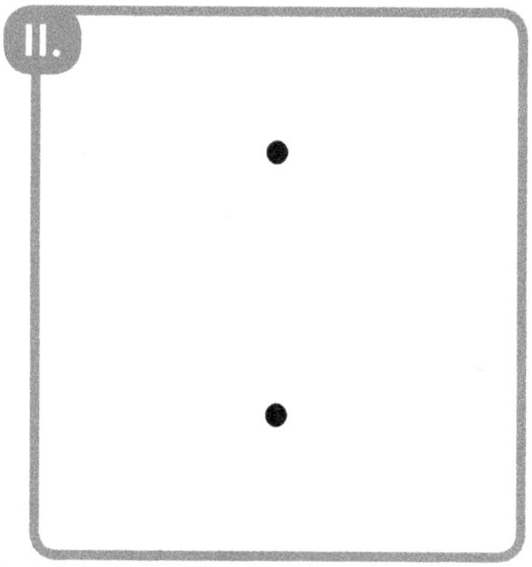

12.
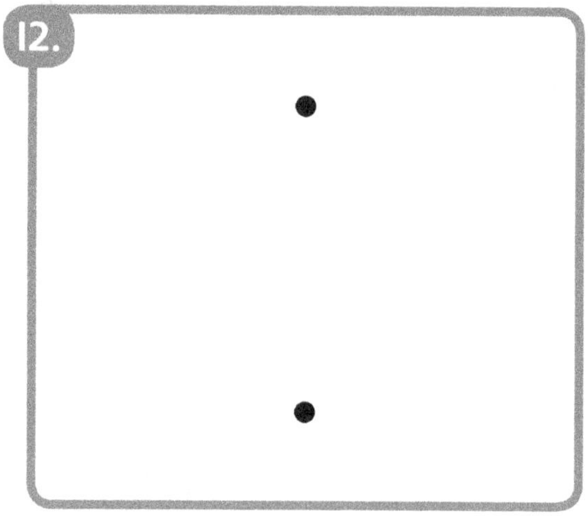

13.
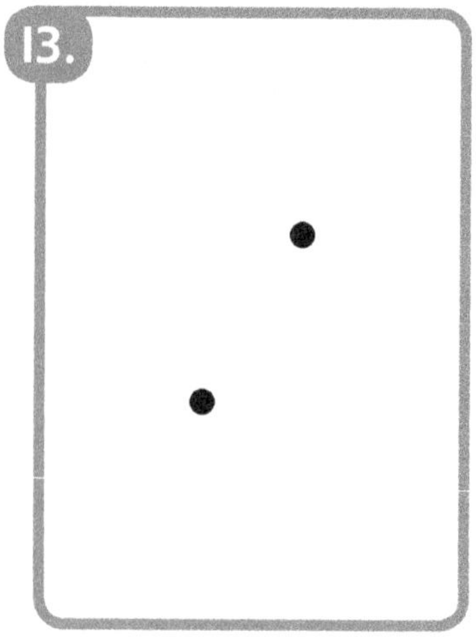

14.
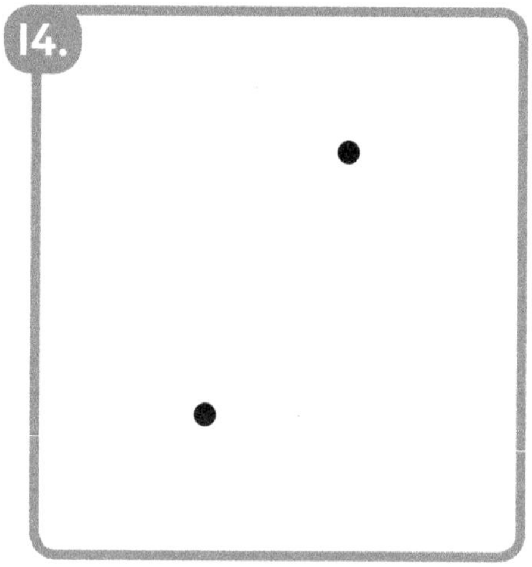

15.
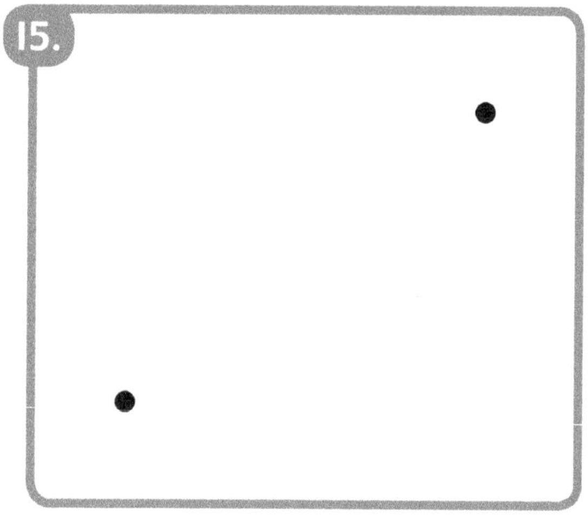

16.
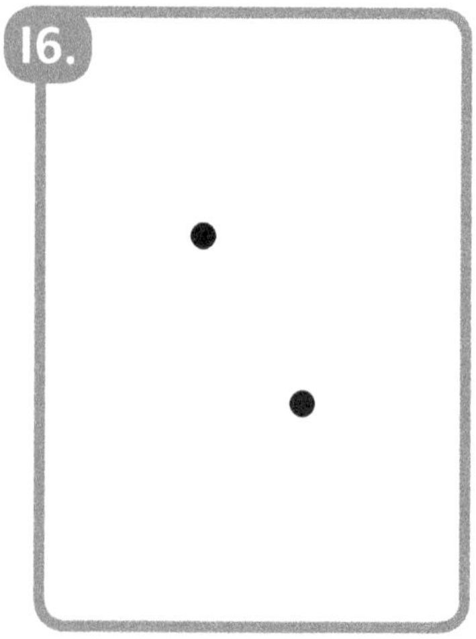

17.
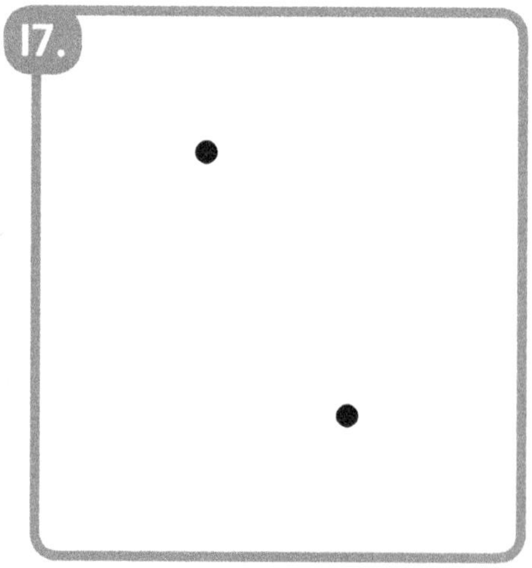

18.
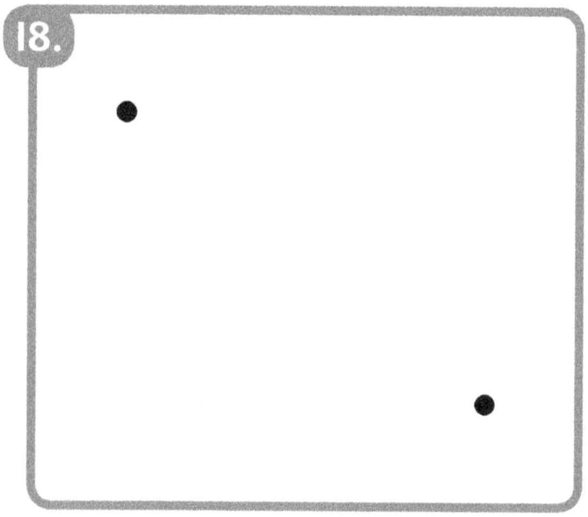

☐ Join the dots.

19.

20.

21.

22.

23.

24.
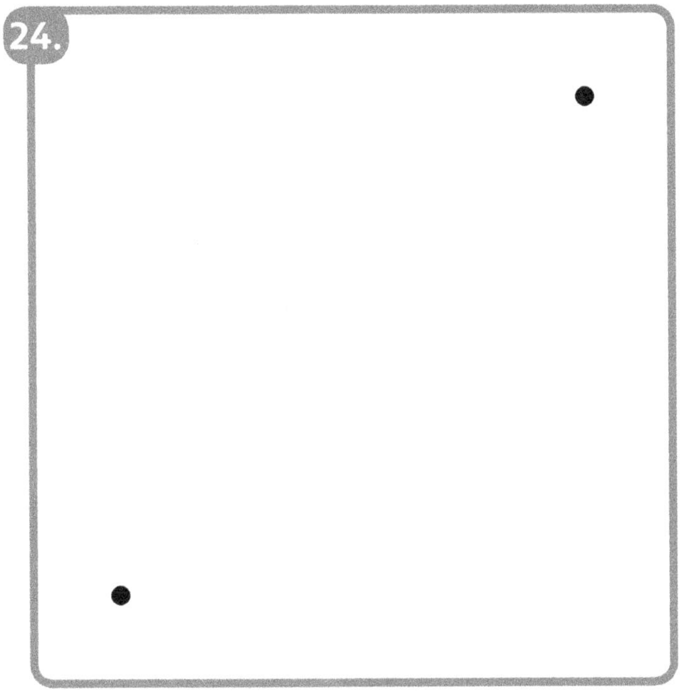

25.

CCK-17 Equal To (Matching)

☐ Glue a  on each .

1.

Draw a line to match each  with a .

2.

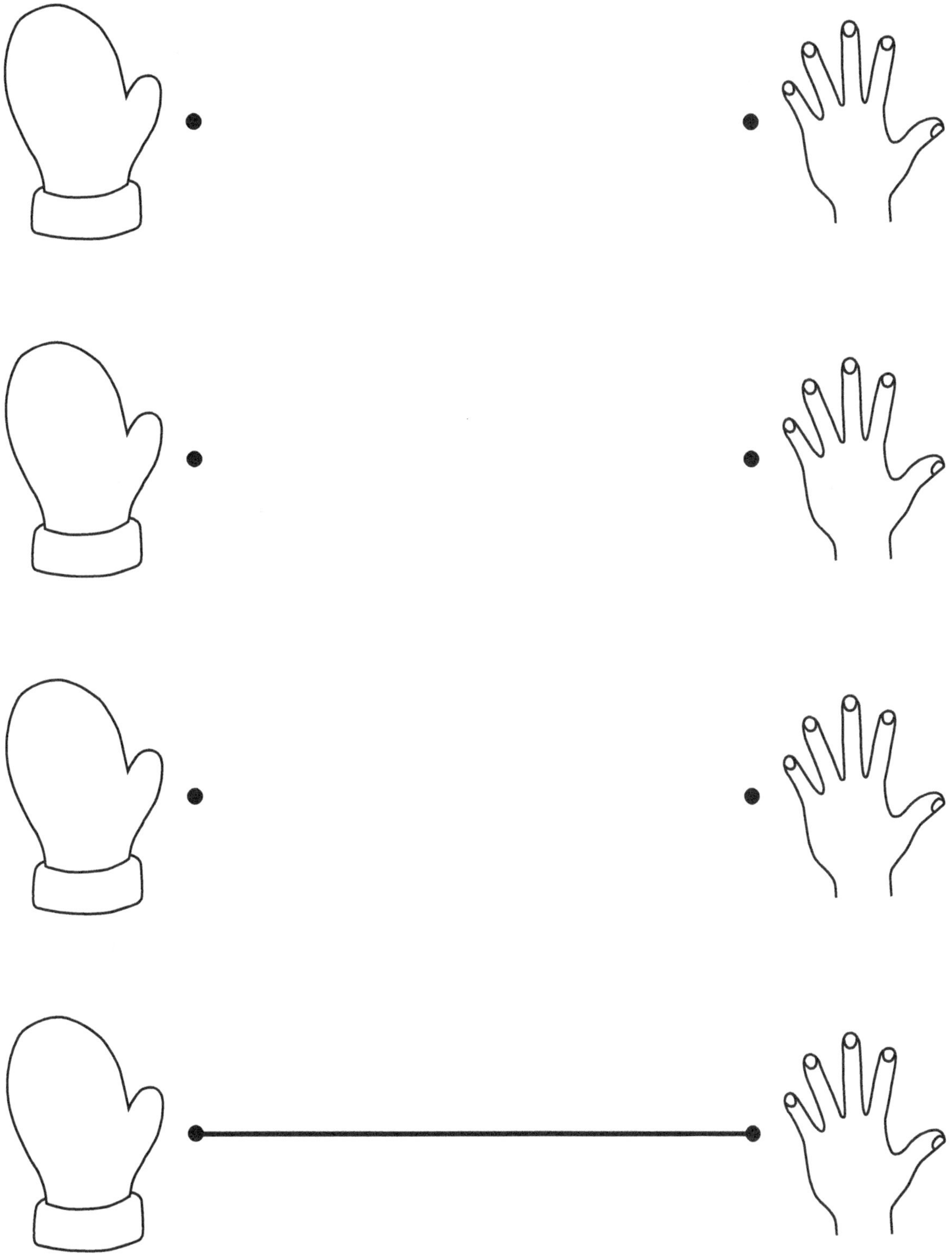

☐ Draw a line to match each foot with a shoe.

3.

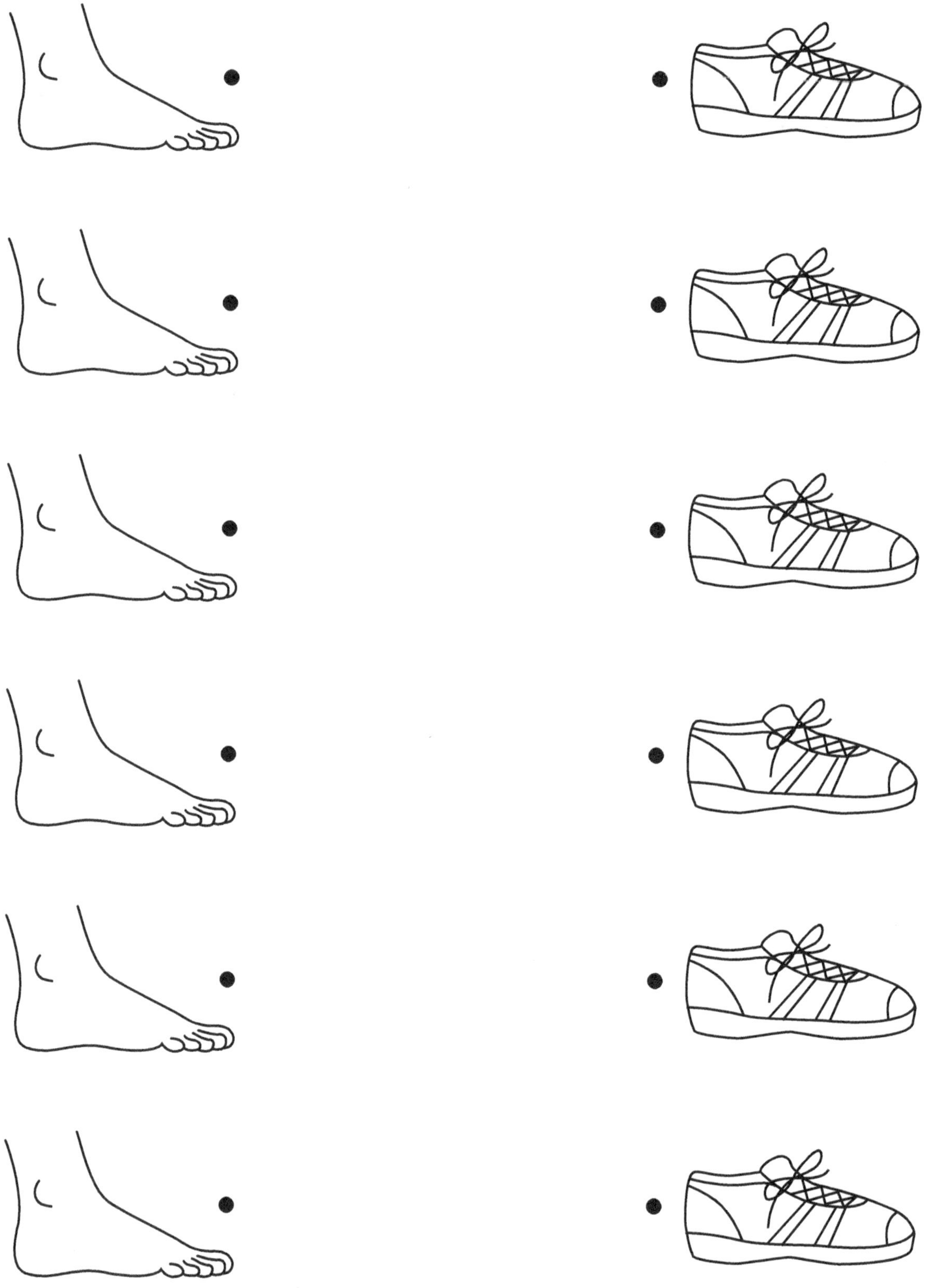

CCK-18 **Equal To (Counting)**

Which numbers are **equal**?

☐ Draw a line.

1\.

3

3

4

2\.

5

2

2

3\.

4

1

1

4\.

5

5

3

5\.

2

4

4

6\.

1

3

3

☐ Count. Circle the number.

☐ Color ☺ for equal. Color ☹ for not equal.

7.

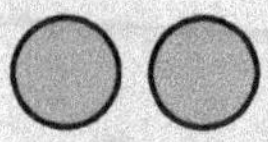
1 (2) 3 4 5

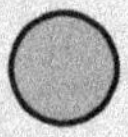
(1) 2 3 4 5

8.

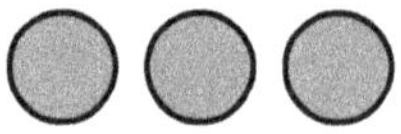
1 2 3 4 5

1 2 3 4 5

9.

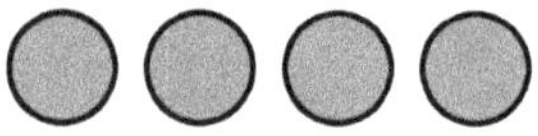
1 2 3 4 5

1 2 3 4 5

- [ ] Count. Circle the number.
- [ ] Color ☺ for equal. Color ☹ for not equal.

10.

1 2 3 4 5

1 2 3 4 5

11.

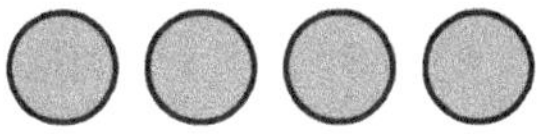

1 2 3 4 5

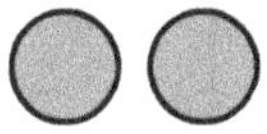

1 2 3 4 5

12.

1 2 3 4 5

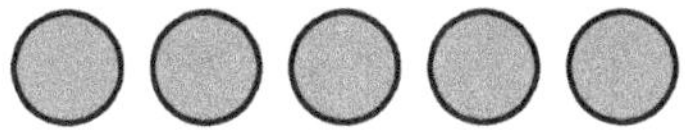

1 2 3 4 5

Greater Than (Matching)

☐ Match by drawing a line.

☐ Color the ☼ on the side that has **more**.

1.

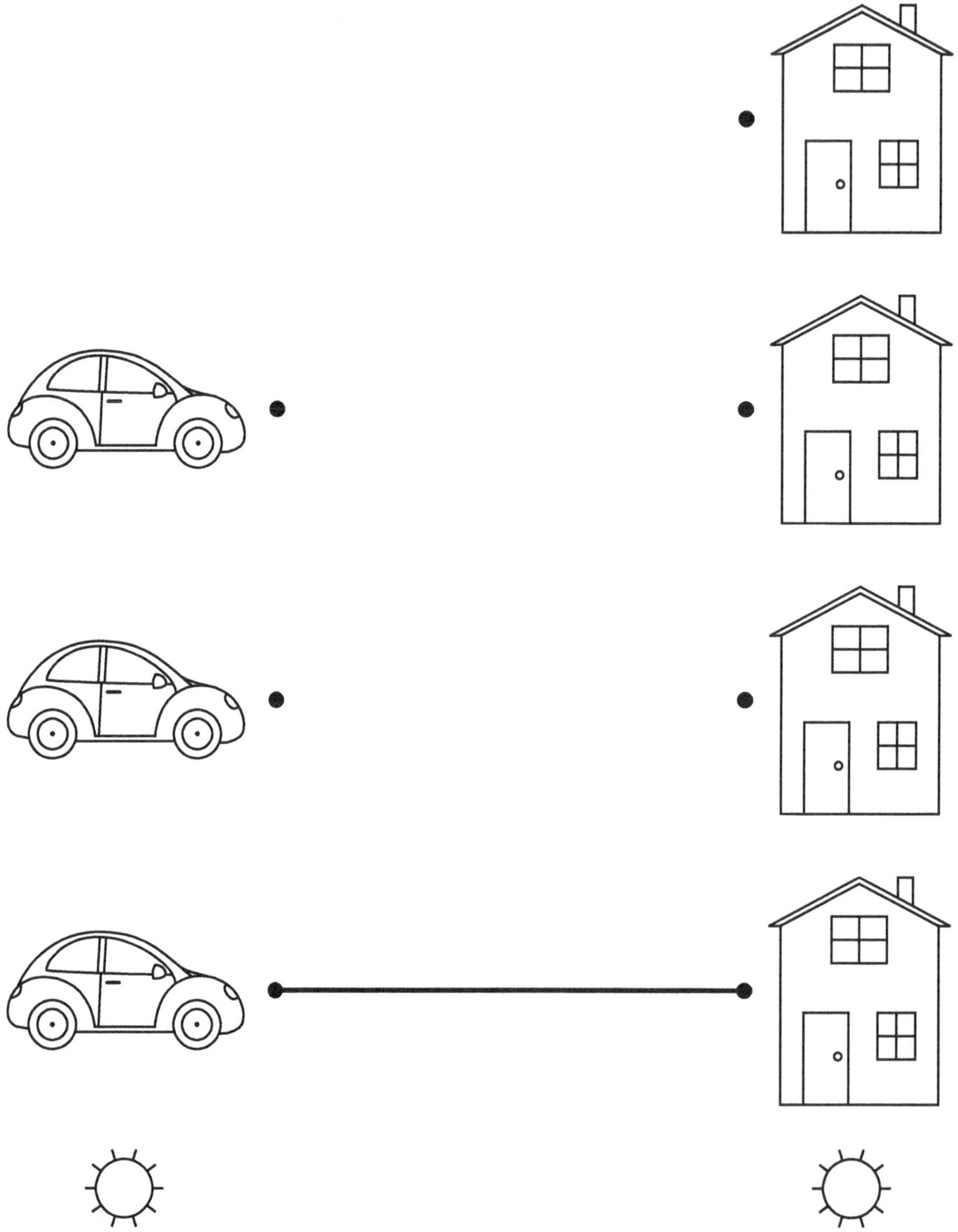

☐ Match by drawing a line.

☐ Color the ☼ on the side that has more.

2.

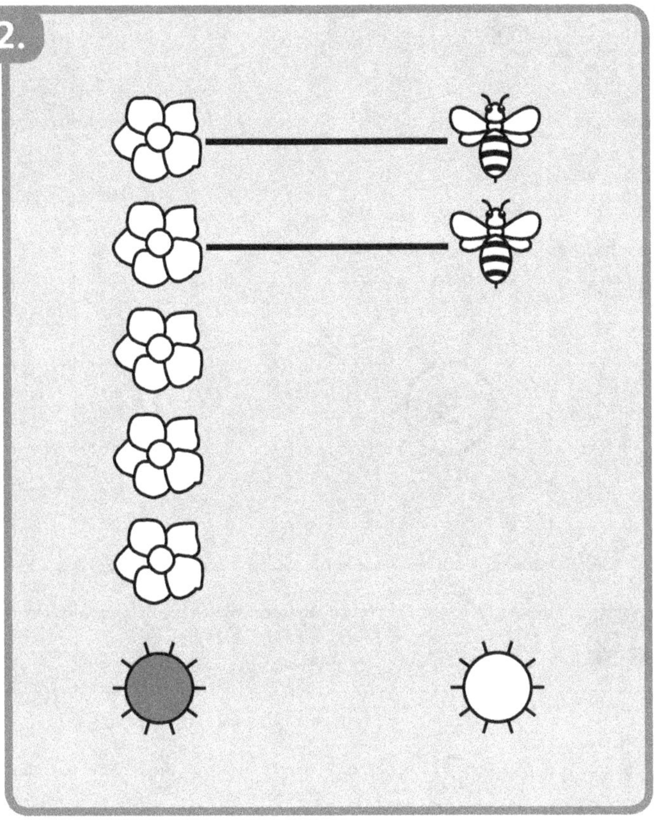

3.

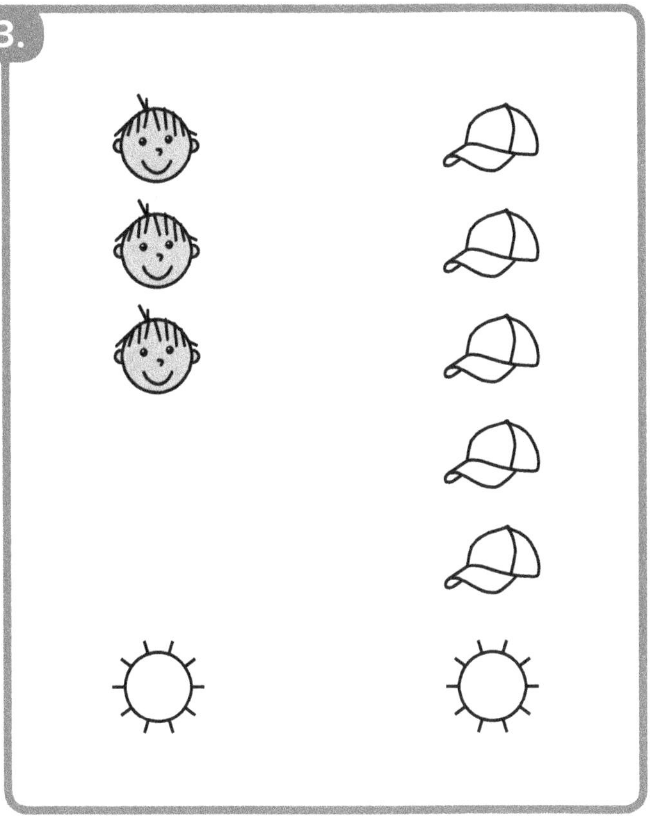

4.

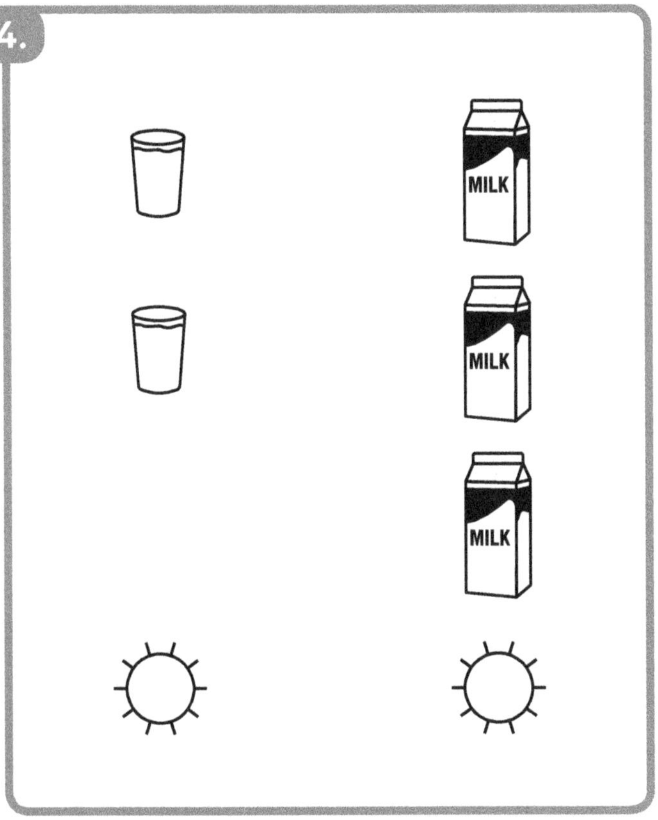

5.

Greater Than (Counting)

1 2 3 4 5

☐ Circle the **greater** number.

1. 2 (4)

2. (3) 1

3. 4 5

4. 2 5

5. 3 2

6. 4 3

7. 5 1

8. 1 4

☐ Count. Circle the number.

☐ Color the ☼ for the greater number.

9.

1 2 3 4 5 ☼

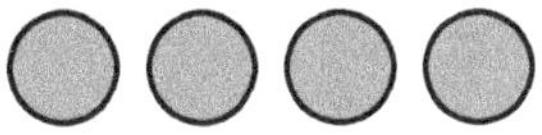

1 2 3 4 5 ☼

10.

1 2 3 4 5 ☼

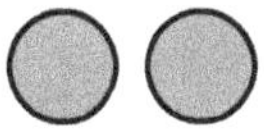

1 2 3 4 5 ☼

11.

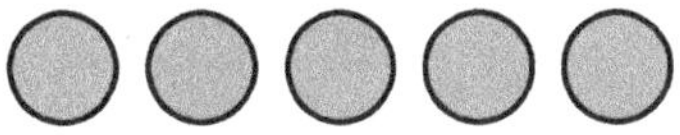

1 2 3 4 5 ☼

1 2 3 4 5 ☼

- [ ] Count. Circle the number.
- [ ] Color the ☼ for the greater number.

12.

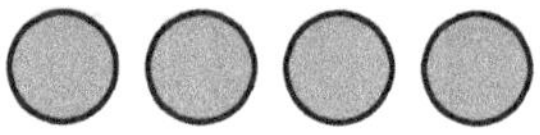

1 2 3 4 5

1 2 3 4 5

13.

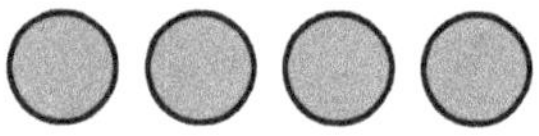

1 2 3 4 5

1 2 3 4 5

14.

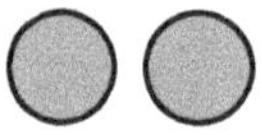

1 2 3 4 5

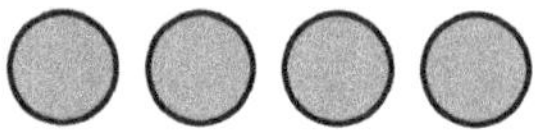

1 2 3 4 5

CCK-21 Less Than (Matching)

☐ Color the ☼ for the group that has **fewer**.

1.

2.

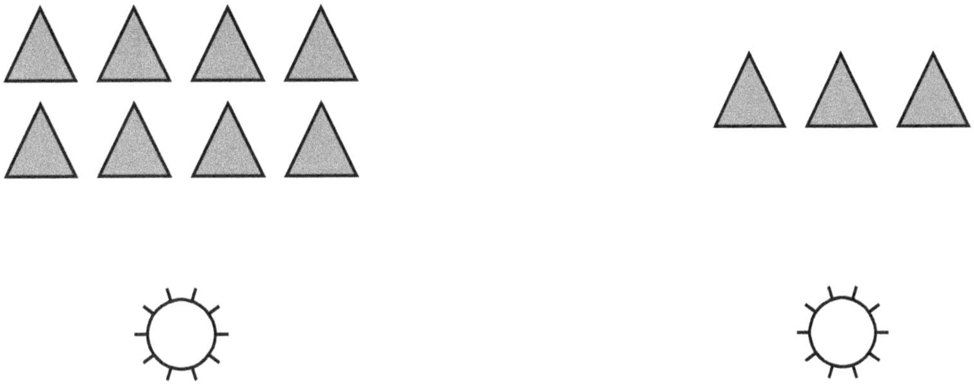

3.

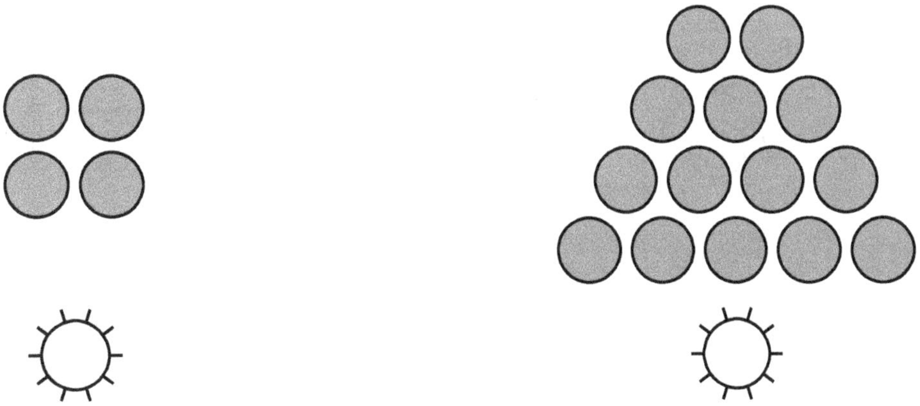

- [ ] Match by drawing a line.
- [ ] Color the ☼ on the side that has fewer.

4.

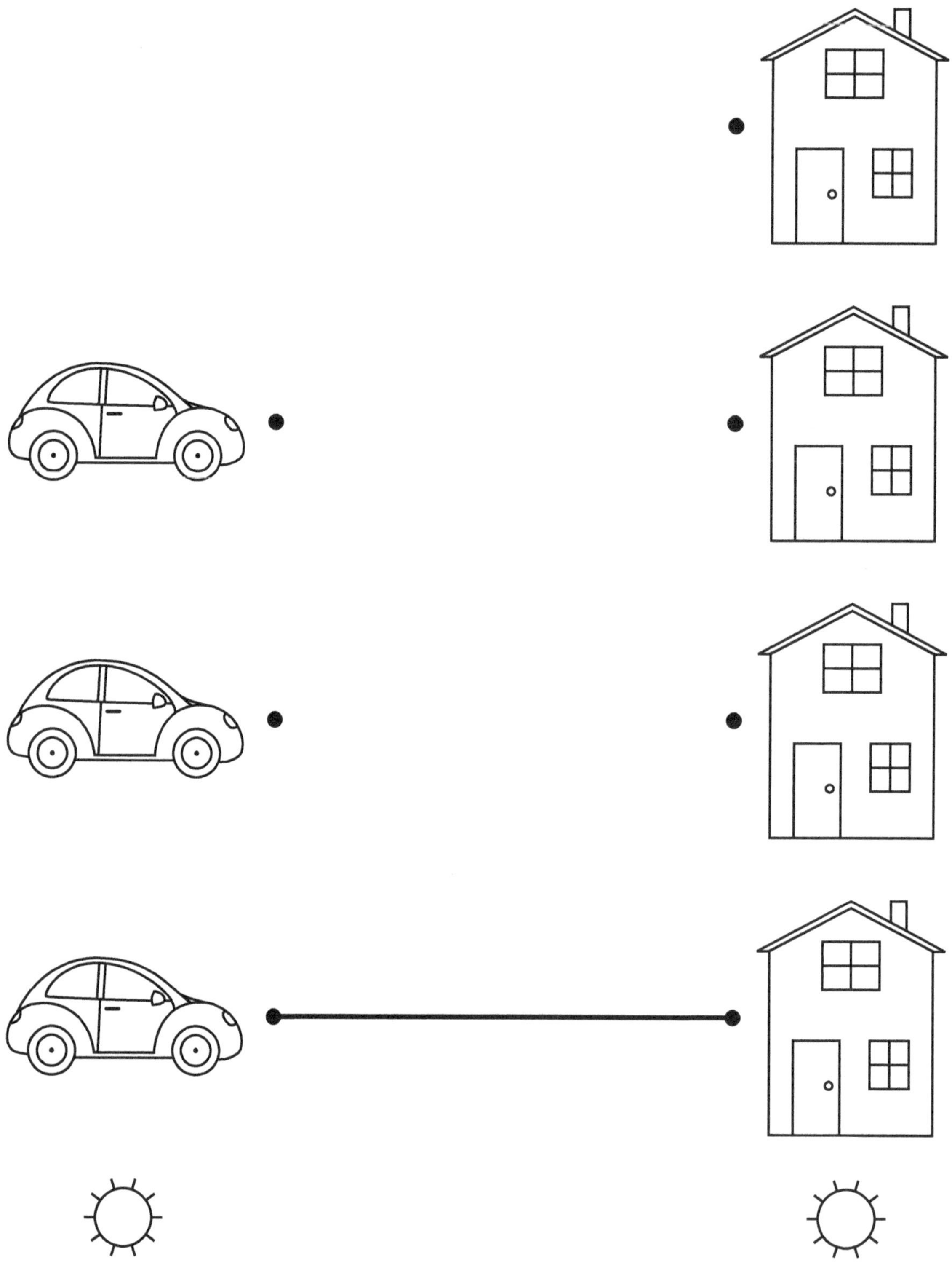

☐ Match by drawing a line.

☐ Color the ☼ on the side that has fewer.

5.

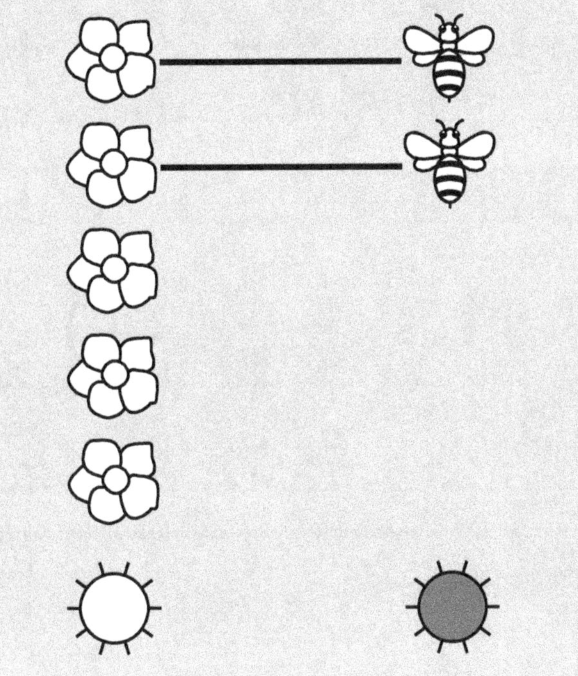

6.

7.

8.

Less Than (Counting)

1 2 3 4 5

☐ Circle the number that is **less**.

1. (2) 4

2. 3 (1)

3. 4 5

4. 2 5

5. 3 2

6. 4 3

7. 5 1

8. 1 4

☐ Count. Circle the number.

☐ Color the ☼ for the number that is less.

9.

 1 2 3 4 5 ☼

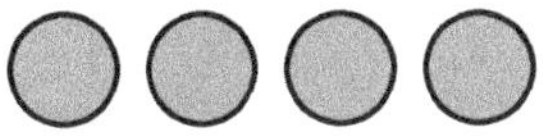 1 2 3 4 5 ☼

10.

 1 2 3 4 5 ☼

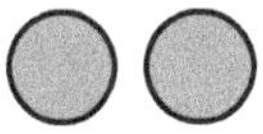 1 2 3 4 5 ☼

11.

 1 2 3 4 5 ☼

 1 2 3 4 5 ☼

☐ Count. Circle the number.

☐ Color the ☼ for the number that is less.

12.

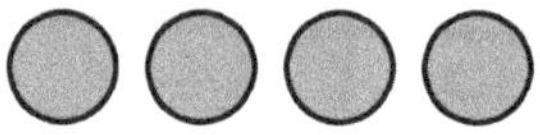 1 2 3 4 5 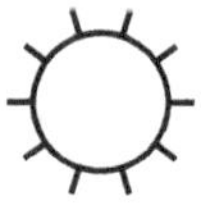

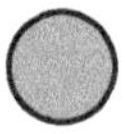 1 2 3 4 5 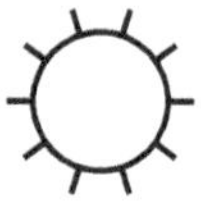

13.

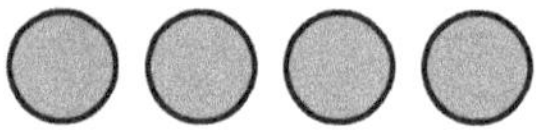 1 2 3 4 5 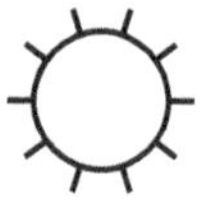

 1 2 3 4 5 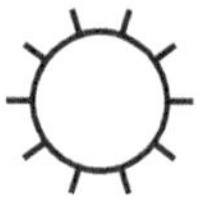

14.

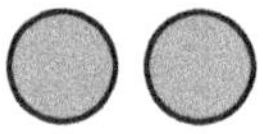 1 2 3 4 5 

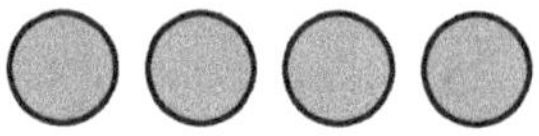 1 2 3 4 5 

CCK-23 **Zero**

☐ Color the ☼ to show which is 0.

1.

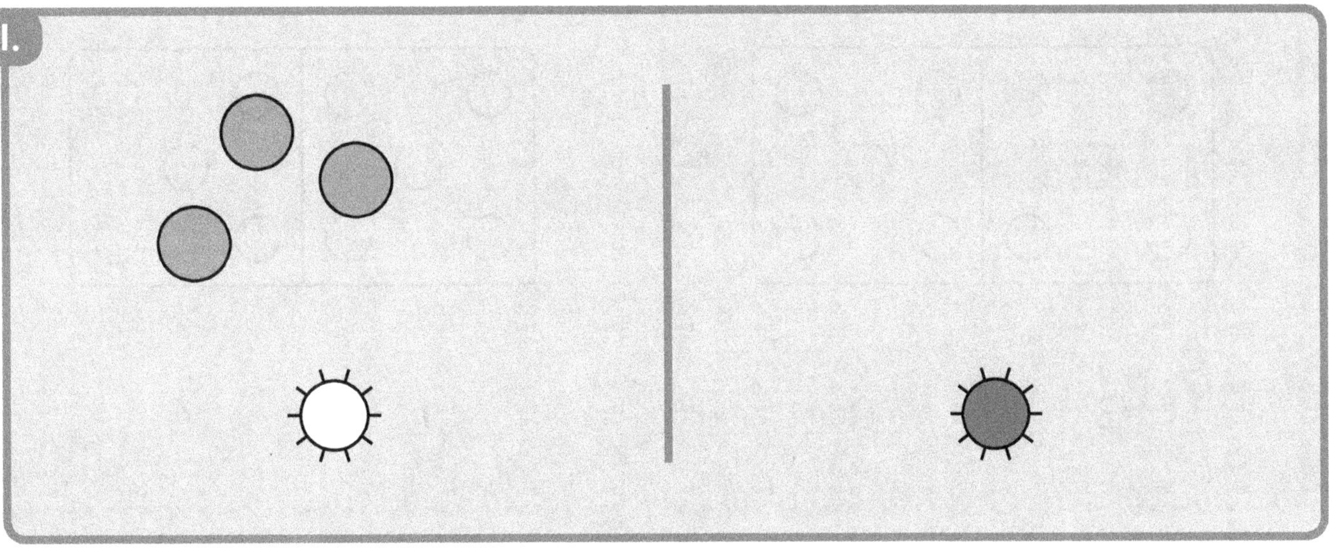

2.

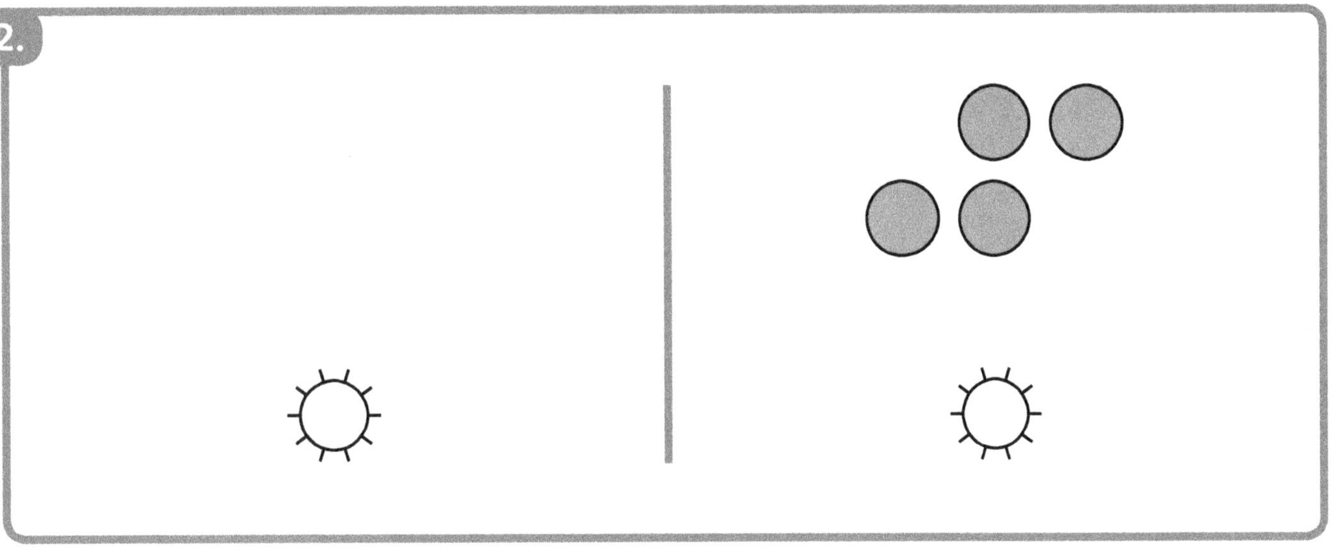

3.

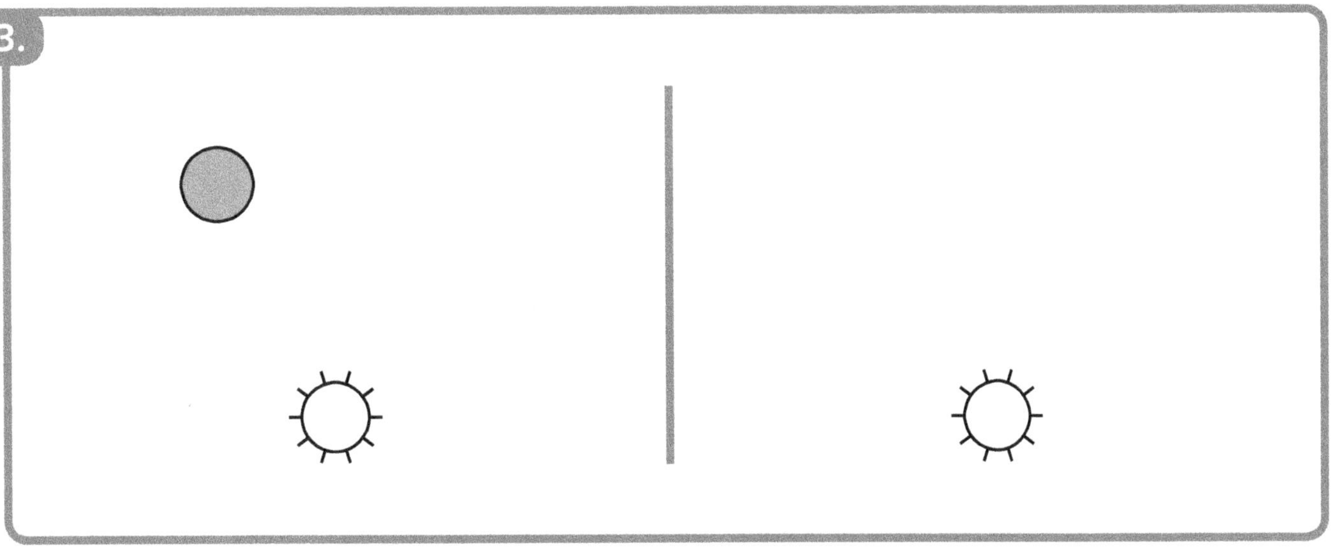

☐ Color dots to show the numbers.

4.

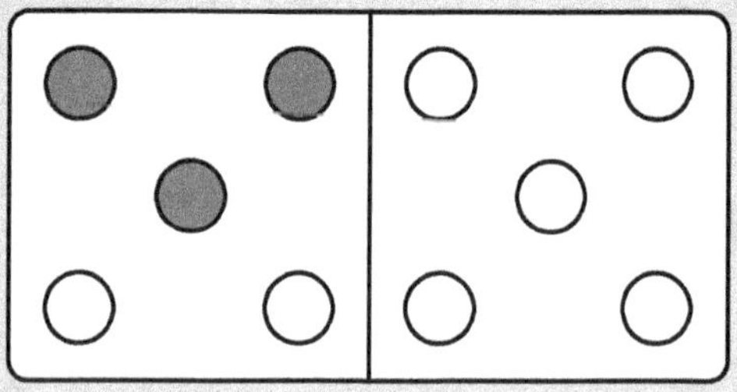

3 0

5.

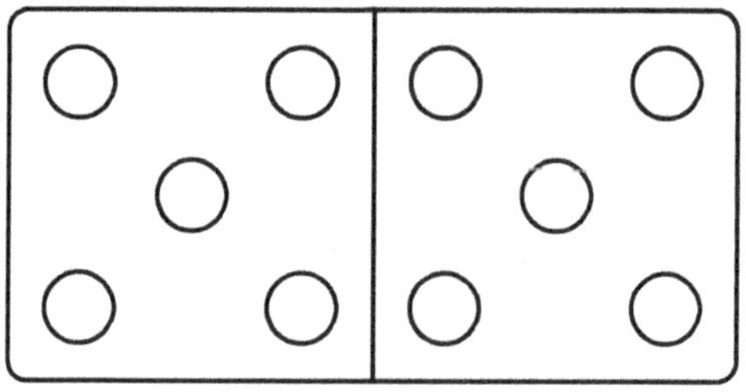

1 4

6.

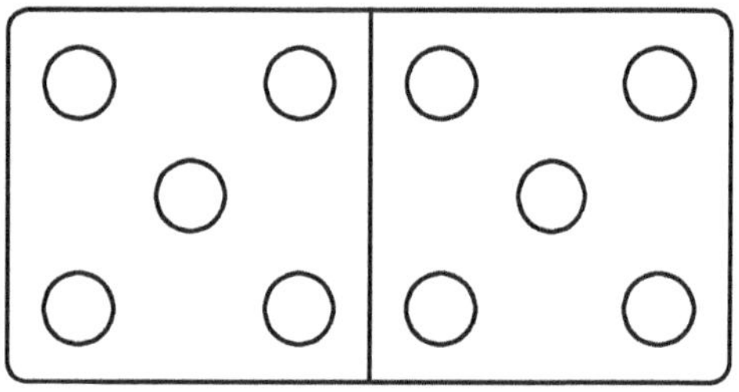

5 1

7.

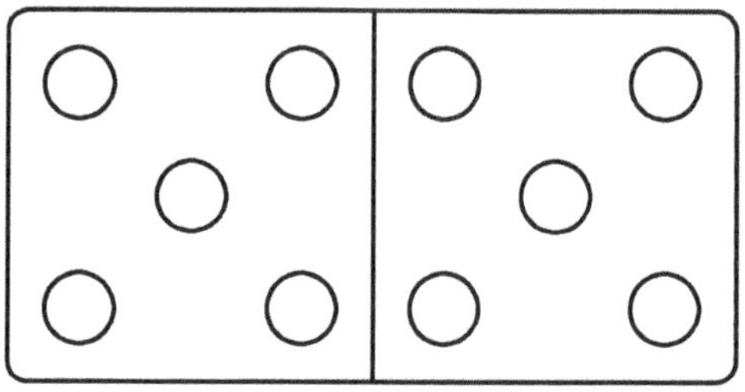

0 2

8.

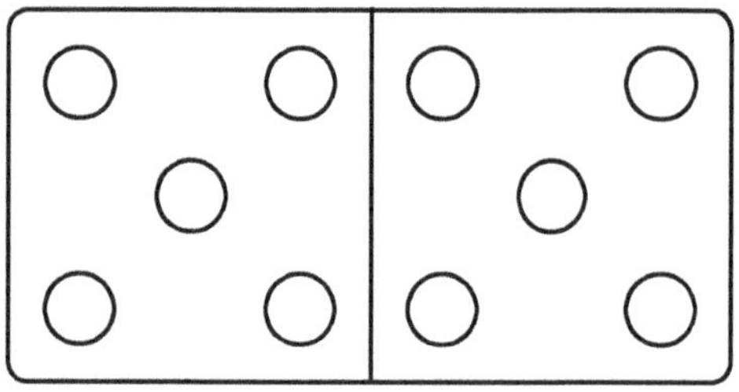

0 4

9.

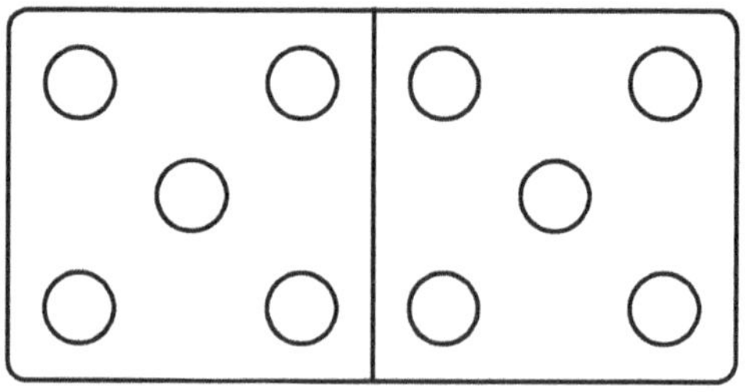

3 5

0 1 2 3 4 5

☐ Circle the number that is **less**.

10.	2	(0)
11.	0	4
12.	0	1
13.	3	1
14.	4	0
15.	2	5
16.	4	5
17.	3	0

☐ Trace.

18.

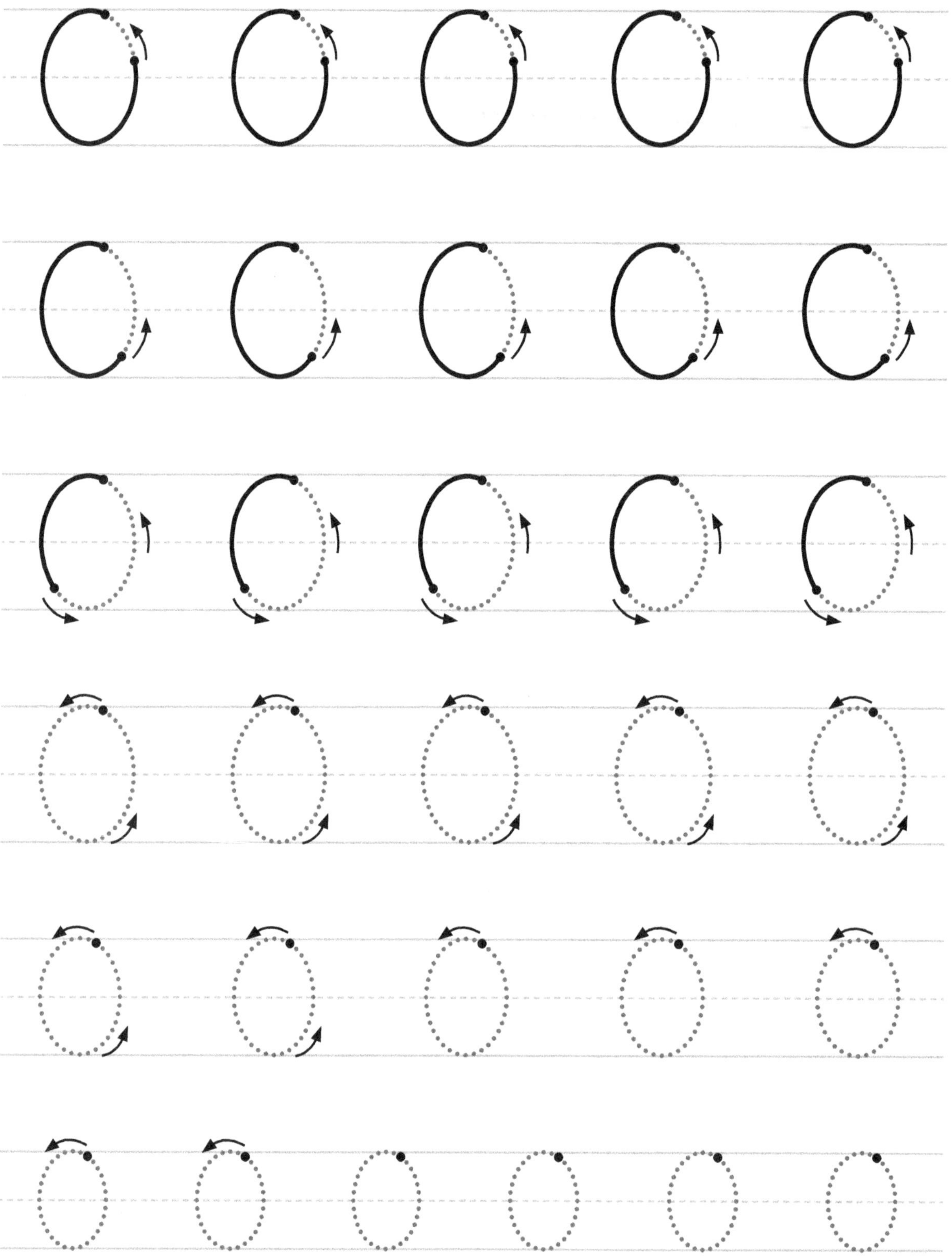

CCK-24 Comparing Numbers I to 5

☐ Color to show the numbers.

☐ Match.

1.

I 2

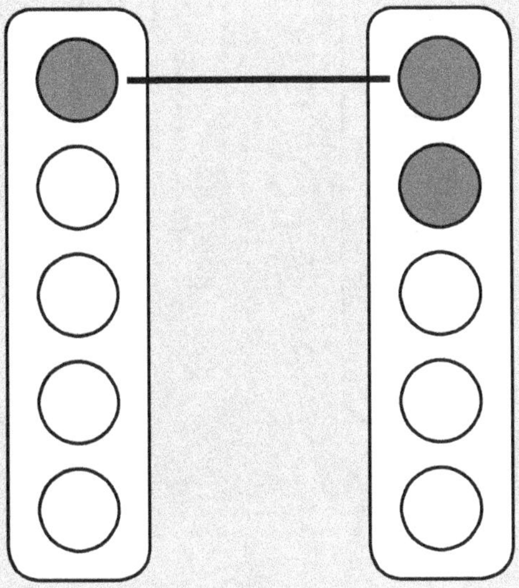

2.

3 I

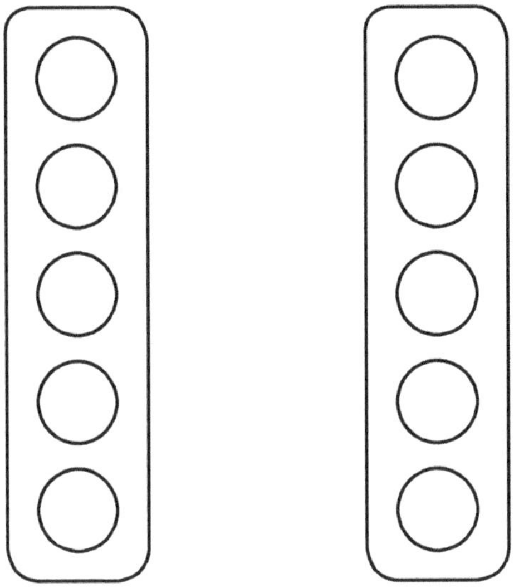

3.

2 5

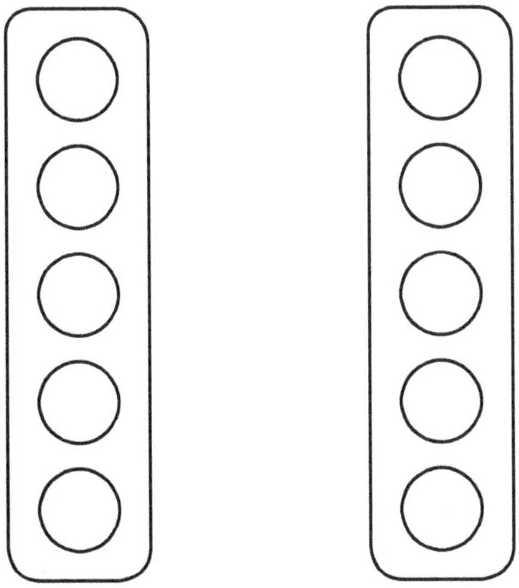

4.

4 3

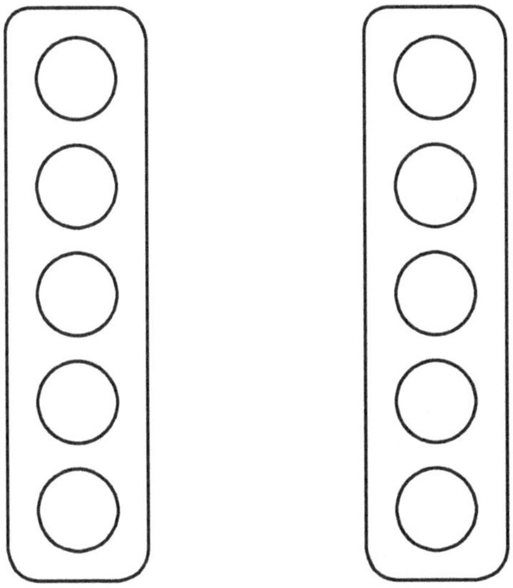

☐ Color to show the numbers. Match.

☐ Color the ☼ for the greater number.

5.

3 2

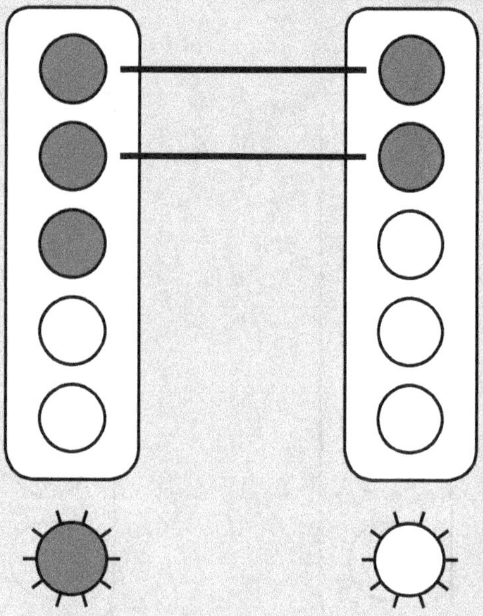

6.

1 4

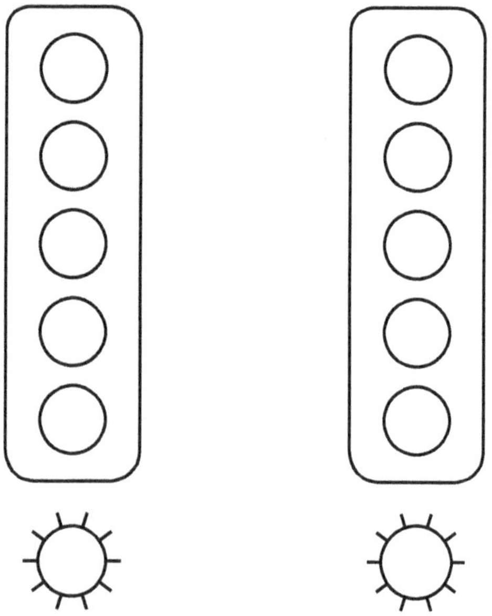

7.

5 2

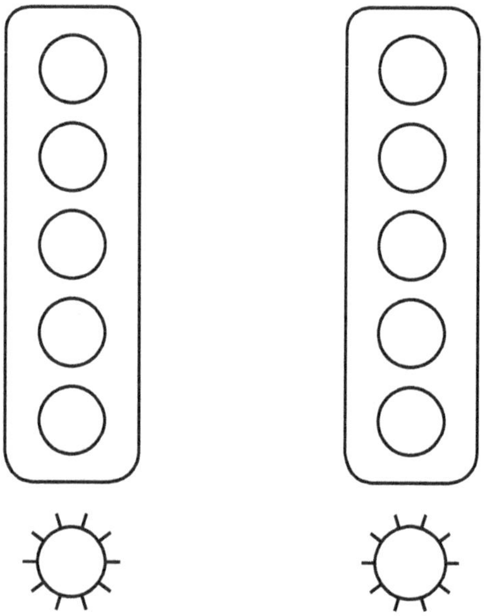

8.

3 5

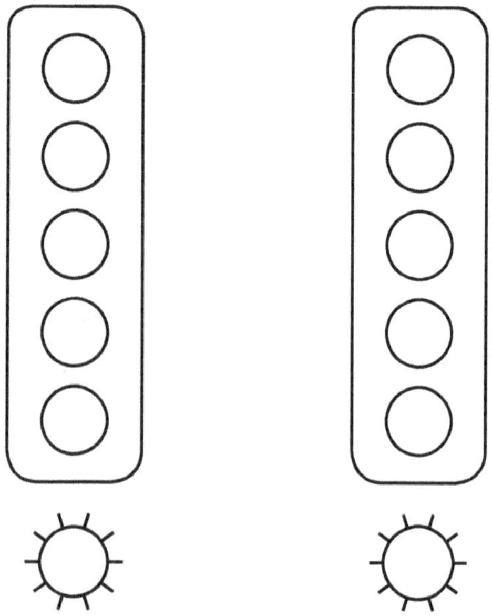

☐ Color to show the numbers. Match.

☐ Color the ☼ for the number that is less.

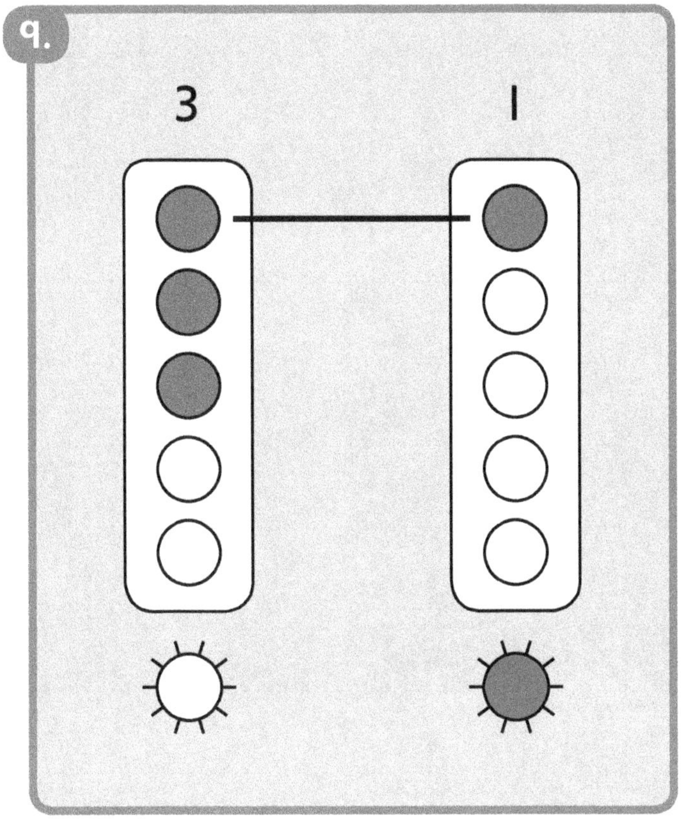

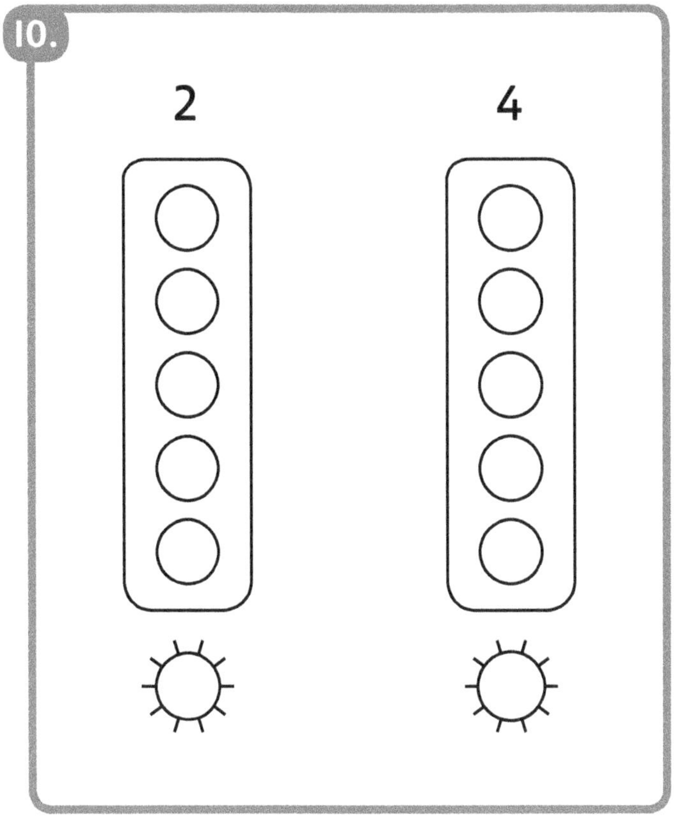

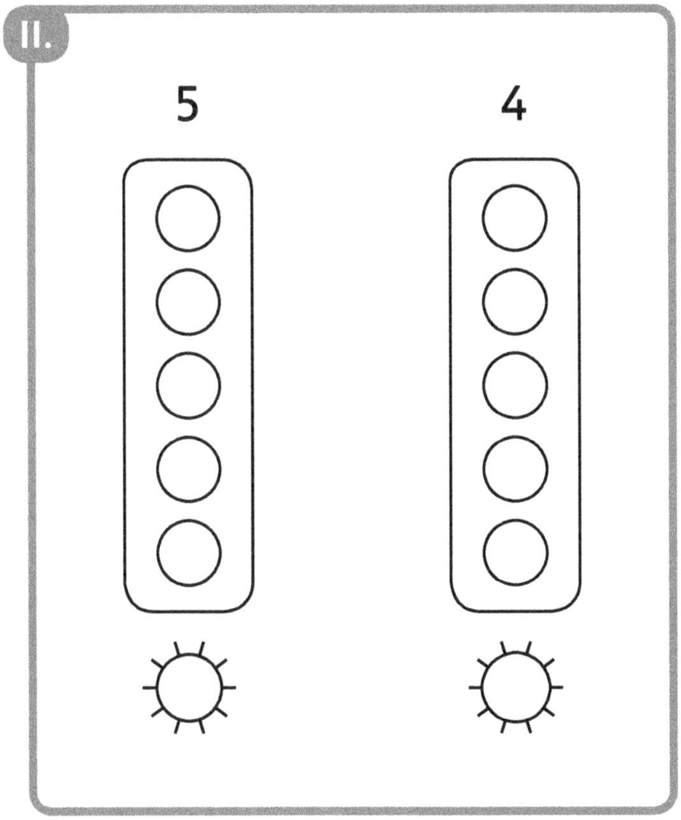

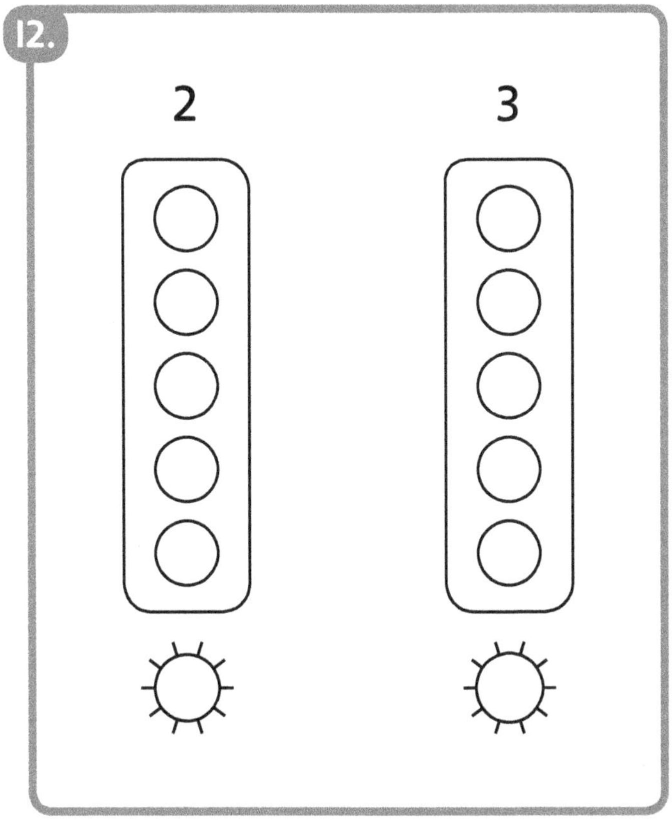

GK-1 Counting to 30

☐ Trace.

1.

20 21 22

23 24 25

26 27 28

29 30

2.

2 2 2 2 2 2 2

☐ Write 2.

3.

GK-2 Circles

☐ Count the ○.

1.

1 2 3 (4) 5

2.

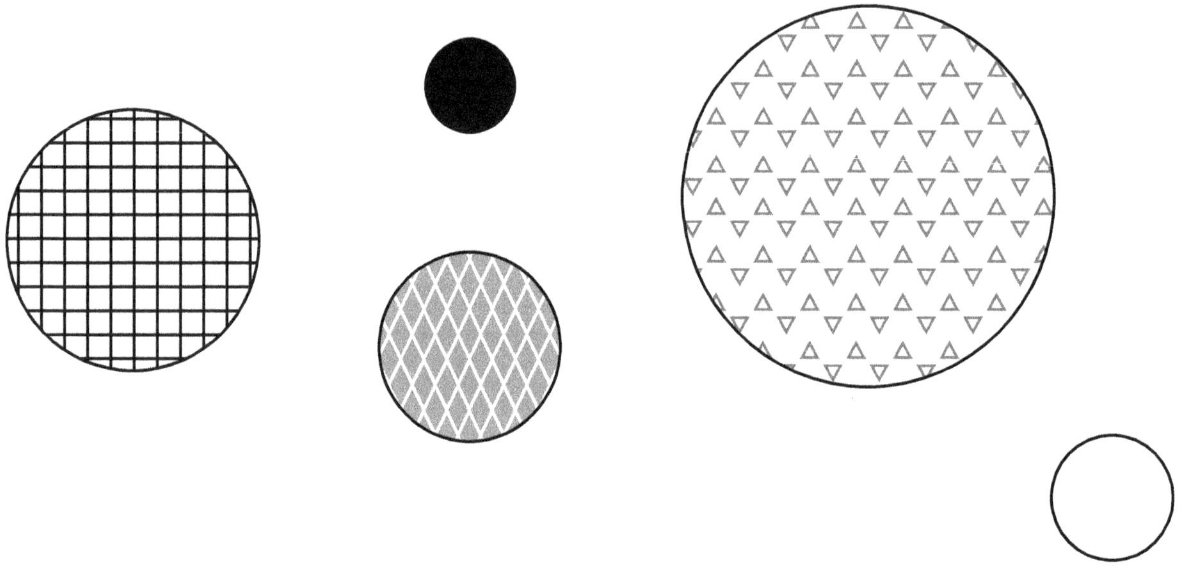

1 2 3 4 5

☐ Color the ○.

☐ Draw × on the other shapes.

3.

4.

☐ Color the ○.

☐ Draw × on the other shapes.

5.

6.

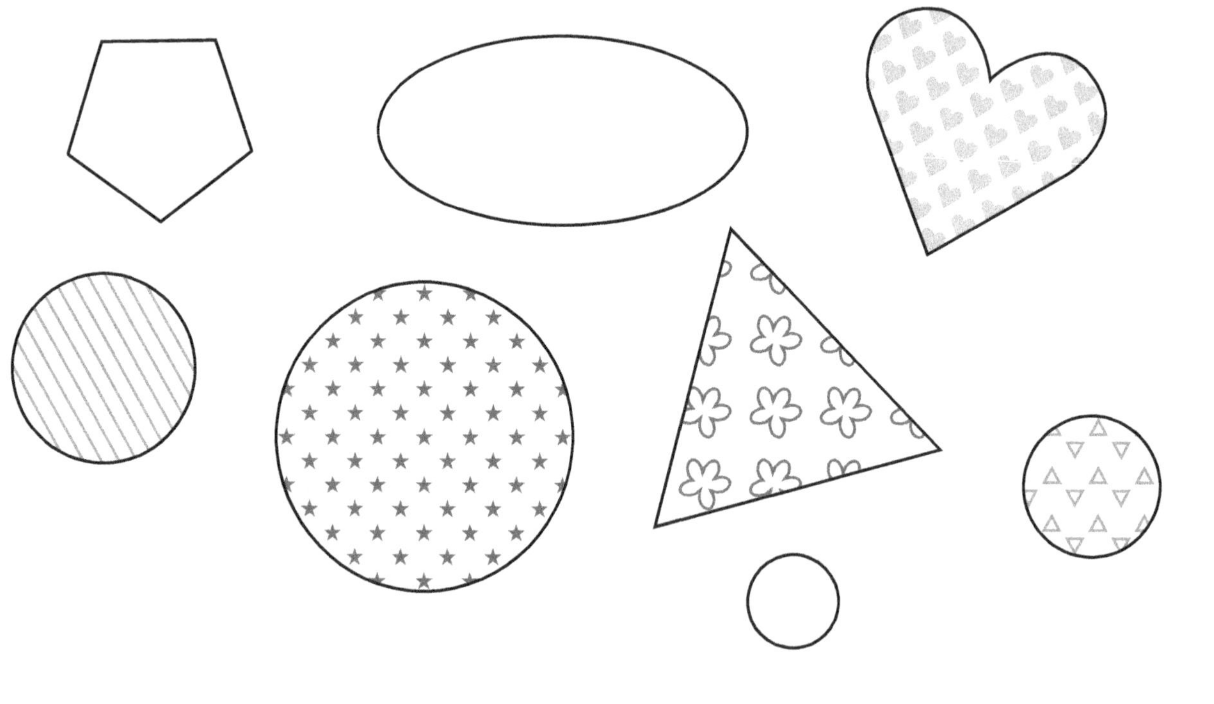

GK-3 Squares

▢ Count the ▢.

1.

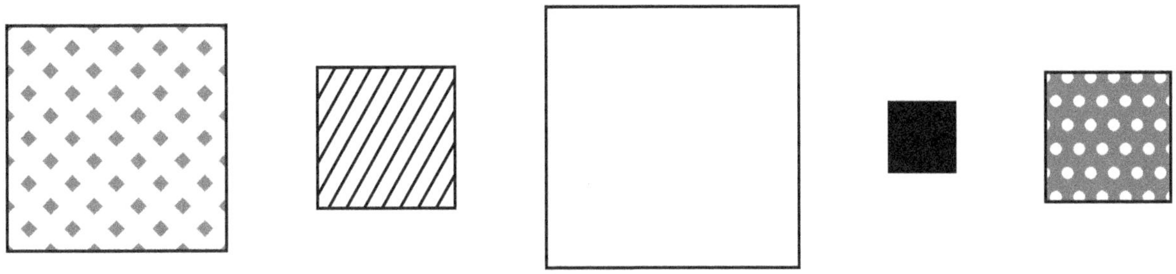

1 2 3 4 5

2.

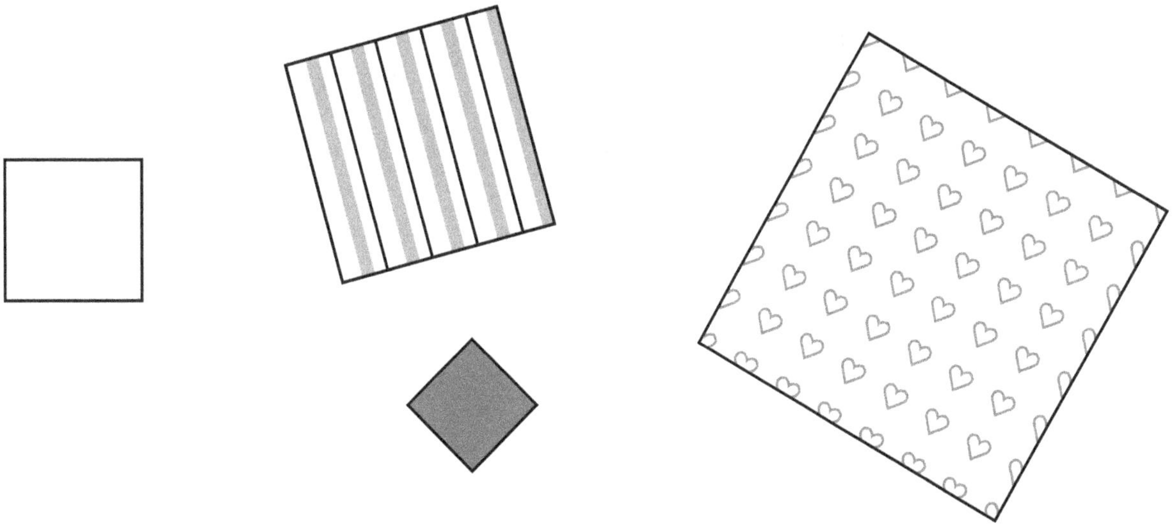

1 2 3 4 5

☐ Color the □.

☐ Draw ✕ on the other shapes.

3.

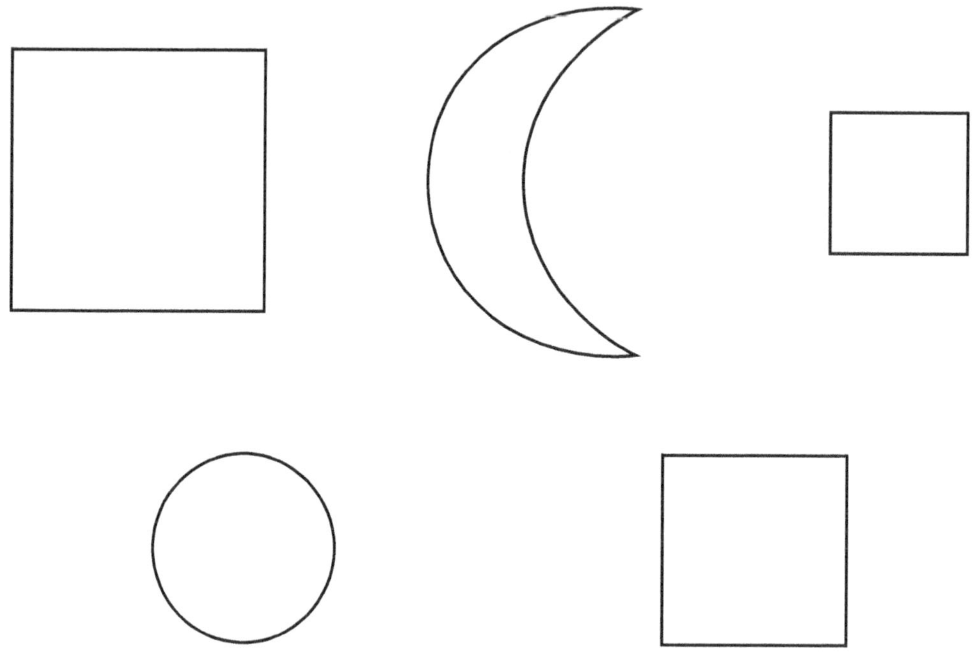

4.

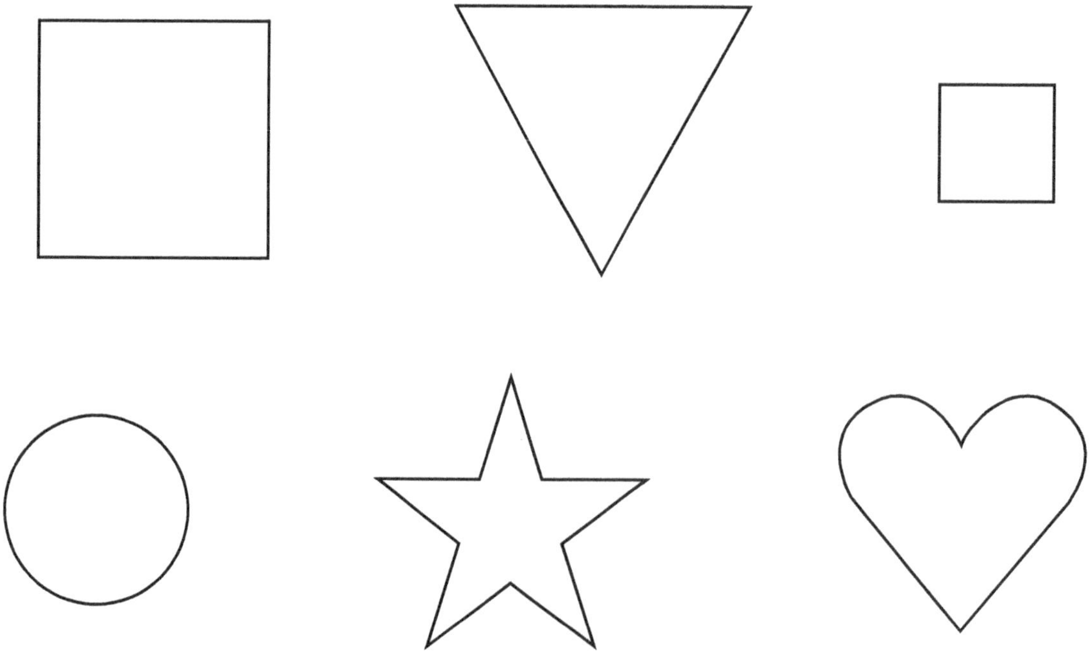

☐ Color the □.

☐ Draw × on the other shapes.

5.

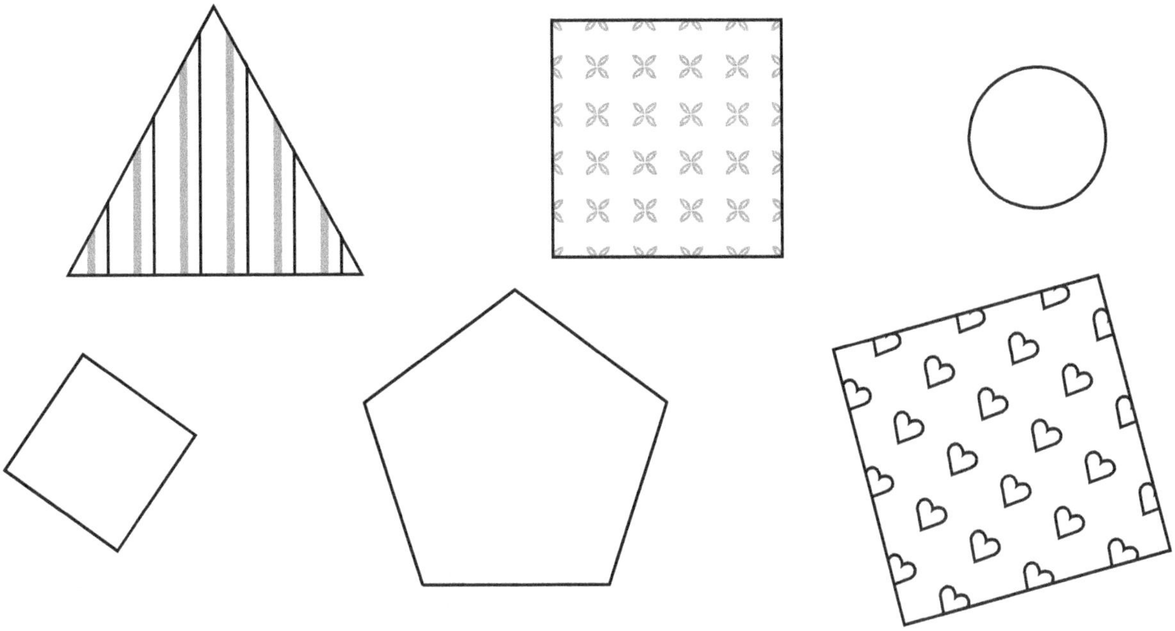

6.

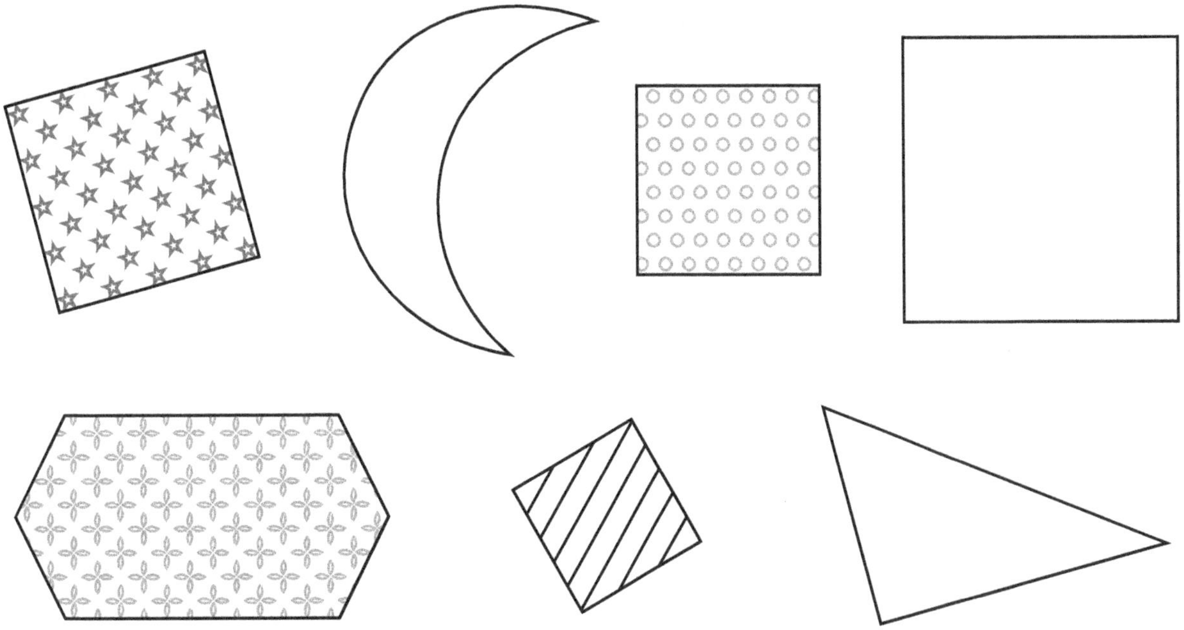

GK-4 Rectangles

☐ Count the ▭.

1.

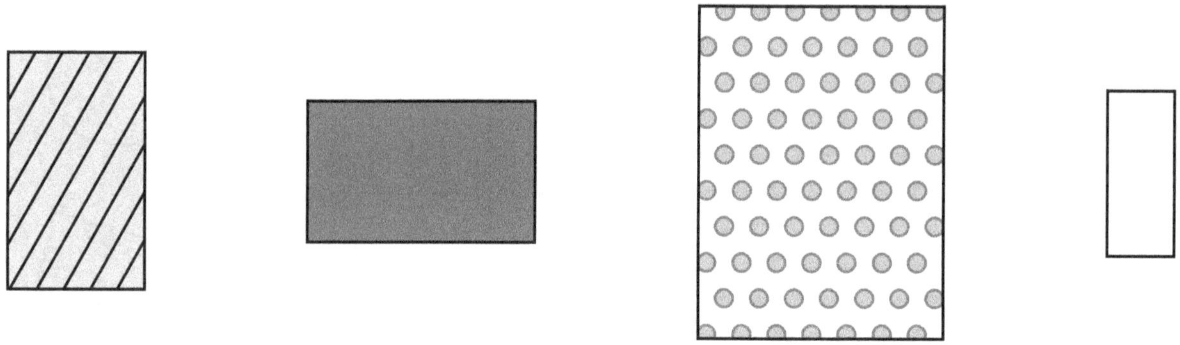

1 2 3 4 5

2.

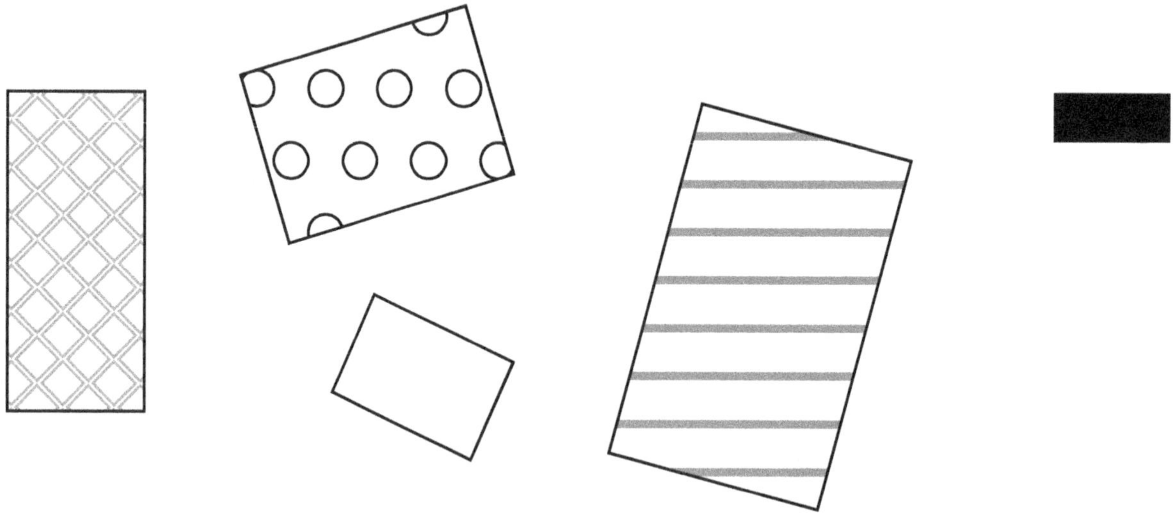

1 2 3 4 5

☐ Color the ▭.

☐ Draw ✕ on the other shapes.

3.

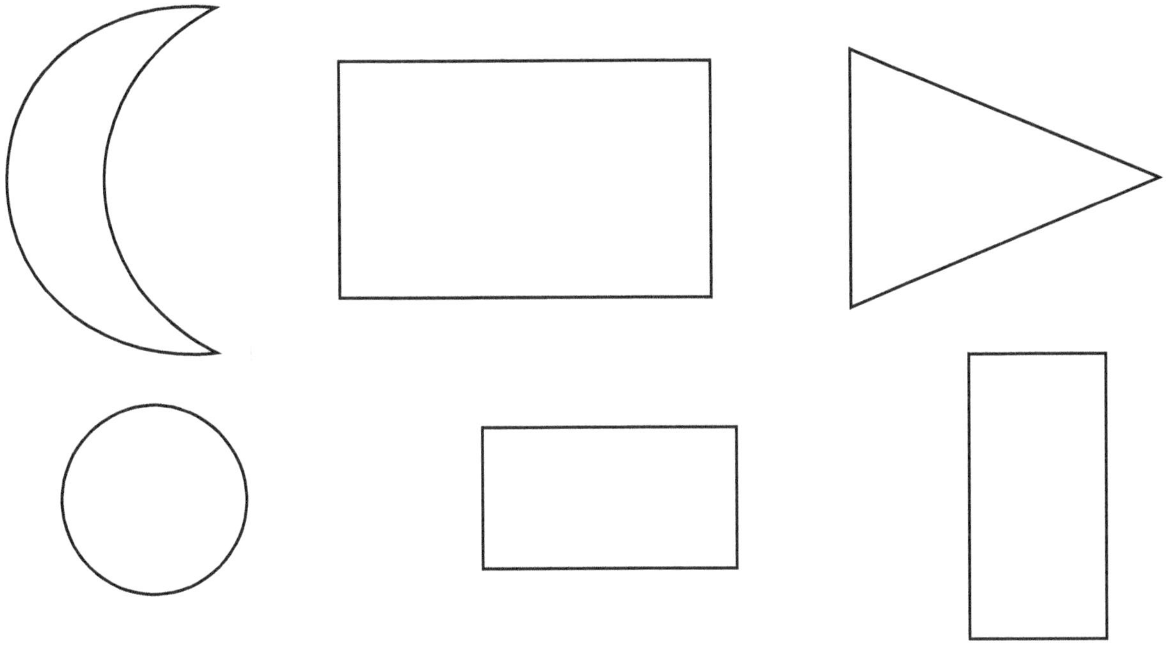

4.

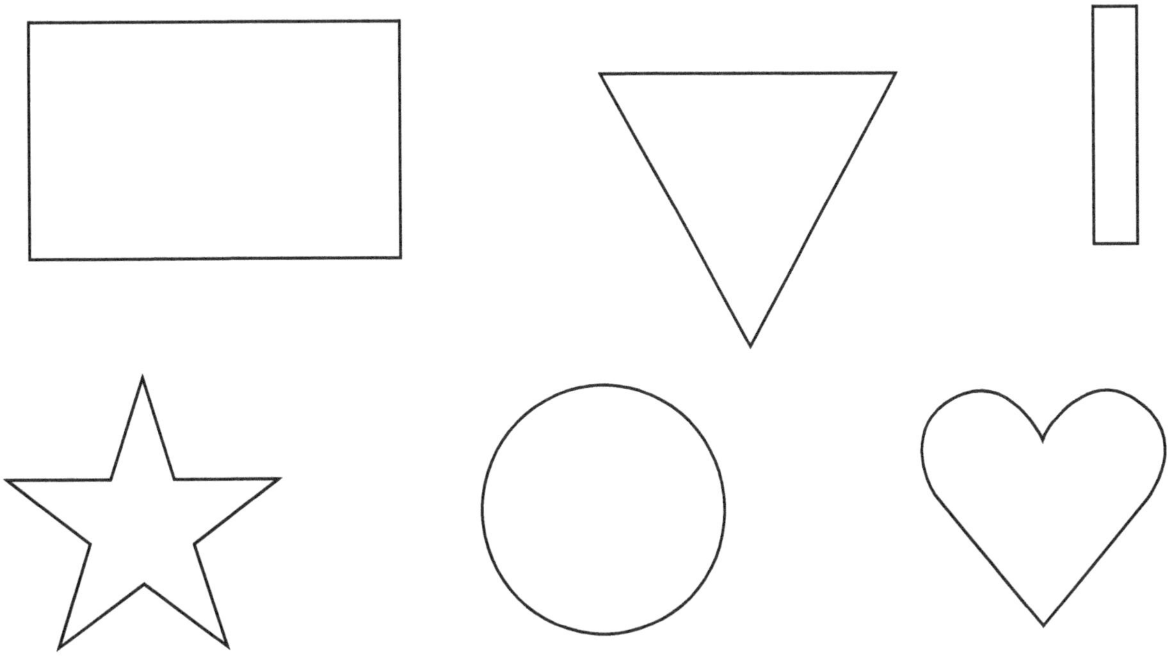

☐ Color the ▭.

☐ Draw × on the other shapes.

5.

6.

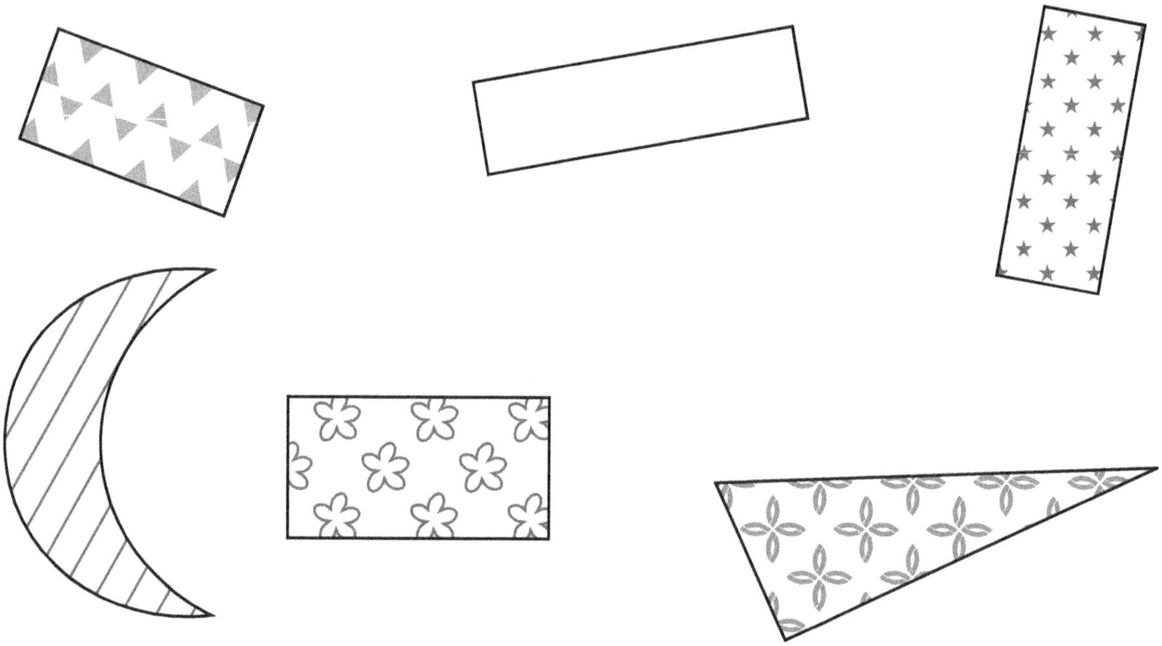

GK-5 Corners and Sides

☐ Draw ● on each corner.

1.

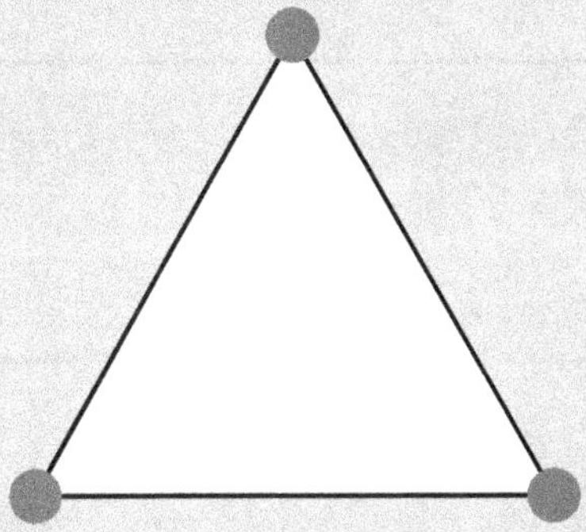

2.

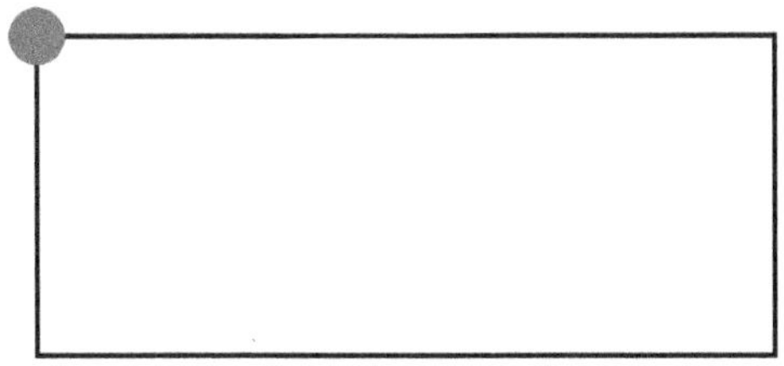

3.

4.

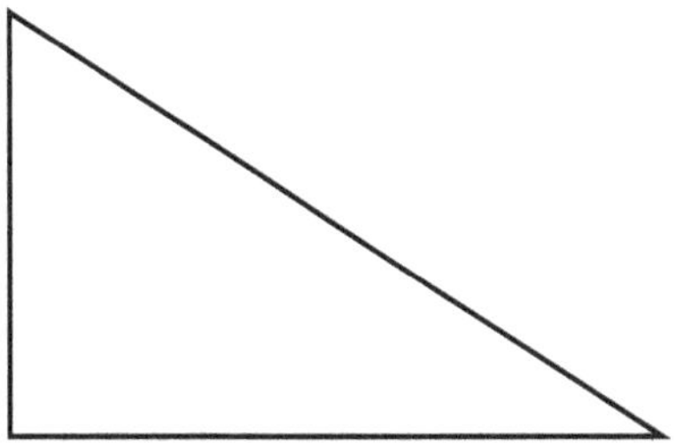

5.

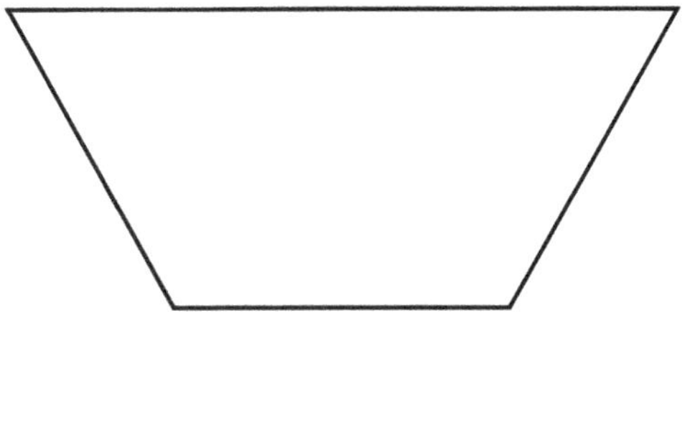

6.

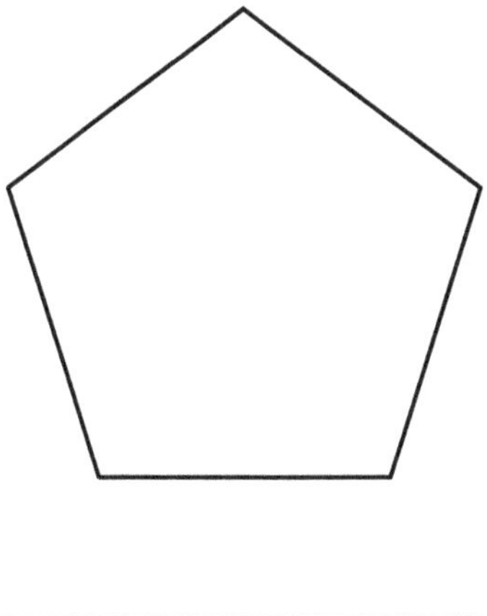

☐ Color the sides.

7.

8.

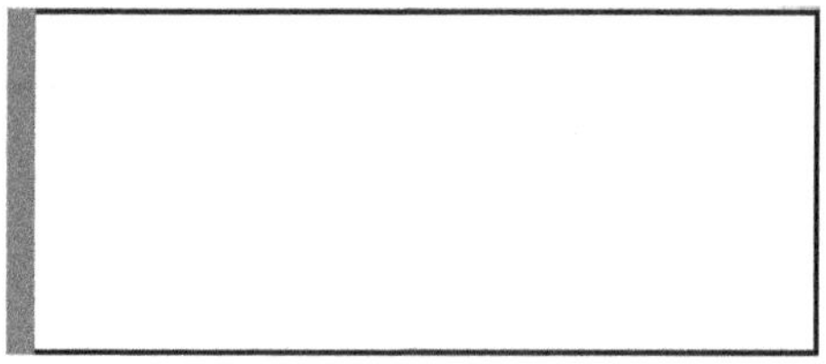

9.

10.

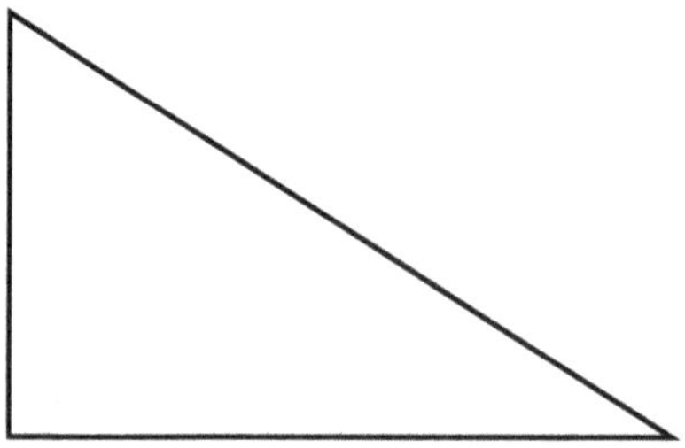

11.

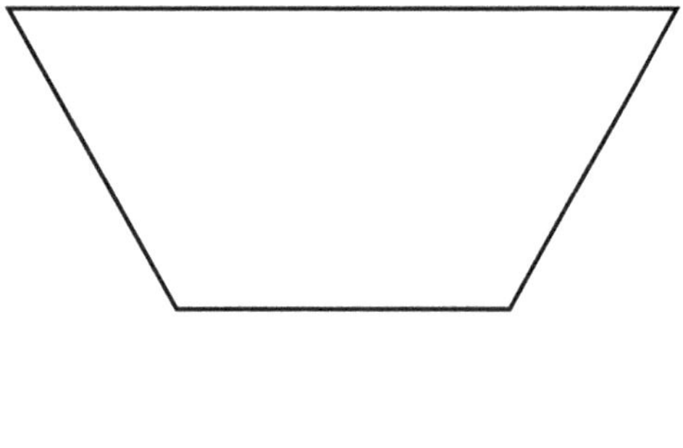

12.

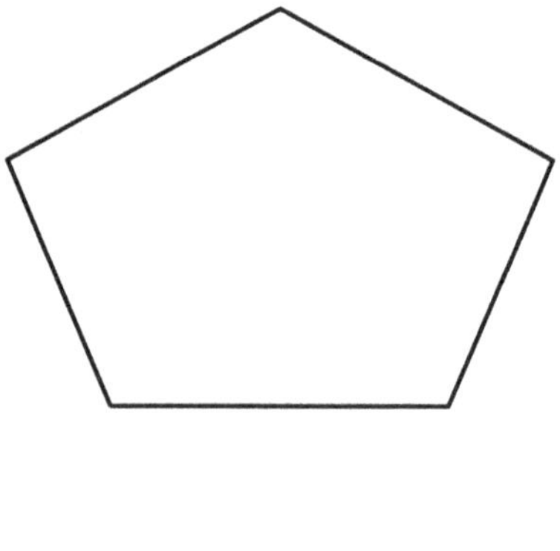

GK-6 Counting Corners and Sides

☐ Draw ● on each corner.

☐ Count the corners.

1.

1 2 3 (4) 5

2.

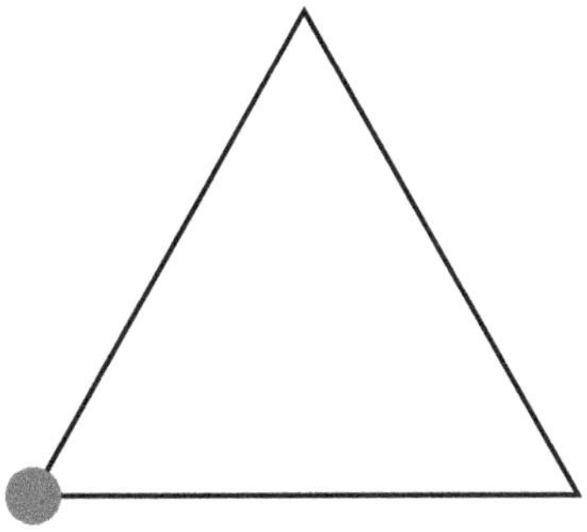

1 2 3 4 5

3.

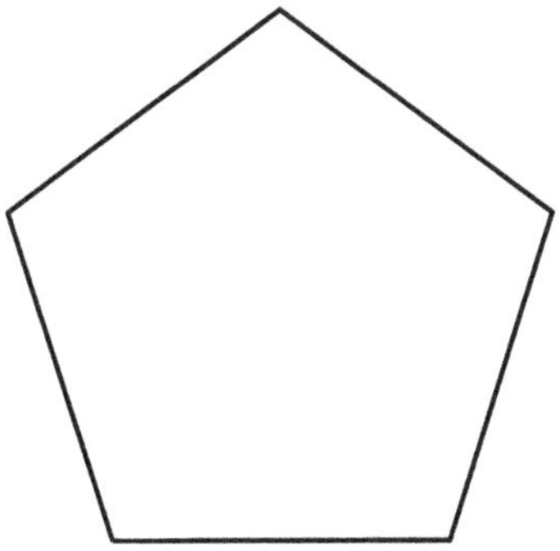

1 2 3 4 5

☐ Draw ● on each corner.

☐ Count the corners.

4.

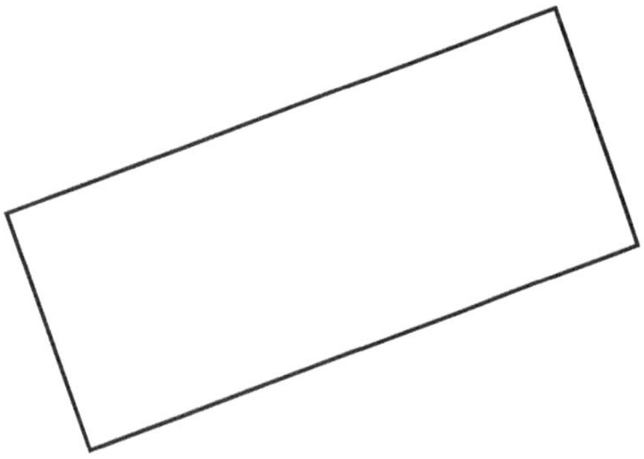

1 2 3 4 5

5.

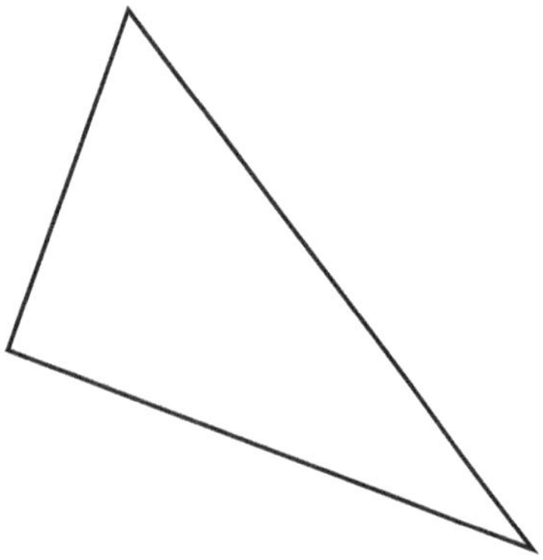

1 2 3 4 5

6.

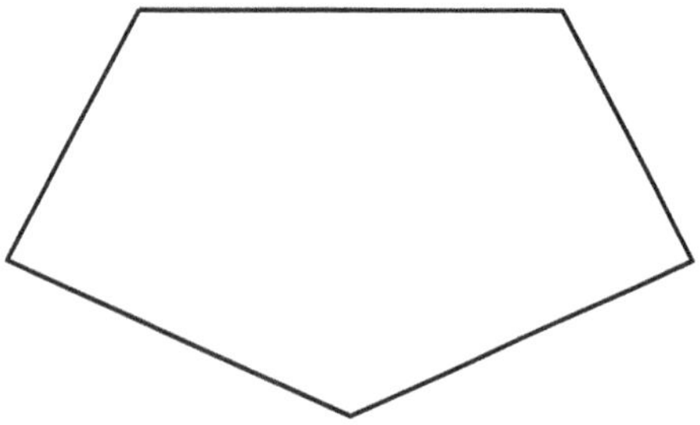

1 2 3 4 5

☐ Color the sides.

☐ Count the sides.

7.

1 2 (3) 4 5

8.

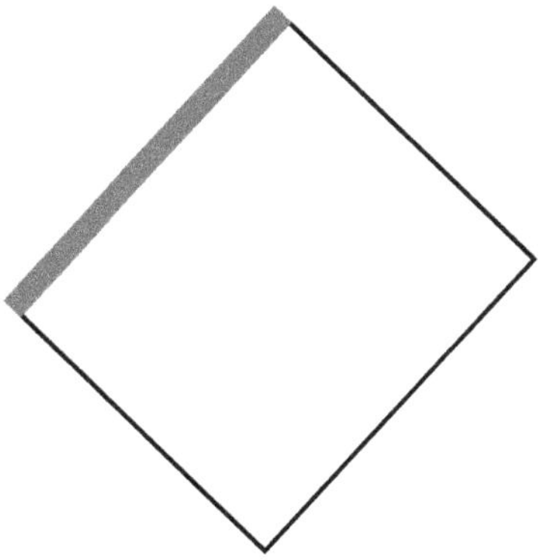

1 2 3 4 5

9.

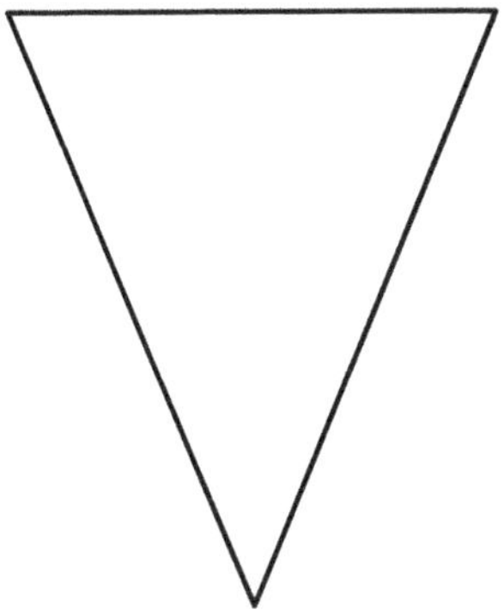

1 2 3 4 5

- [ ] Color the sides.
- [ ] Count the sides.

10.

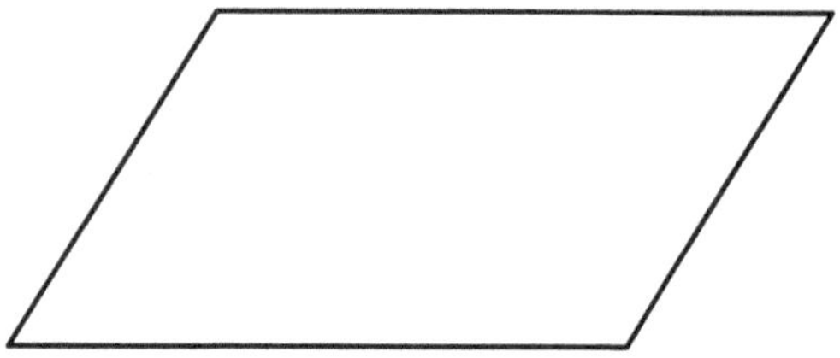

1 2 3 4 5

11.

1 2 3 4 5

12.

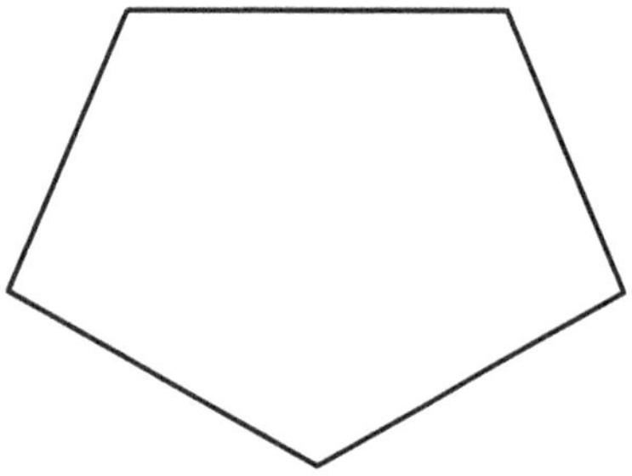

1 2 3 4 5

GK-7 More Squares and Rectangles

☐ Count the ☐.

1.

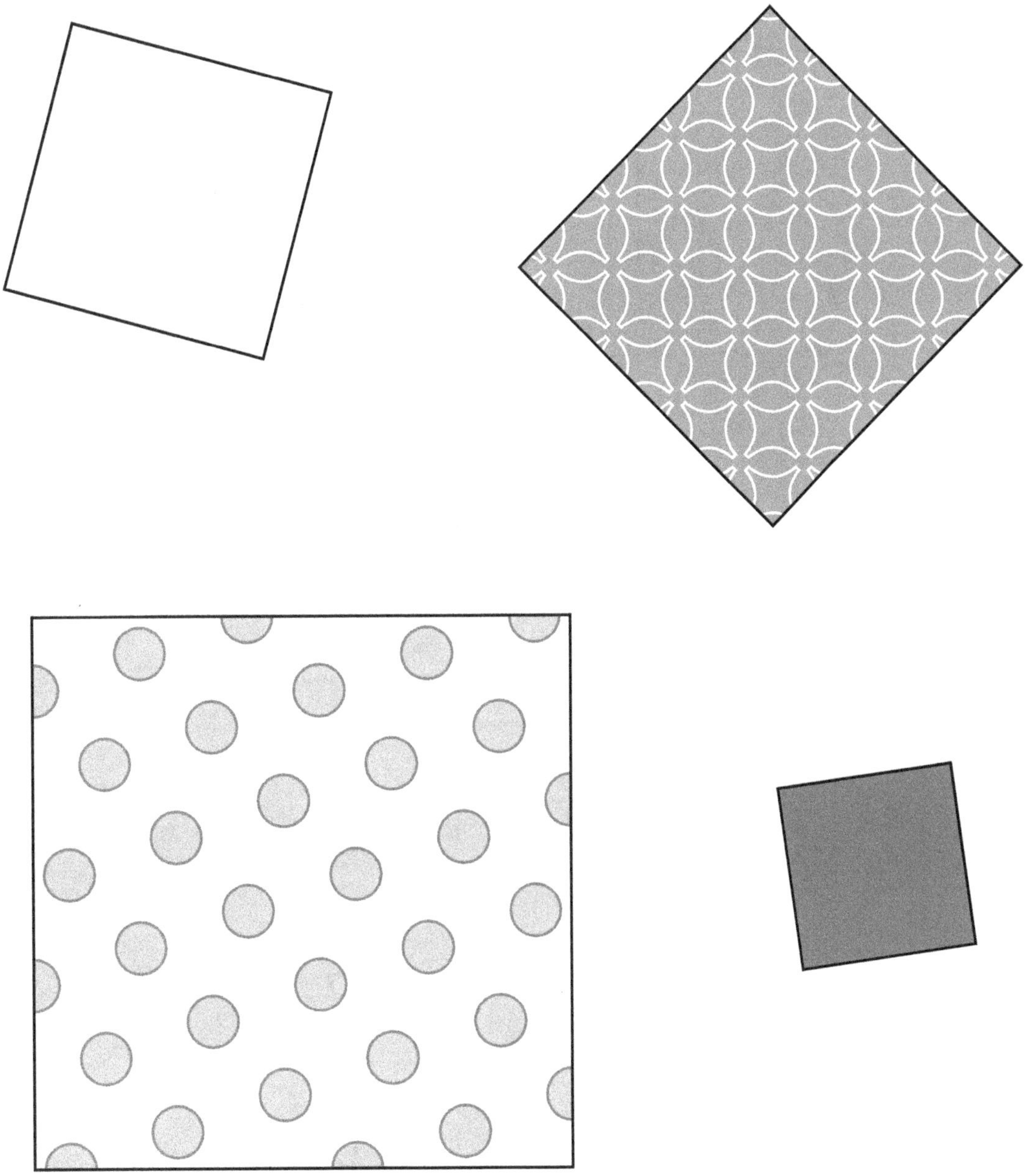

1 2 3 4 5

☐ Color the □.

☐ Draw × on the other shapes.

2.

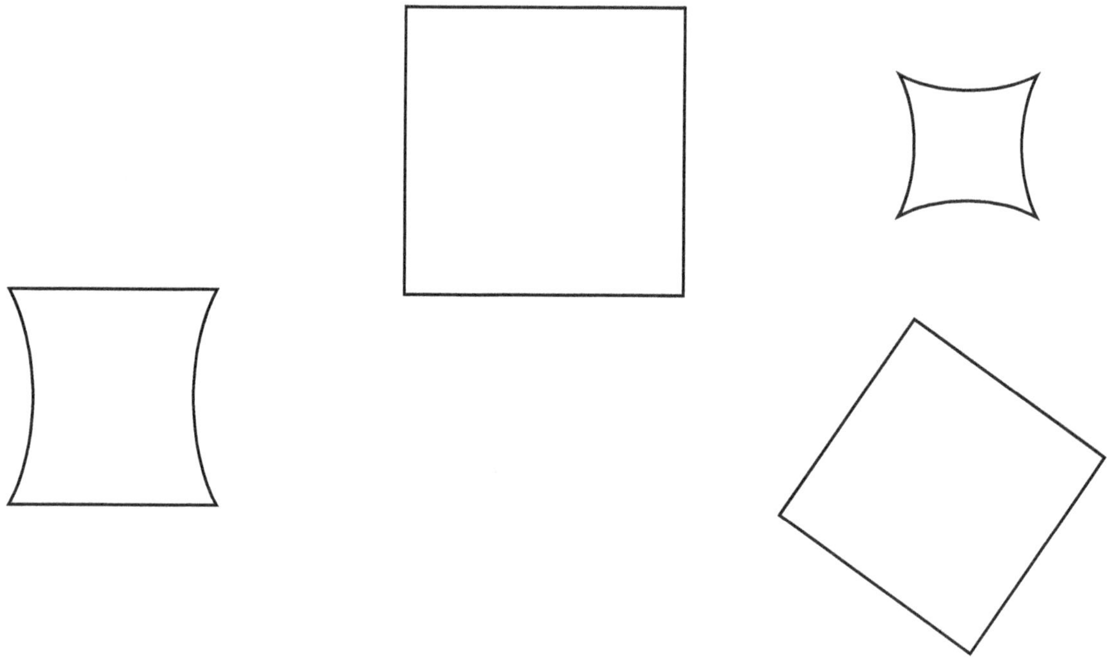

3.

☐ Count the ▭.

4.

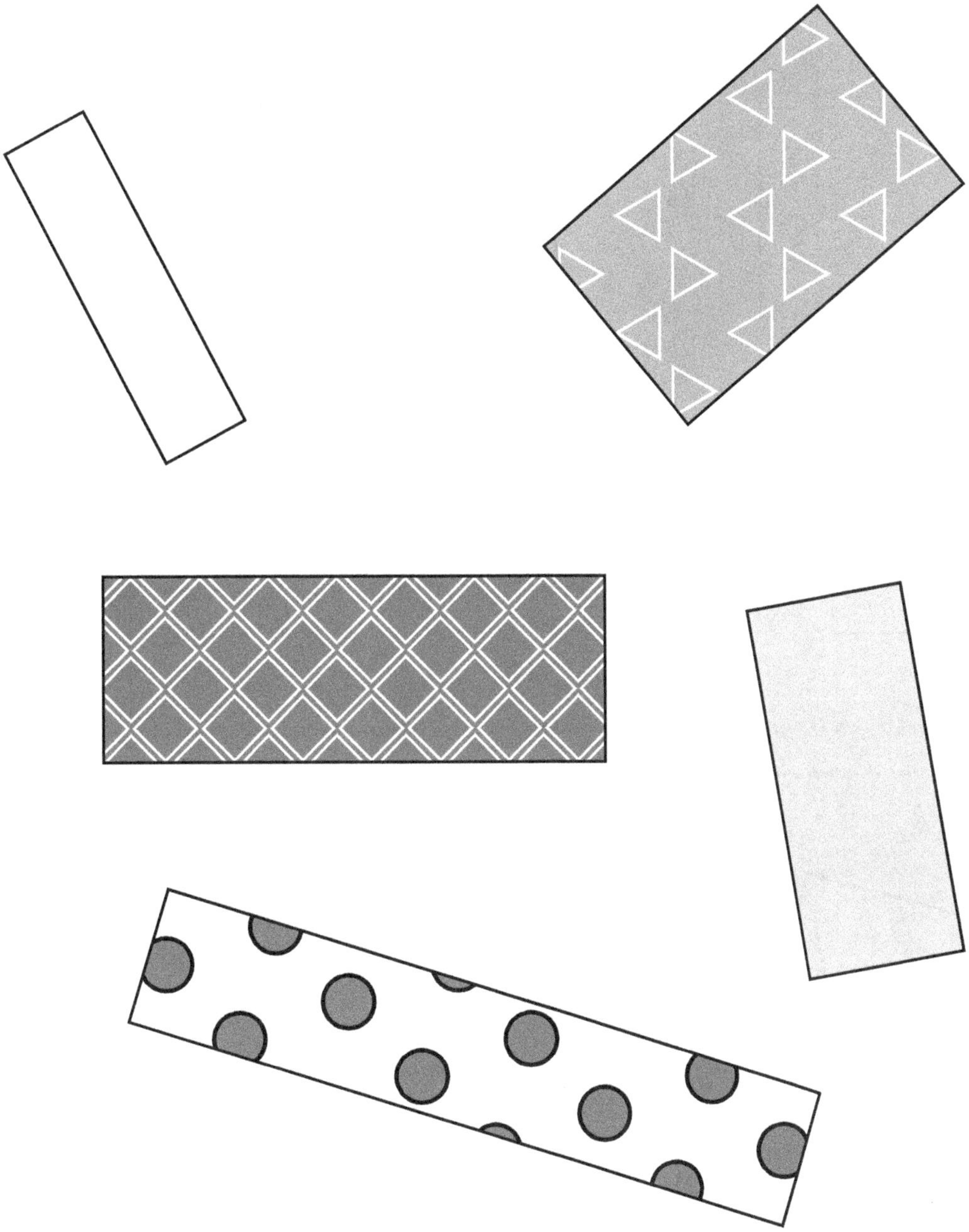

1 2 3 4 5

☐ Color the ▭.

☐ Draw X on the other shapes.

5.

6.

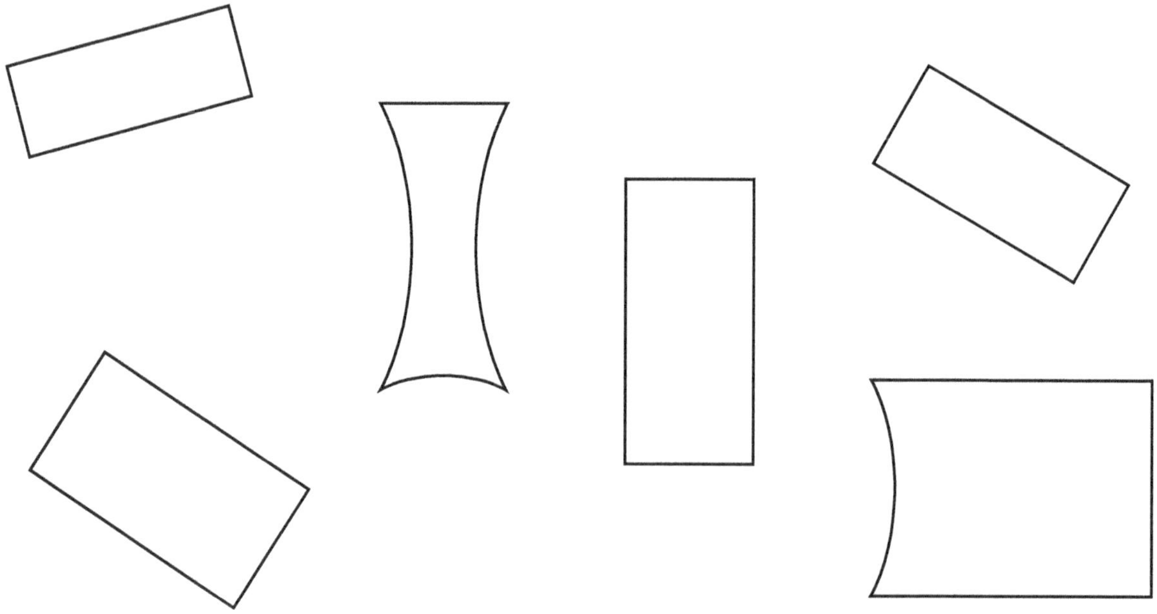

GK-8 Triangles

☐ Count the △.

1.

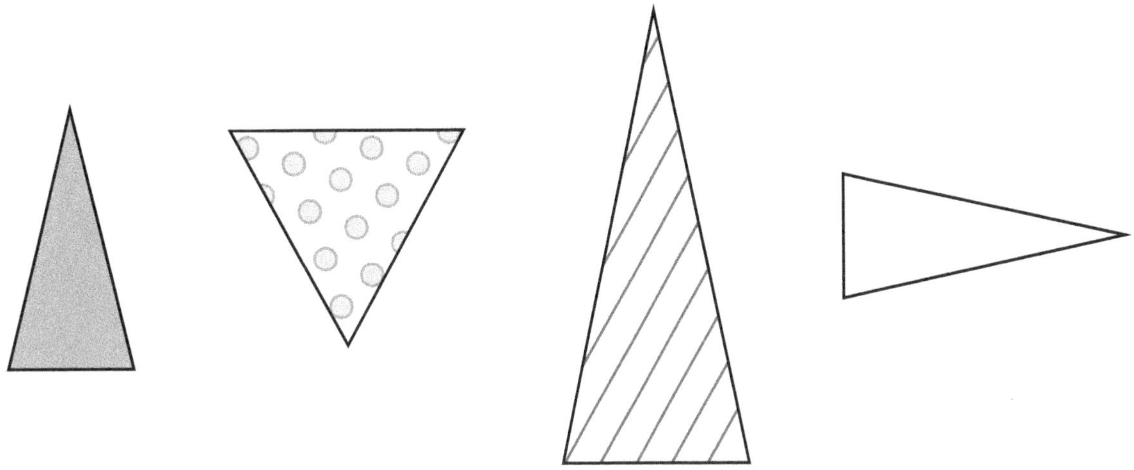

1 2 3 4 5

2.

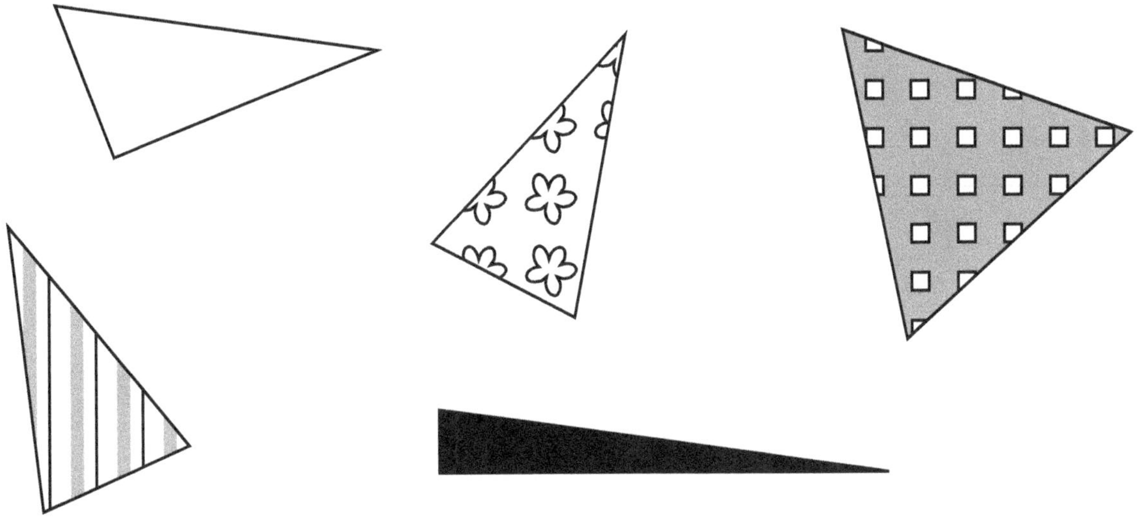

1 2 3 4 5

☐ Color the △.

☐ Draw ✕ on the other shapes.

3.

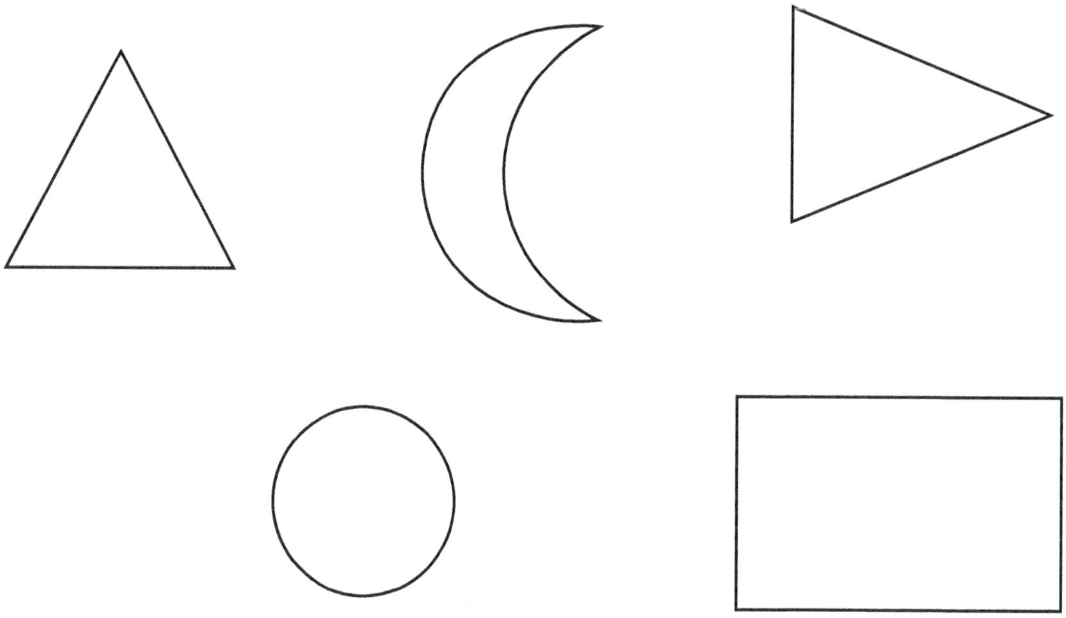

4.

☐ Color the △.

☐ Draw × on the other shapes.

5.

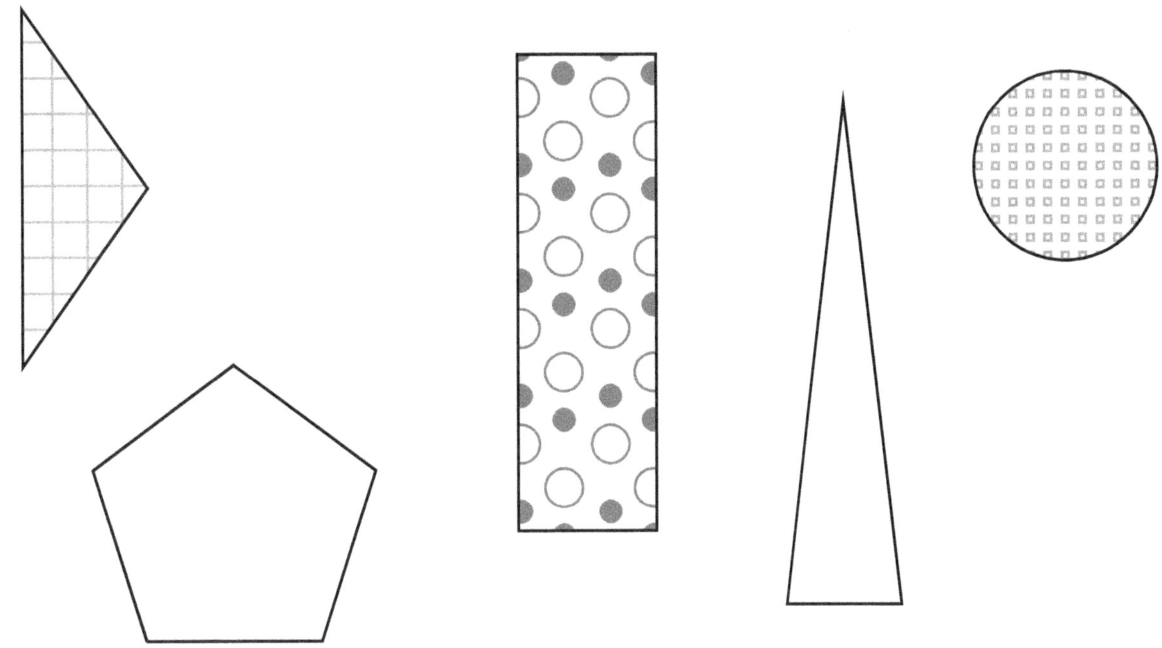

6.

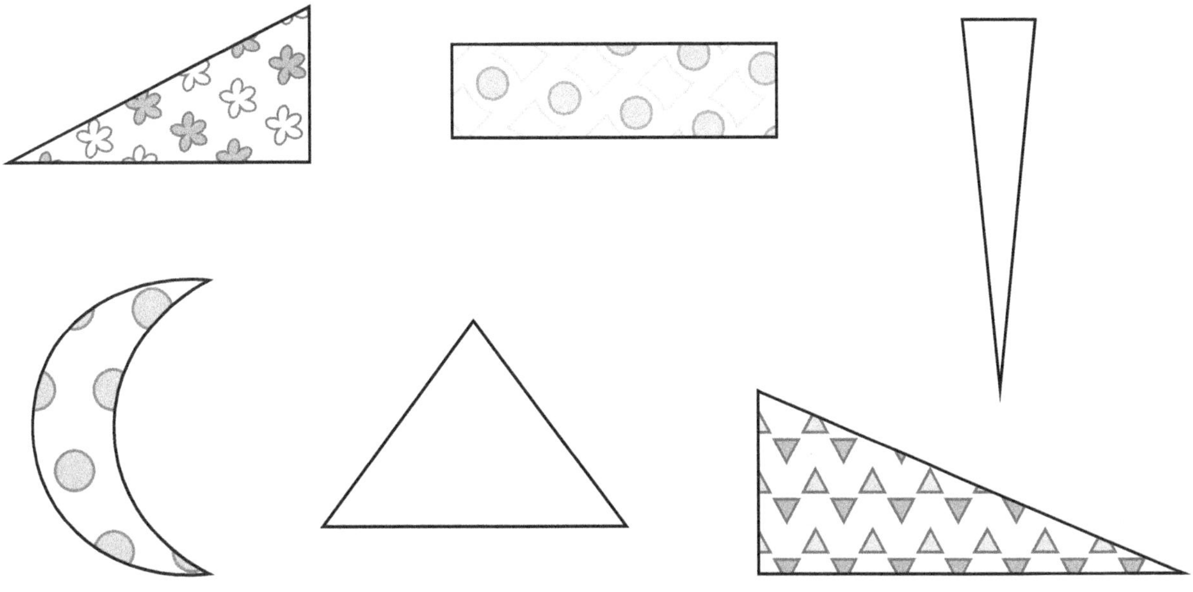

GK-9 Describing and Comparing Shapes

☐ Circle the shapes that are the **same**.

1.

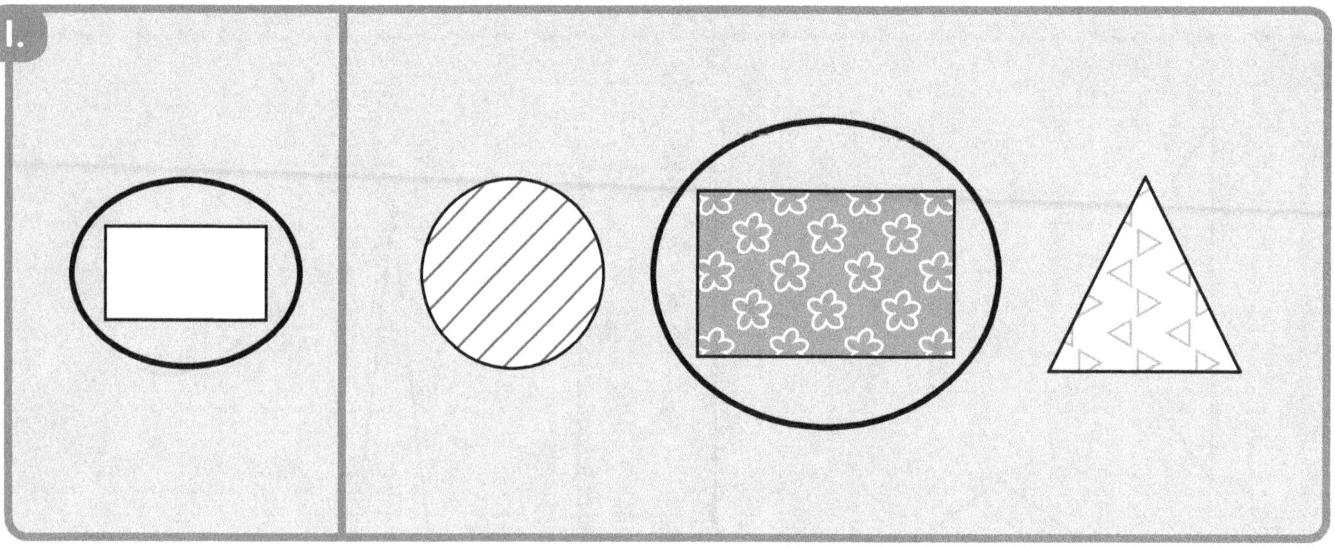

2.

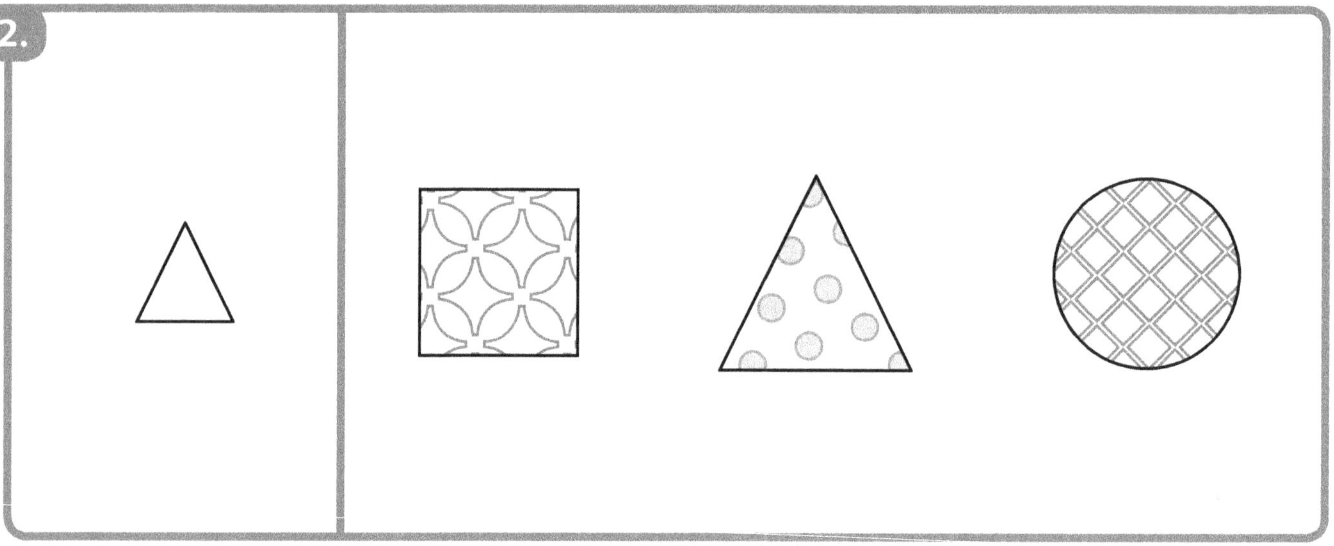

3.

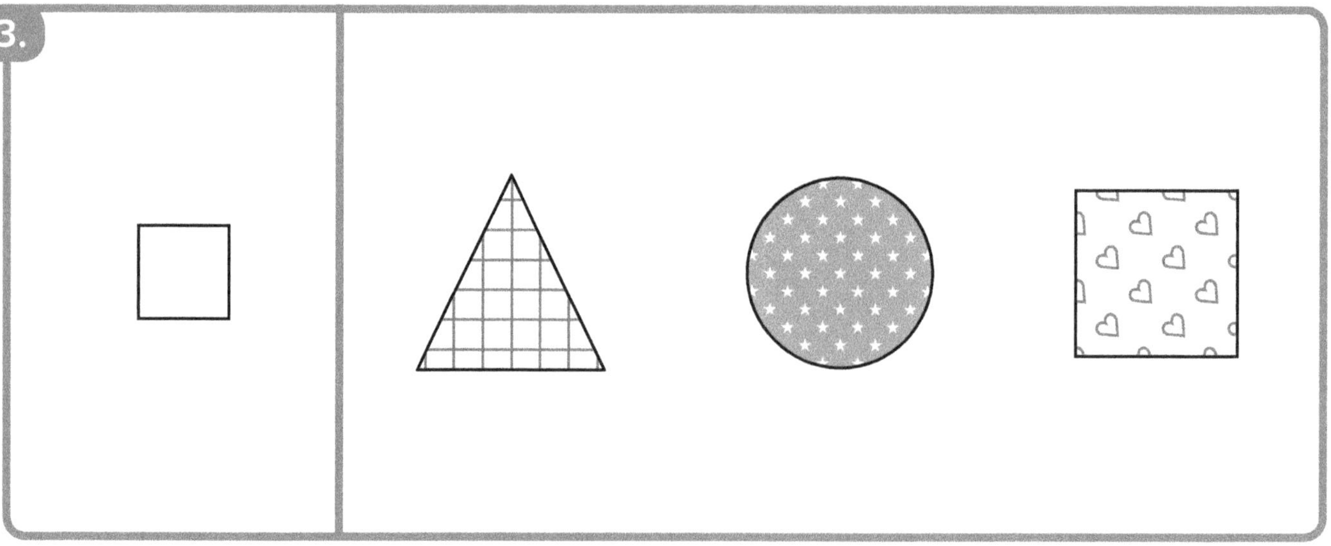

☐ Circle the shapes that are the same.

4.

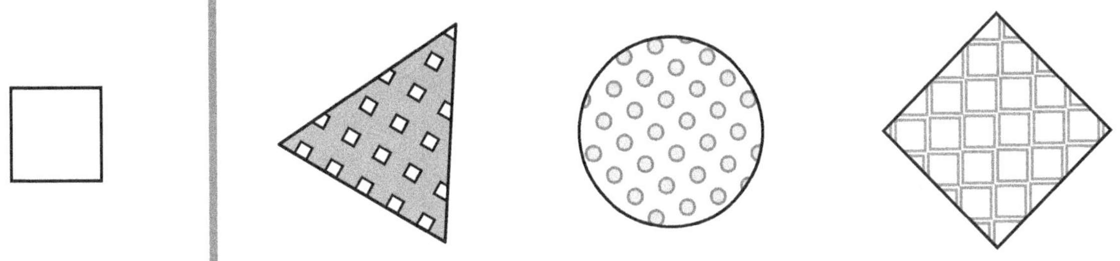

5.

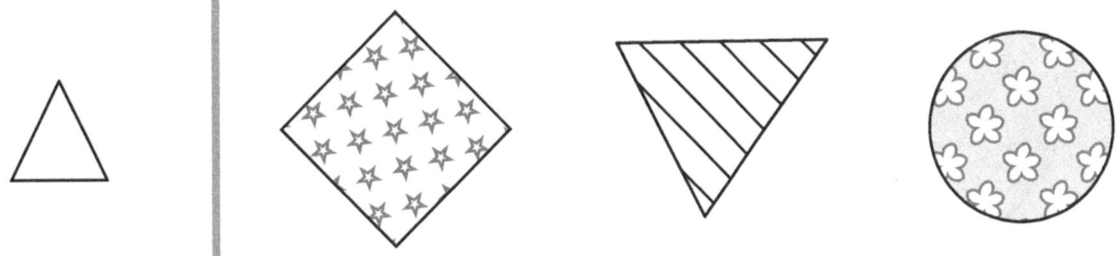

6.

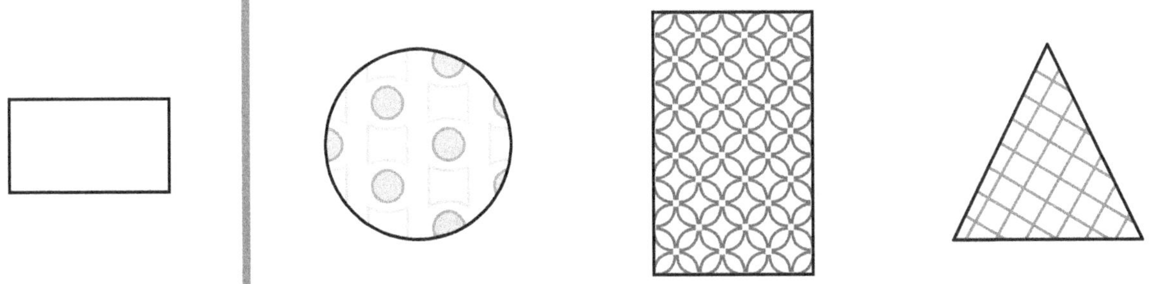

GK-10 Open Shapes and Closed Shapes

☐ Color the **closed shapes.**

☐ Draw X on the **open shapes.**

1.

☐ Color the closed shapes.

☐ Draw X on the open shapes.

2.

GK-11 Above

☐ Circle the shape that is **above**.

1.

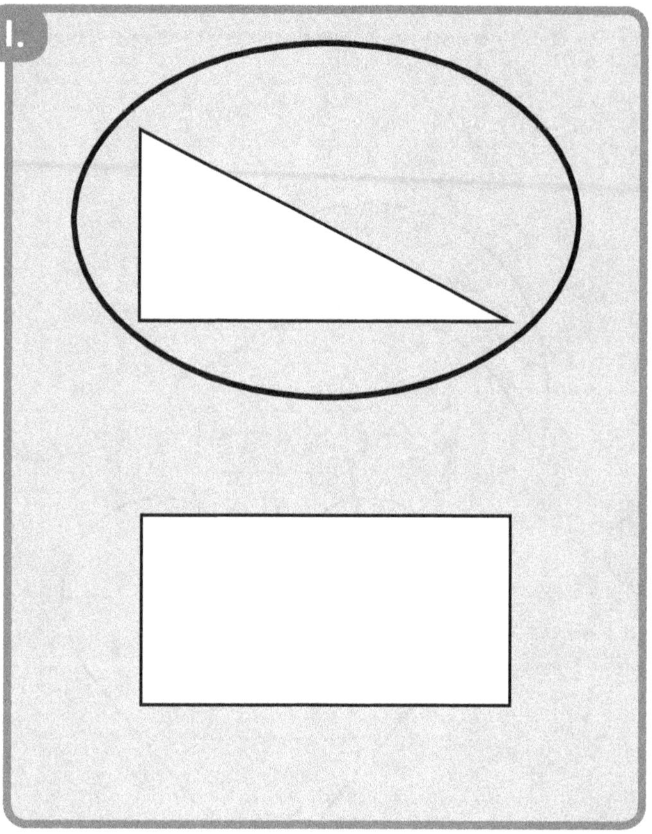

2.

3.

4.

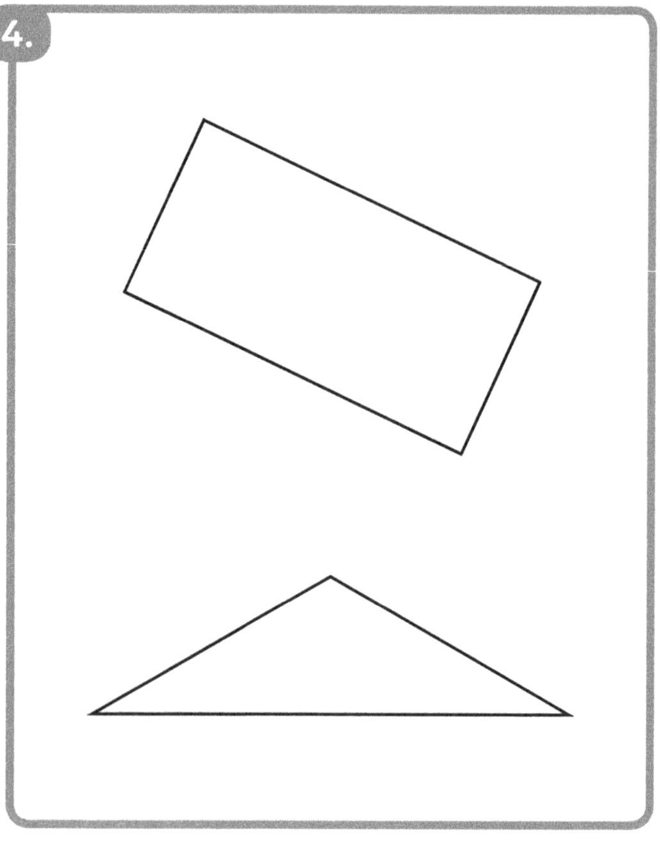

☐ How many shapes are above the line?

5.

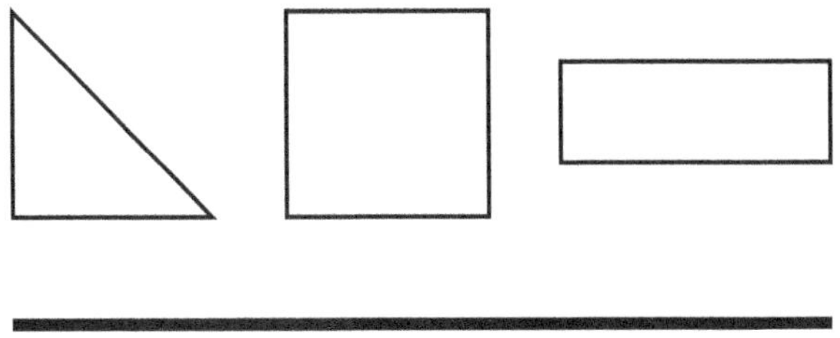

1 2 3 4 5

6.

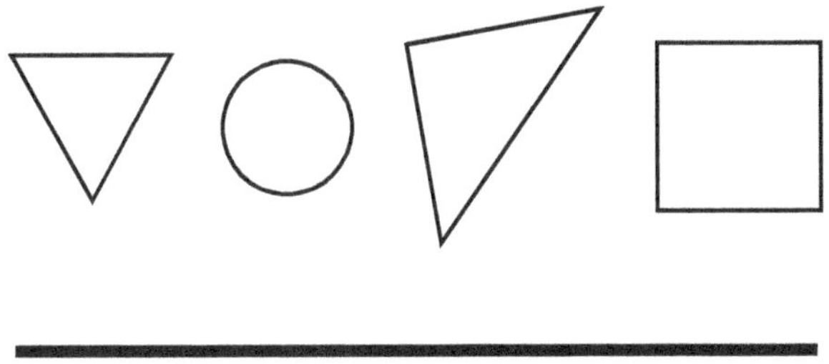

1 2 3 4 5

7.

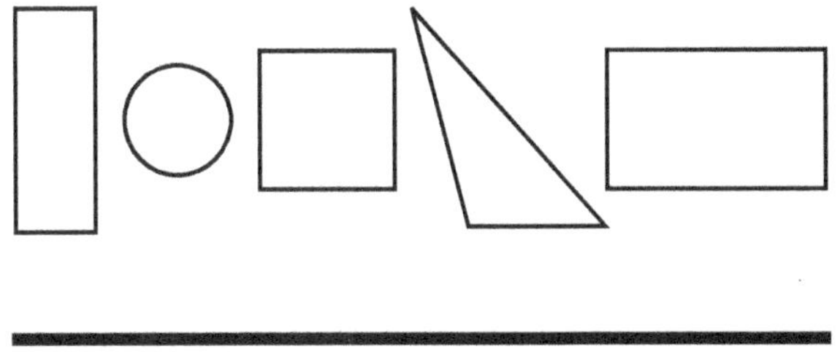

1 2 3 4 5

☐ How many shapes are above the line?

8.

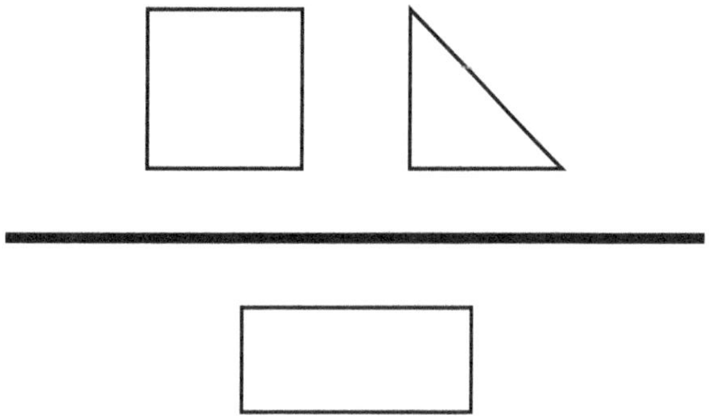

1 2 3 4 5

9.

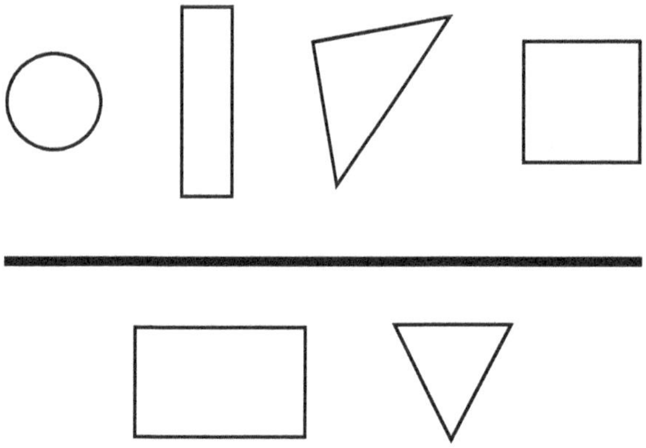

1 2 3 4 5

10.

1 2 3 4 5

GK-12 Below

☐ Circle the shape that is **below**.

1.

2.

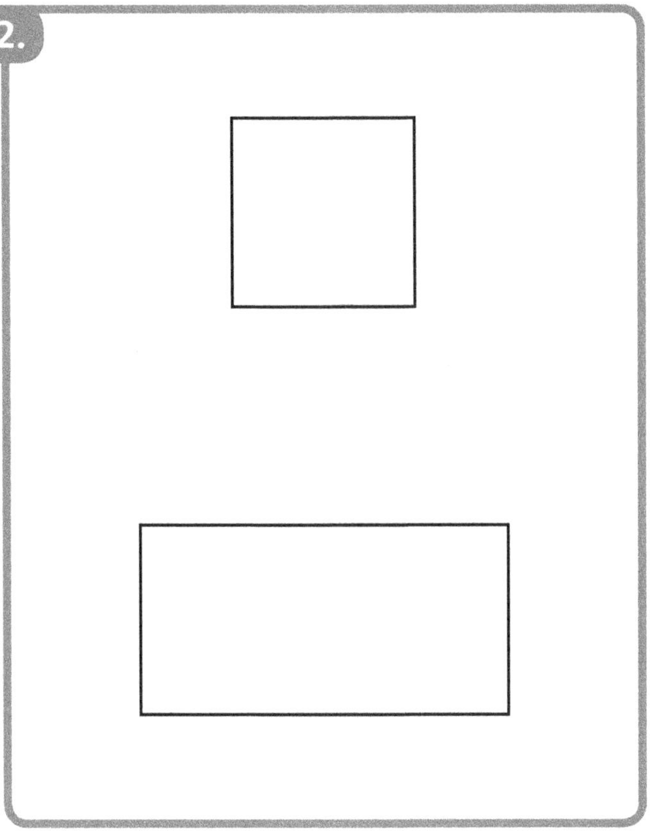

3.

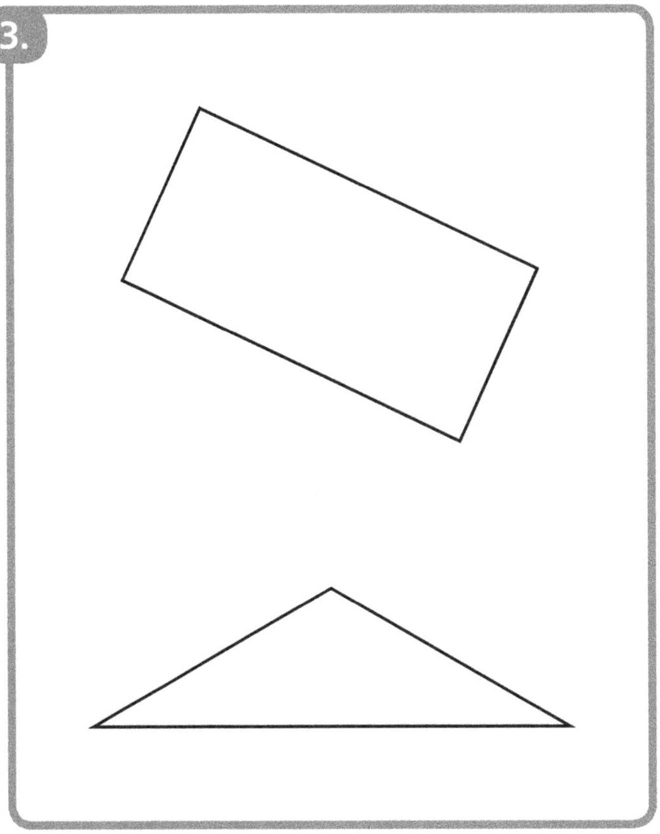

4.

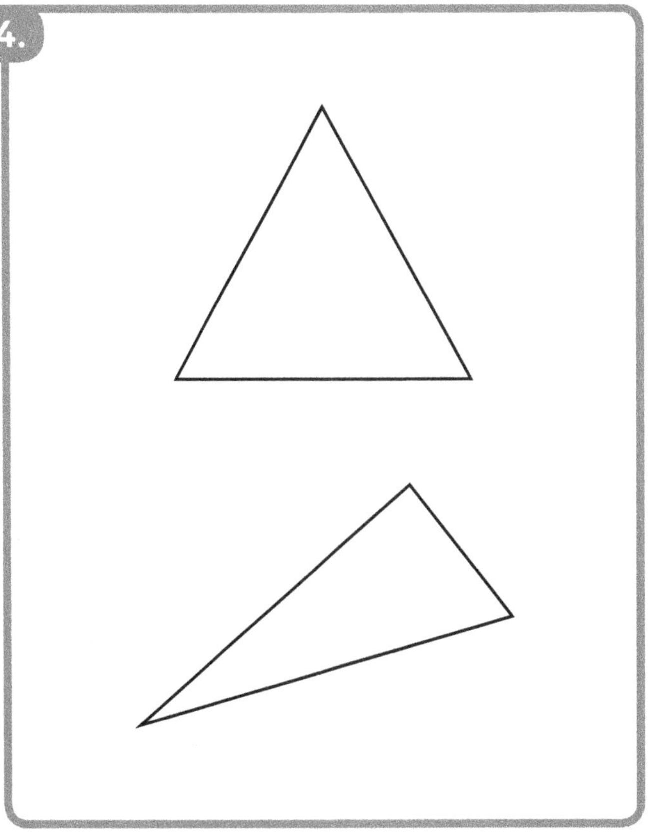

☐ How many shapes are below the line?

5.

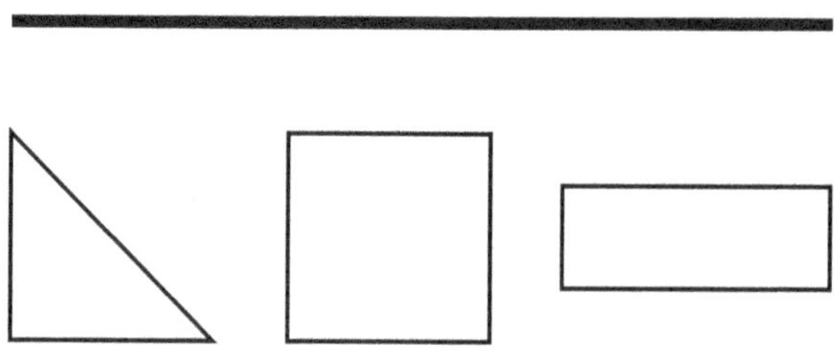

1 2 3 4 5

6.

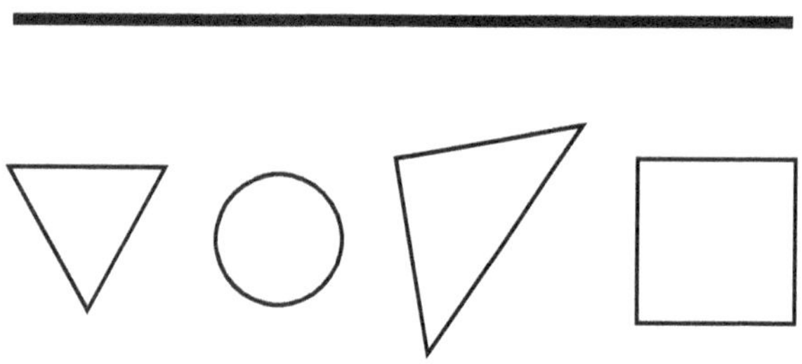

1 2 3 4 5

7.

1 2 3 4 5

☐ How many shapes are below the line?

8.

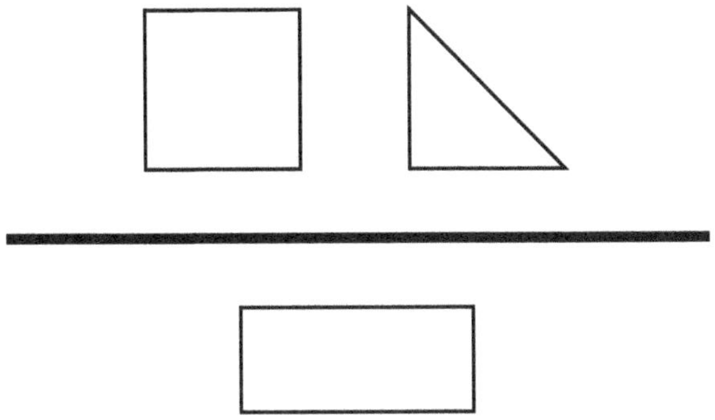

1 2 3 4 5

9.

1 2 3 4 5

10.

1 2 3 4 5

GK-13 Beside

☐ Draw ✕ on the shape **beside** the ○.

1.

2.

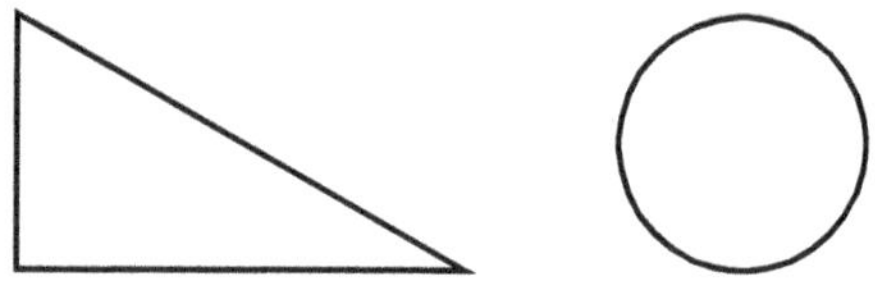

3.

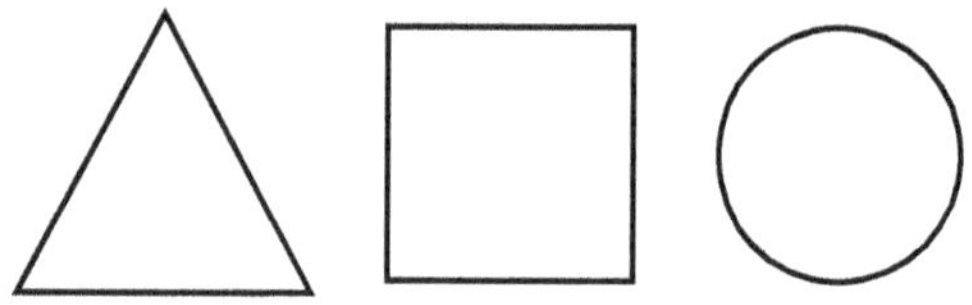

4.

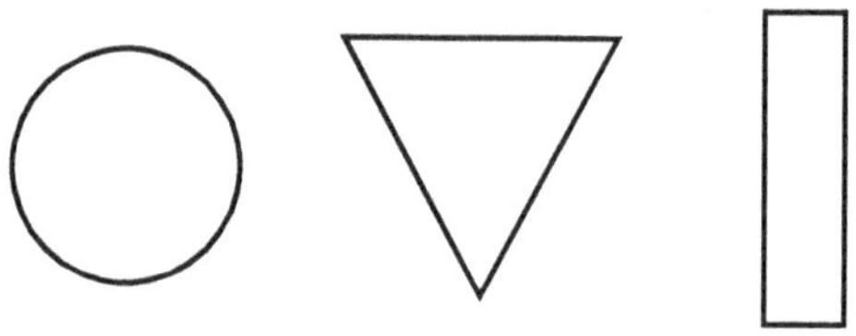

5.

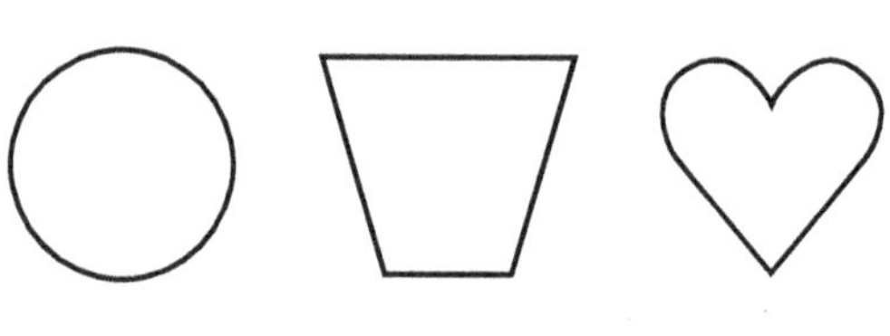

6.

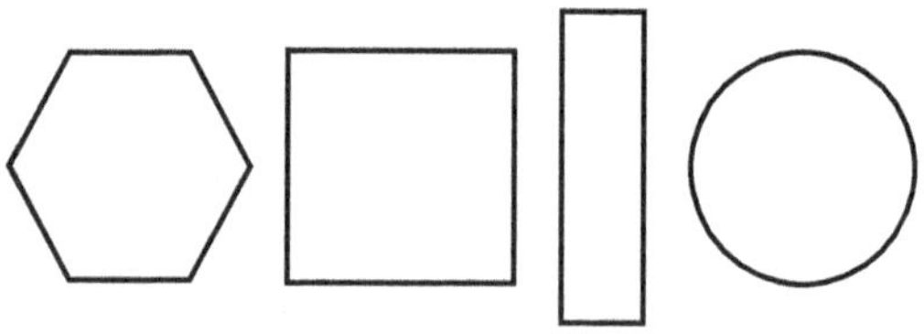

☐ Draw ✕ on the shapes beside the ◯.

7.

8.

9.

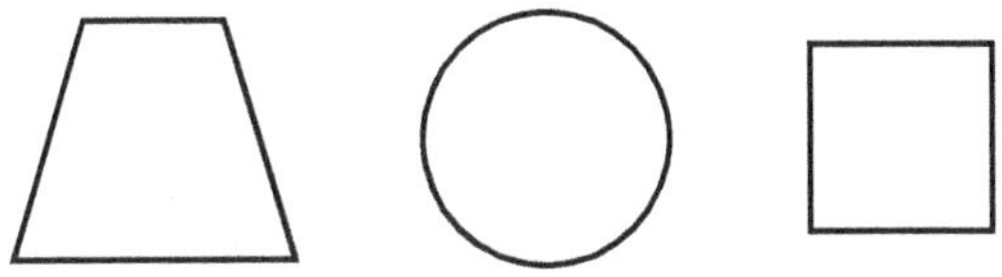

10.

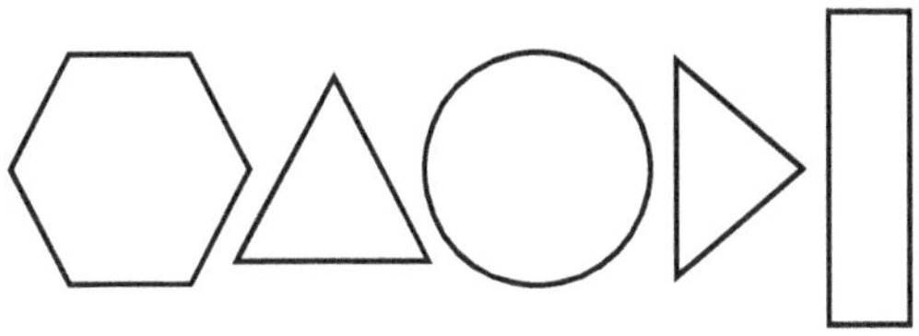

11.

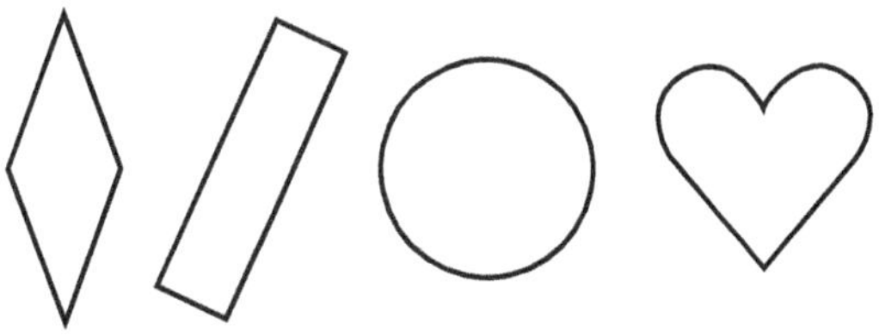

12.

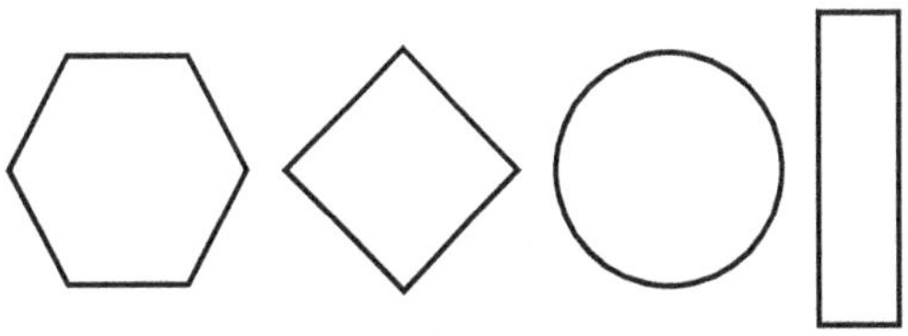

GK-14 Combining Shapes

☐ Use **2** pattern blocks to cover the shape.

1.

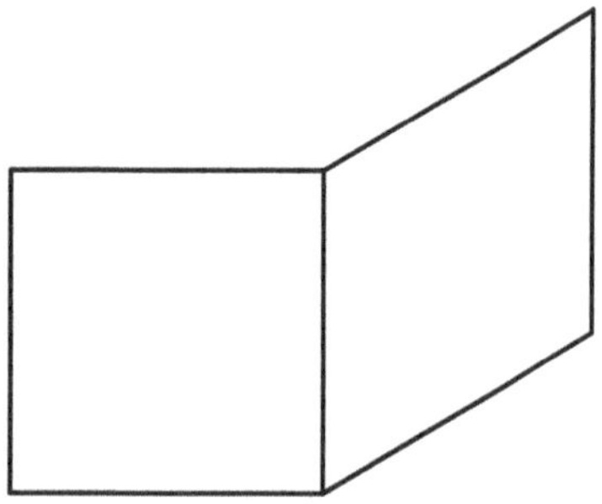

2.

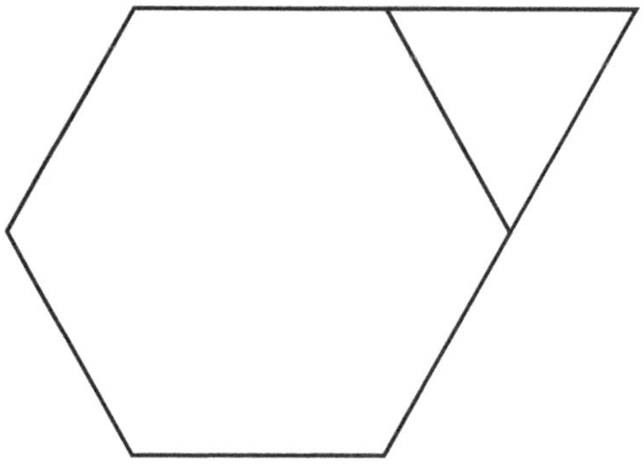

3.

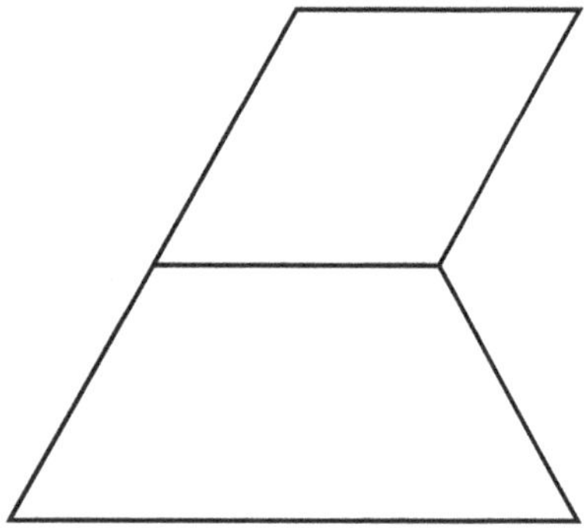

4.

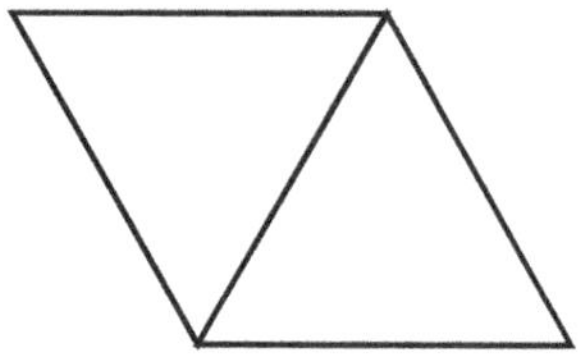

5.

6.

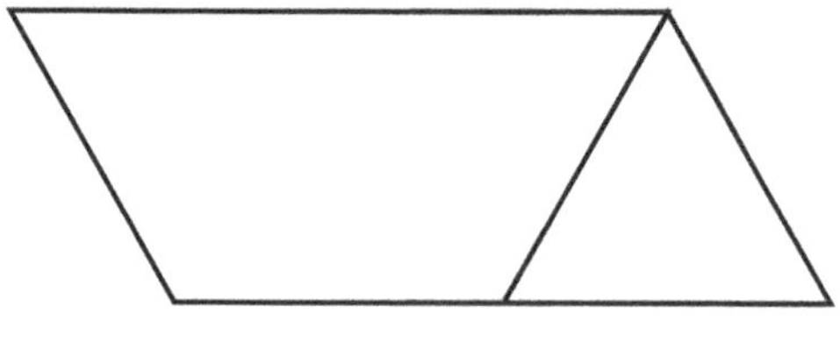

☐ Use pattern blocks to cover the shape.

7.

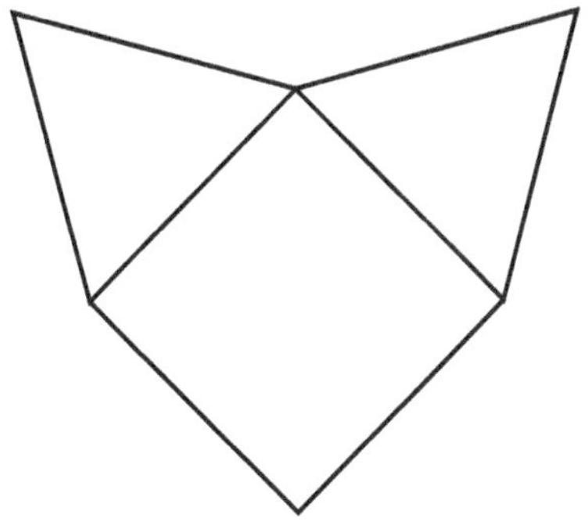

8.

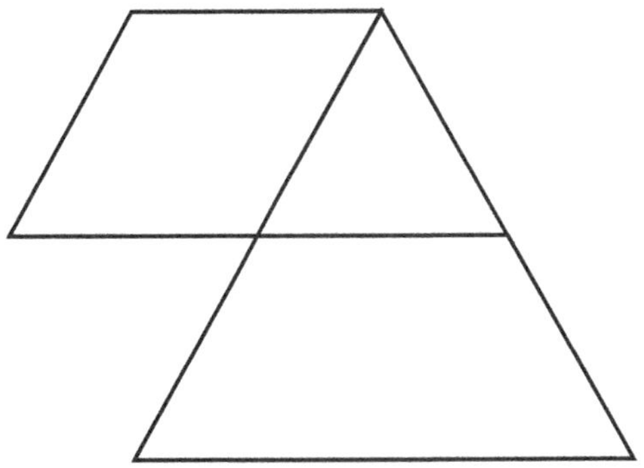

9.

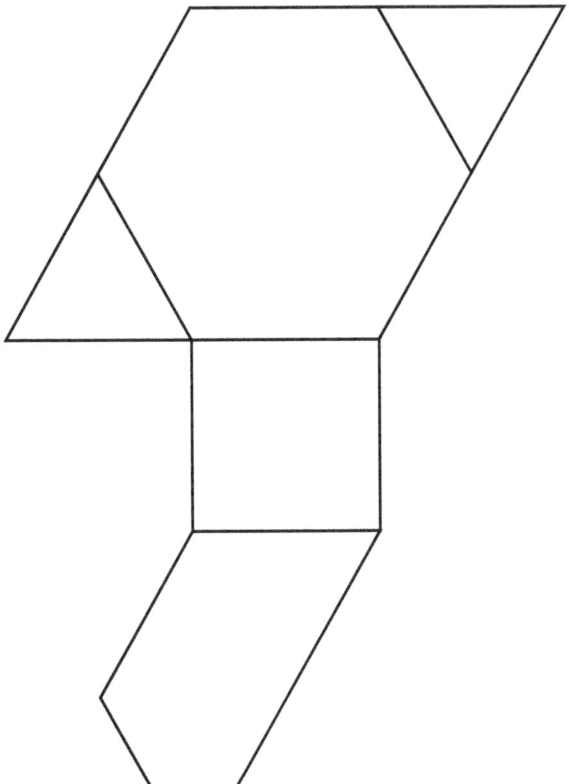

10.

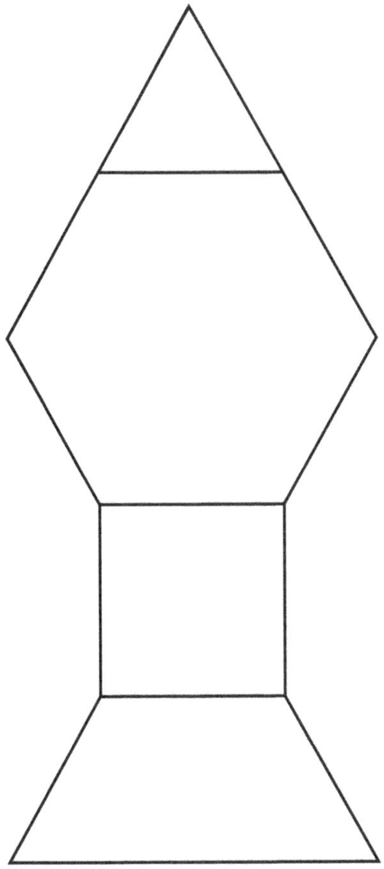

☐ Use pattern blocks to cover the shape.

11.

12.

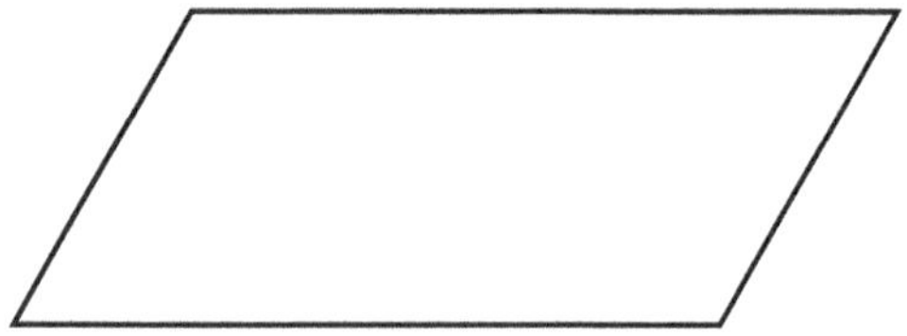

13.

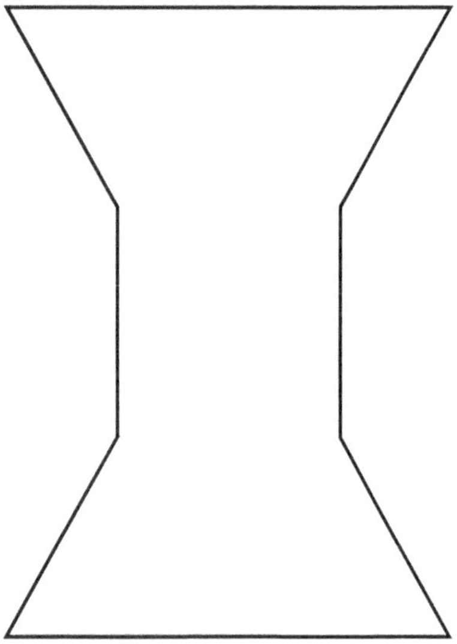

14.

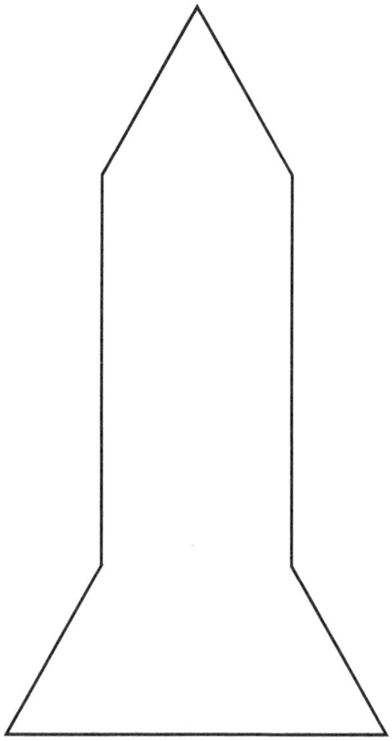

CCK-25 Counting to 40

☐ Trace.

1.

30 31 32

33 34 35

36 37 38

39 40

2.

3 3 3 3 3 3 3

☐ Write 3.

3.

CCK-26 Counting 6 and 7

How many?

☐ Count. Circle the number.

1.

1 (2) 3 4 5 6 7

2.

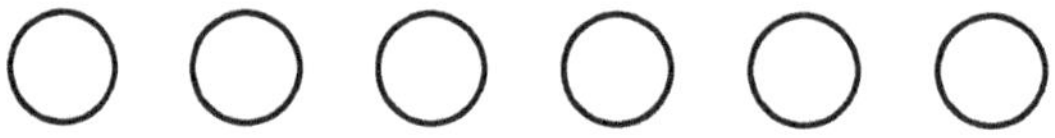

1 2 3 4 5 6 7

3.

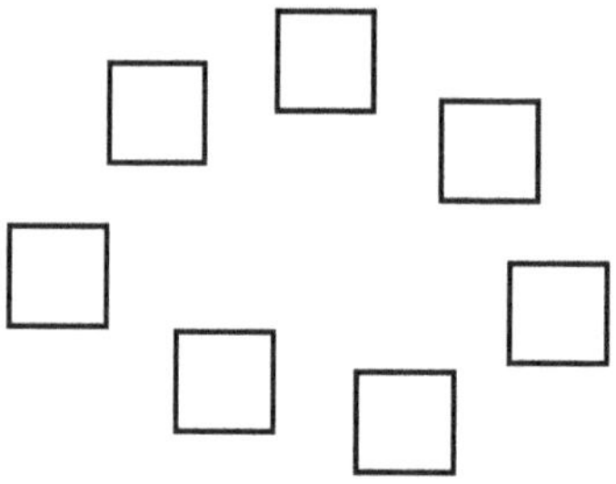

1 2 3 4 5 6 7

4.

1 2 3 4 5 6 7

How many?

☐ Count. Circle the number.

5.

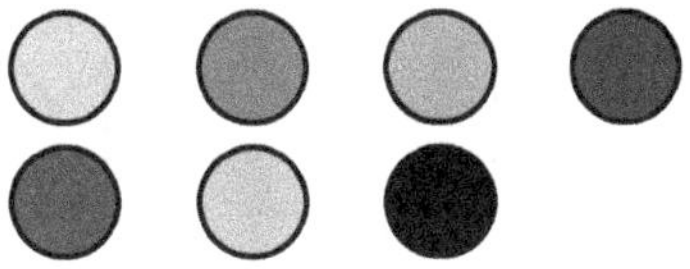

1 2 3 4 5 6 7

6.

1 2 3 4 5 6 7

7.

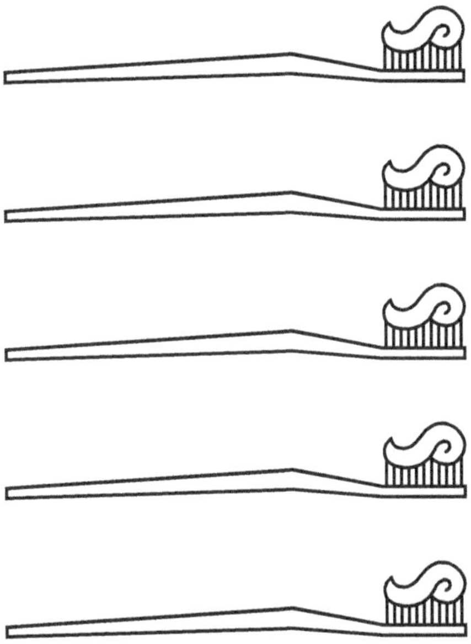

1 2 3 4 5 6 7

☐ Show counting out.

8.

2

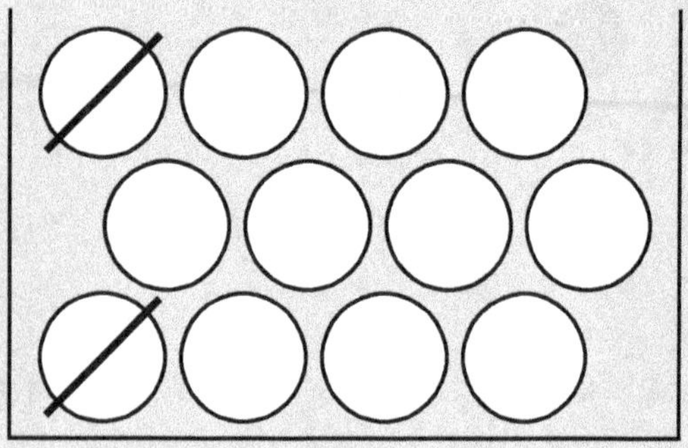

9.

5

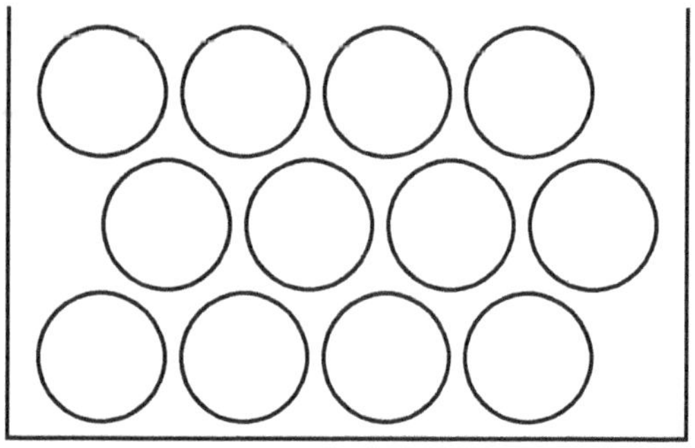

10.

3

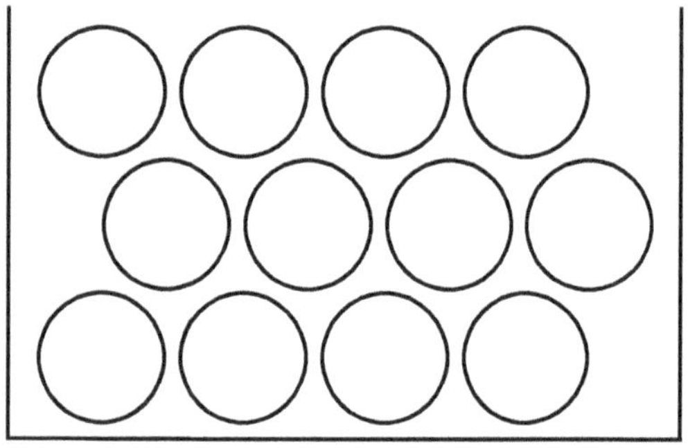

11.

6

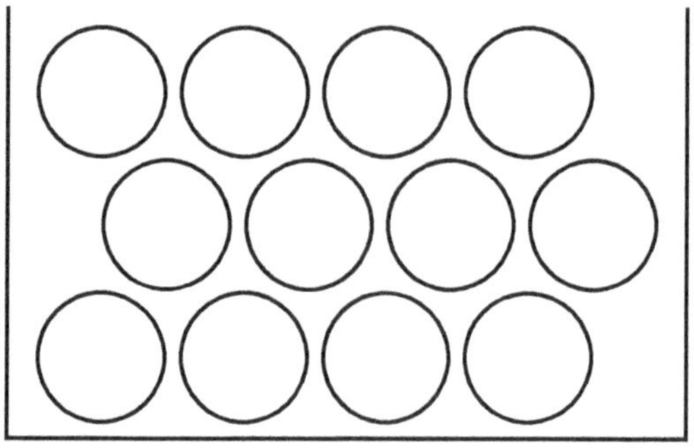

12.

7

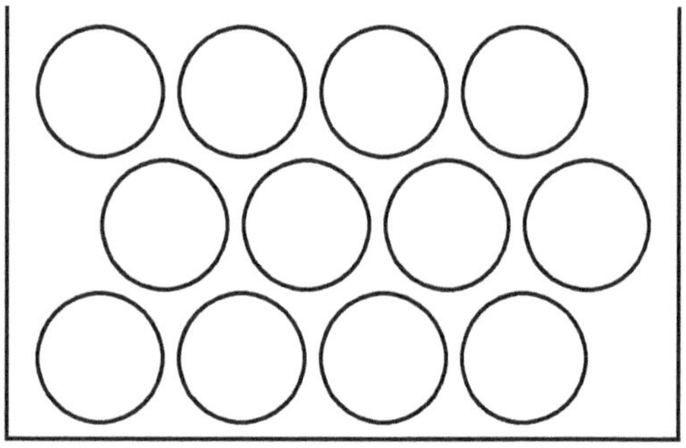

13.

4

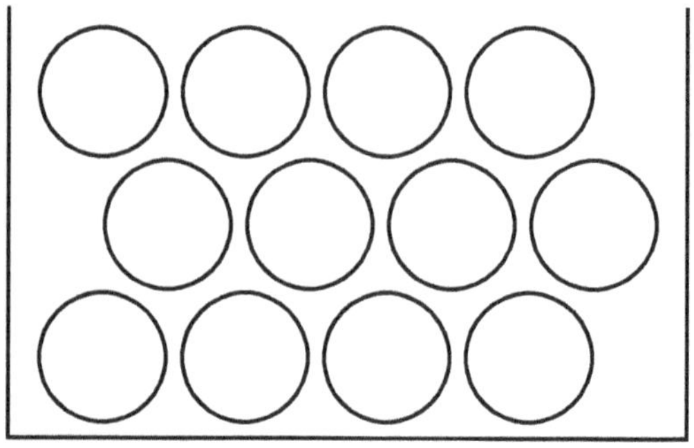

CCK-27 The Numbers 6 and 7

☐ Match by drawing lines.

1.

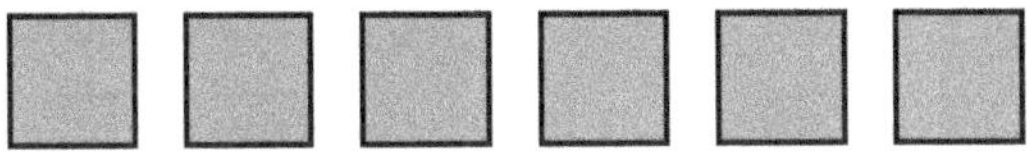 •   • 4

 •   • 6

2.

 •   • 5

 •   • 7

3.

 •   • 6

 •   • 7

4.

 •   • 5

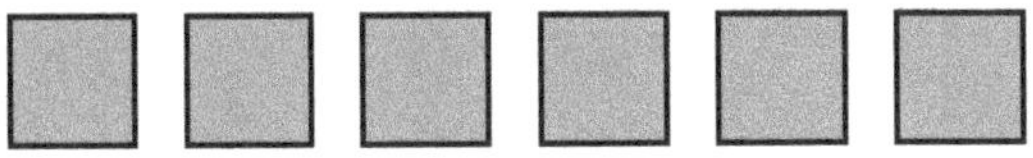 •   • 6

☐ Match by drawing lines.

5.

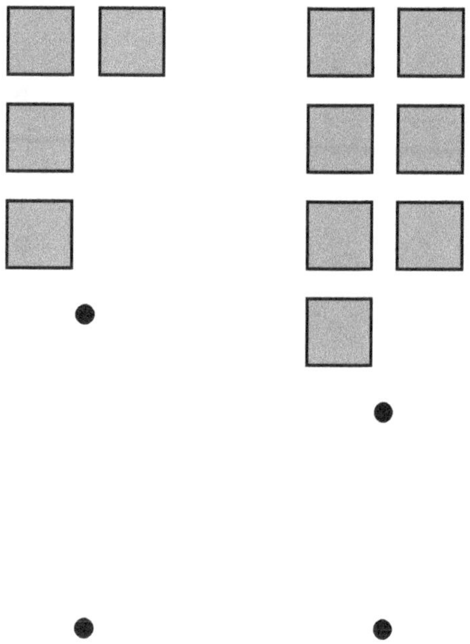

4 7

6.

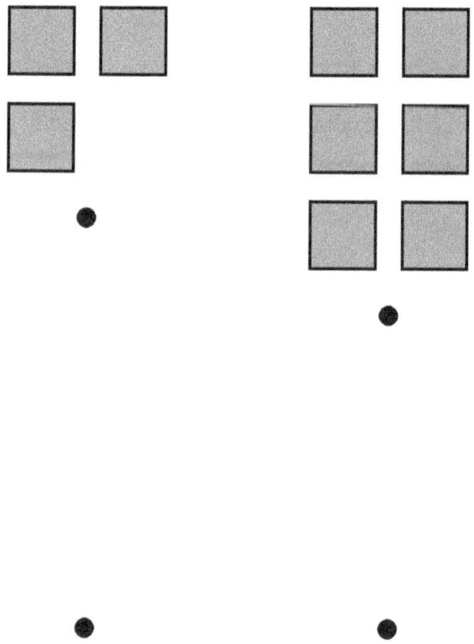

6 3

7.

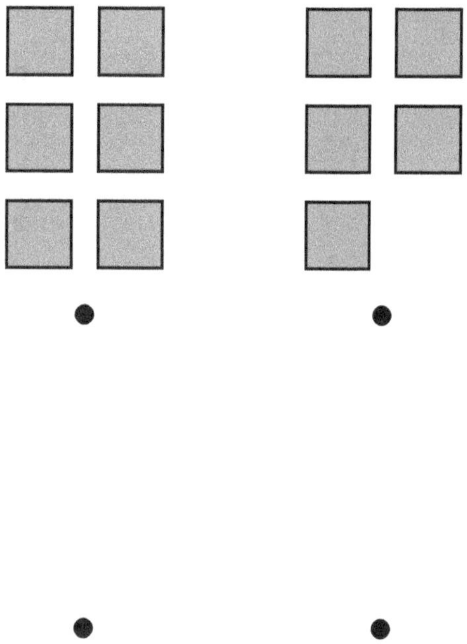

5 6

8.

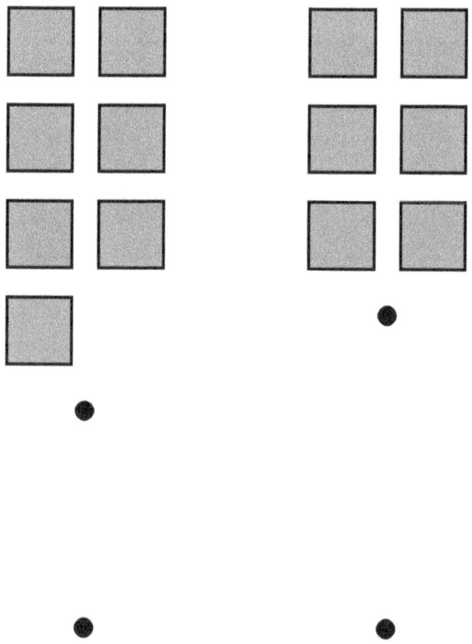

7 6

☐ Match by drawing lines.

9.

 • 3

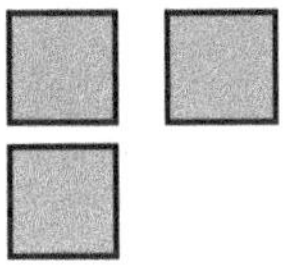 • 7

10.

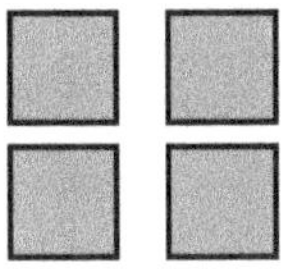 • 4

 • 5

11.

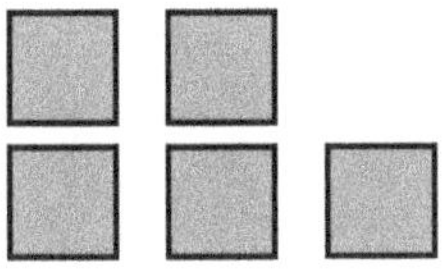 • 6

 • 5

12.

 • 7

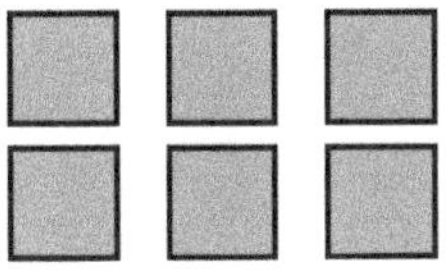 • 6

CCK-28 Writing 6 and 7

☐ Trace.

1.

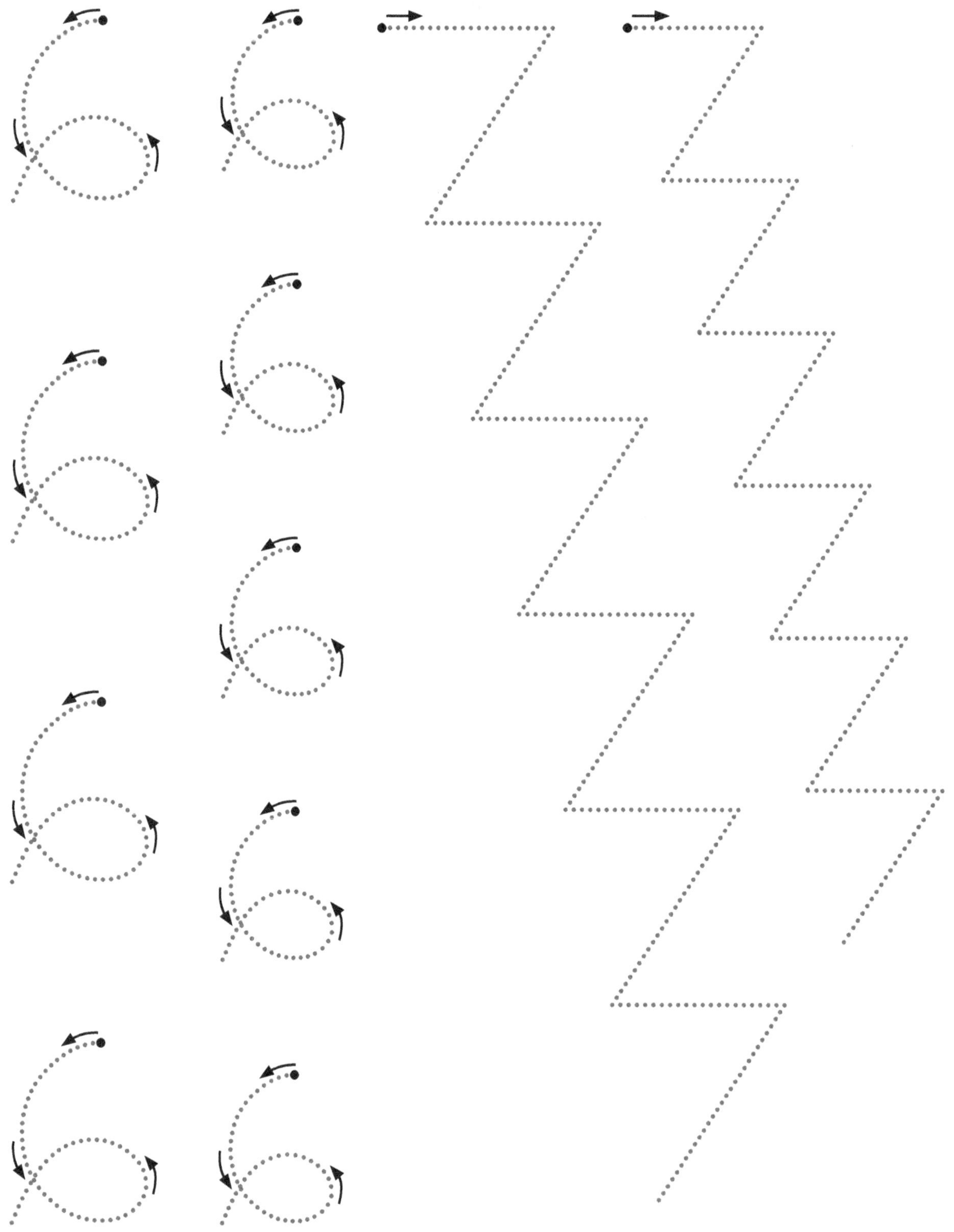

☐ Trace.

2.

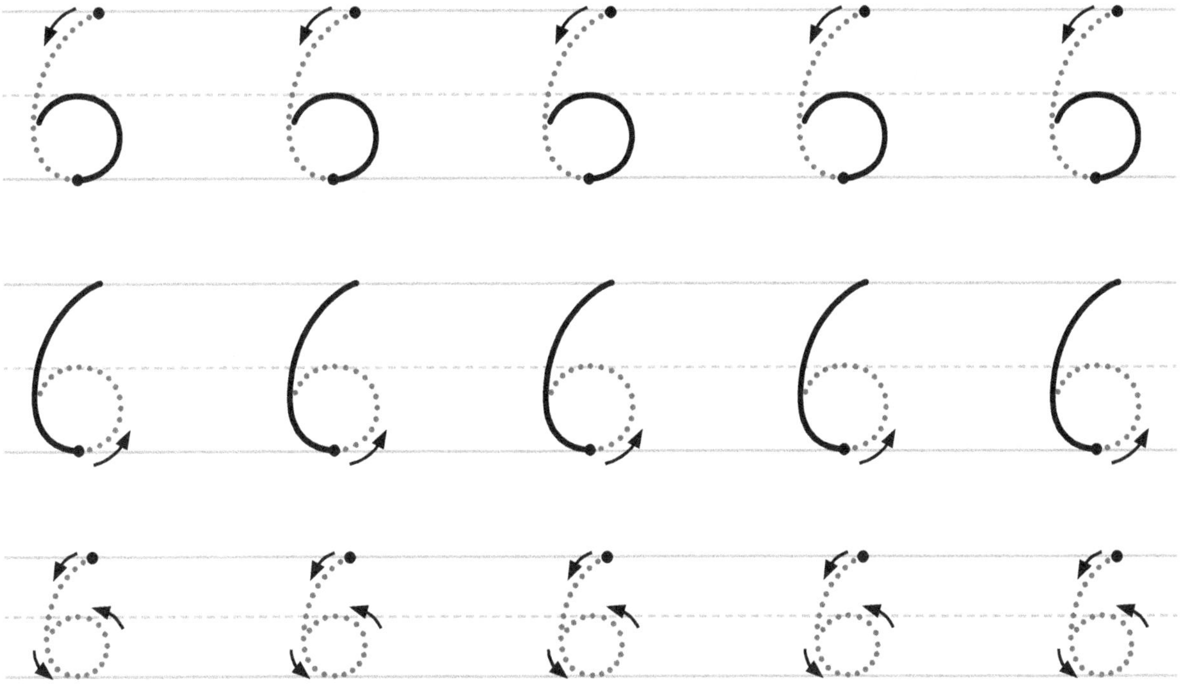

3.

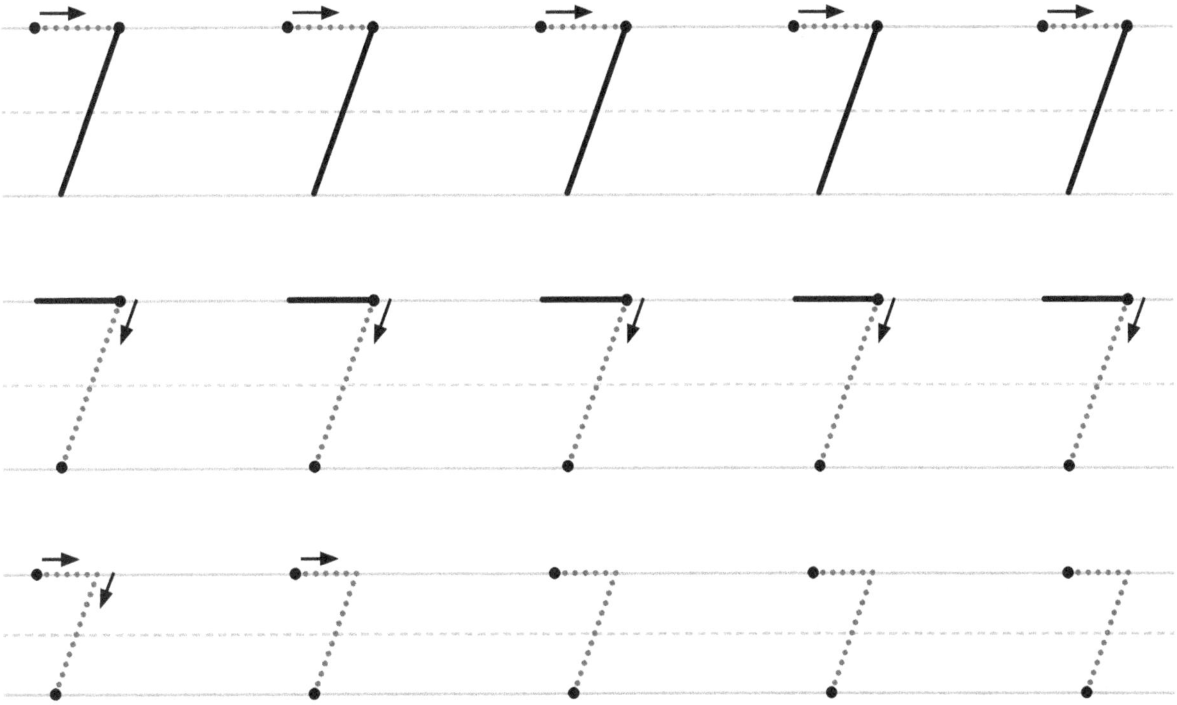

CCK-29 Counting 8 and 9

☐ Show counting out.

1.

4

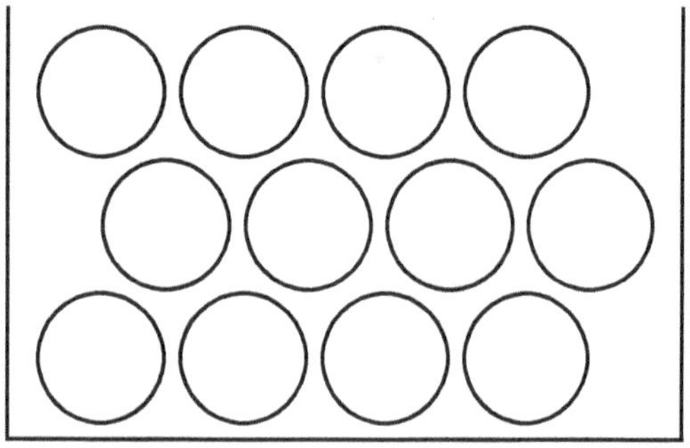

2.

6

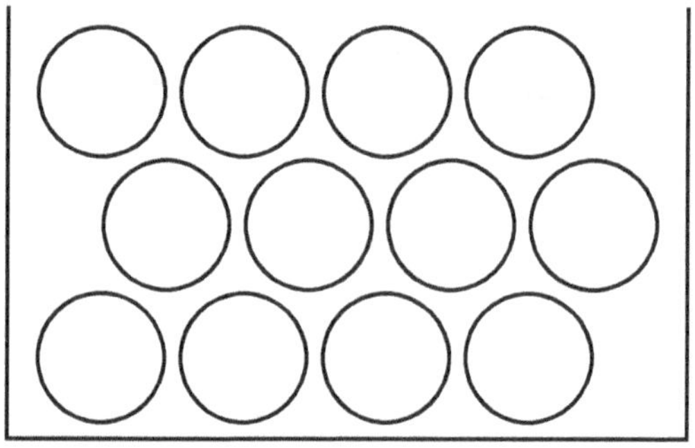

3.

9

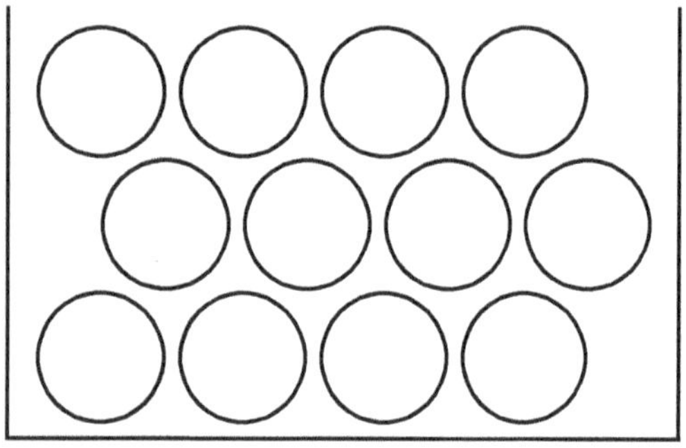

4.

8

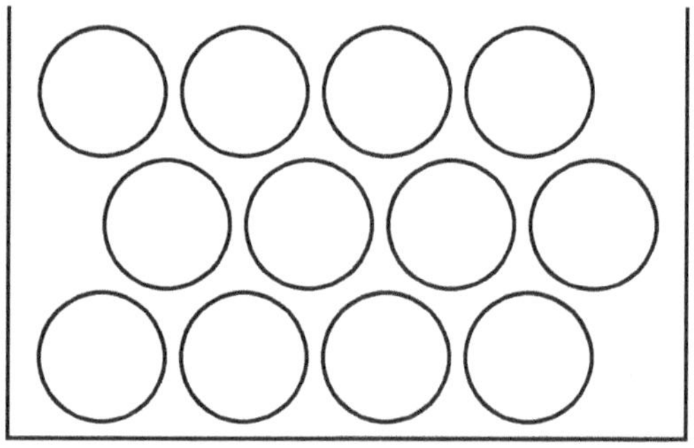

5.

7

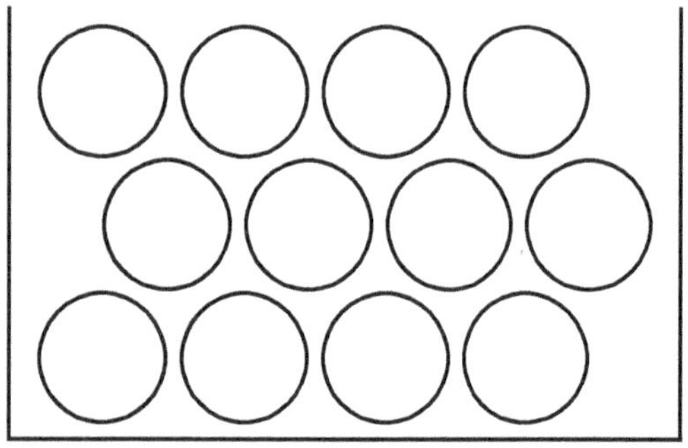

6.

5

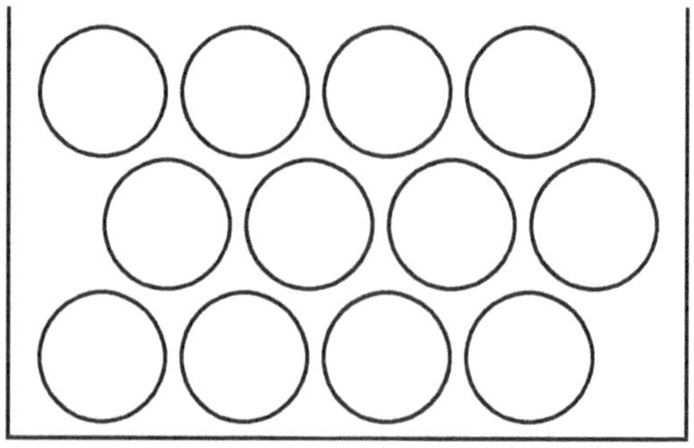

☐ Use ■.

☐ Move and count each ■.

☐ Circle the number.

7.

8 9

8.

8 9

- [ ] Use ■.
- [ ] Move and count each ■.
- [ ] Circle the number.

9.

8 9

10.

8 9

CCK-30 The Numbers 8 and 9

☐ Match by drawing lines.

1.

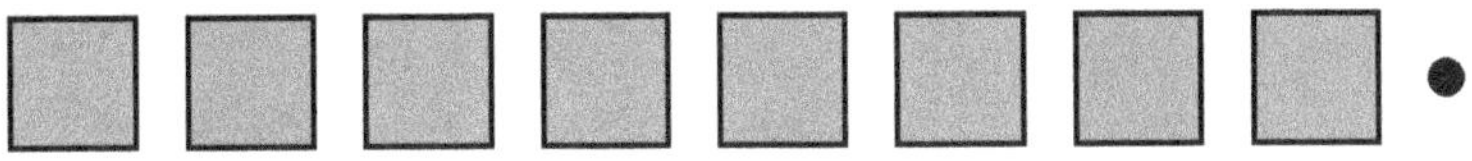

• 8

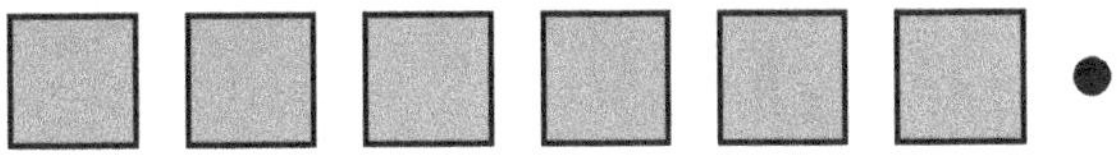

• 6

2.

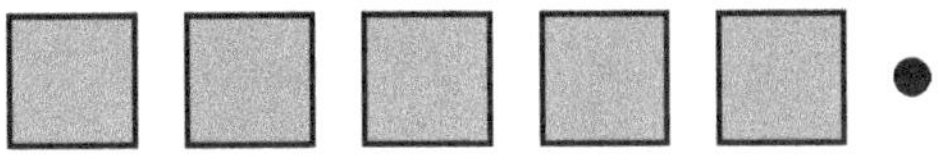

• 5

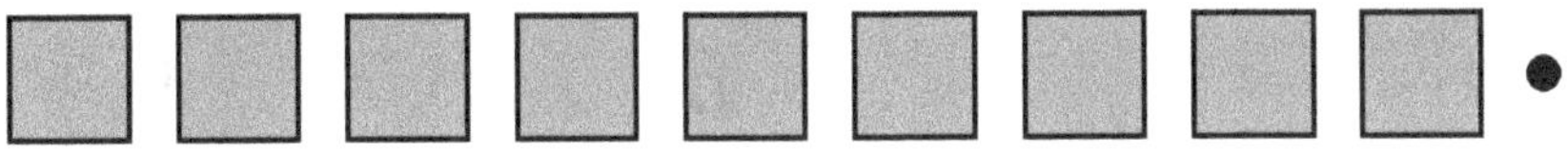

• 9

3.

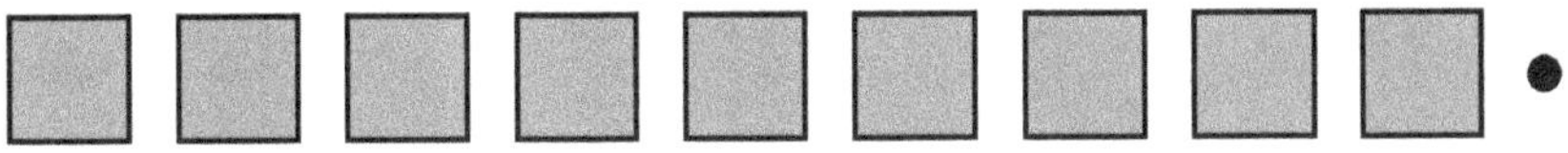

• 7

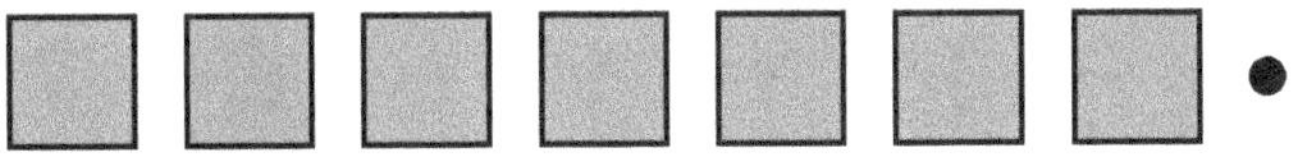

• 9

4.

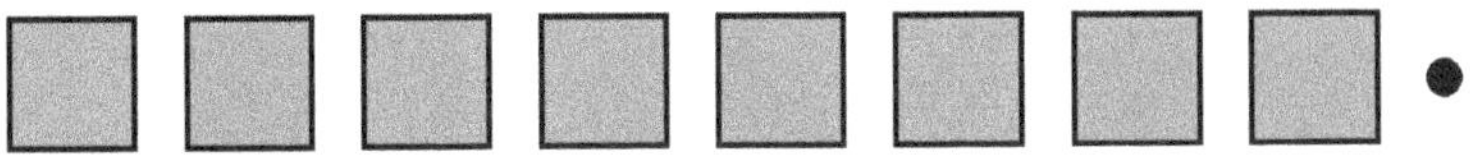

• 7

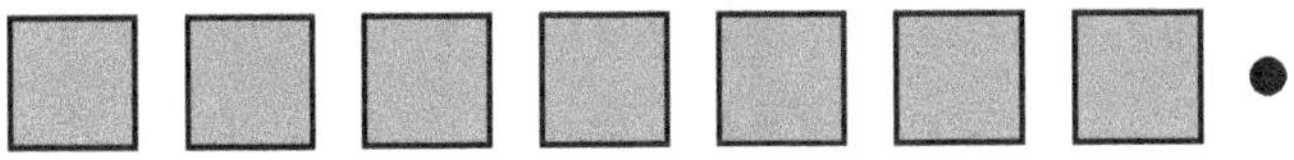

• 8

☐ Match by drawing lines.

5.

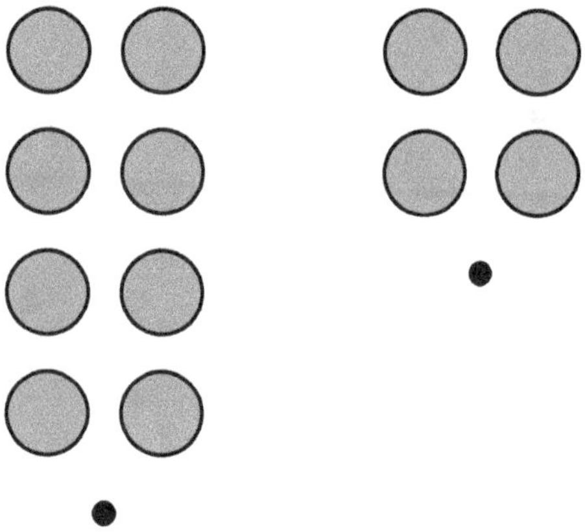

4 8

6.

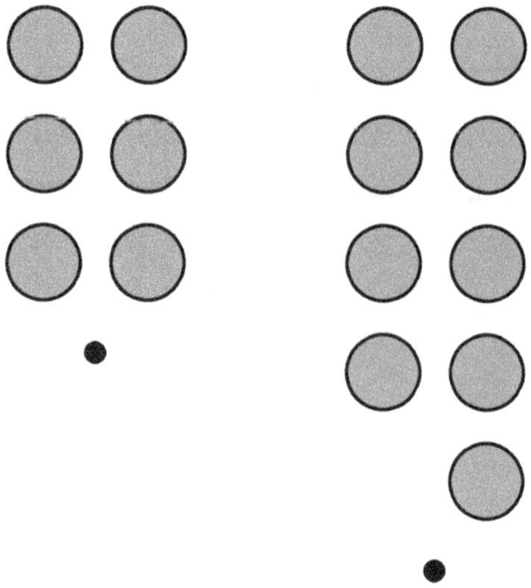

6 9

7.

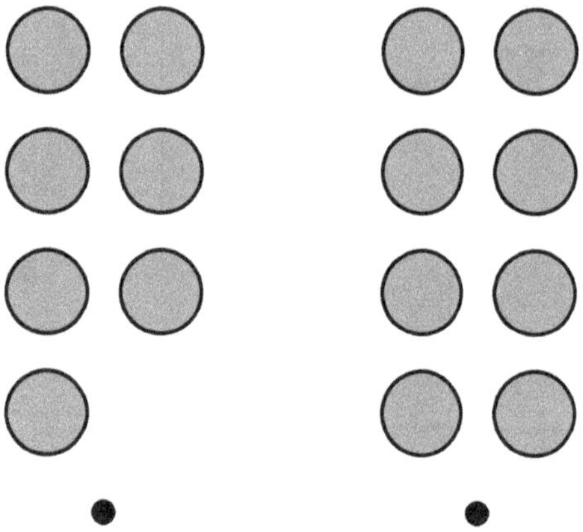

8 7

8.

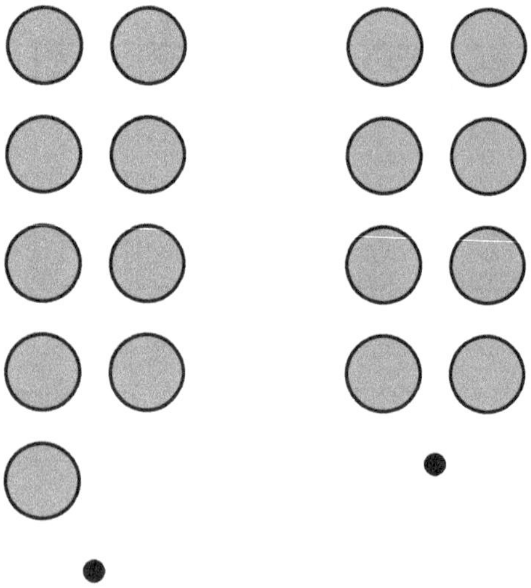

9 8

☐ **BONUS:** Match by drawing lines.

9.

 • | • 8

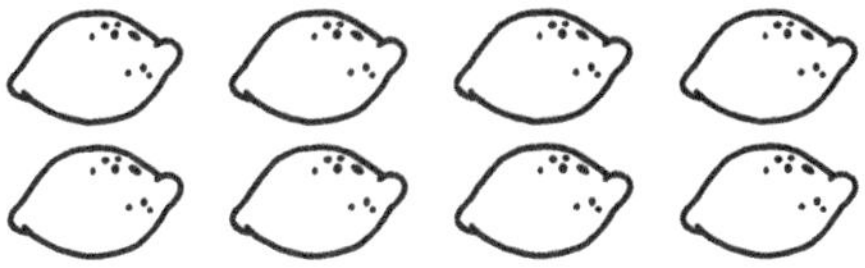 • | • 4

10.

 • | • 9

 • | • 5

11.

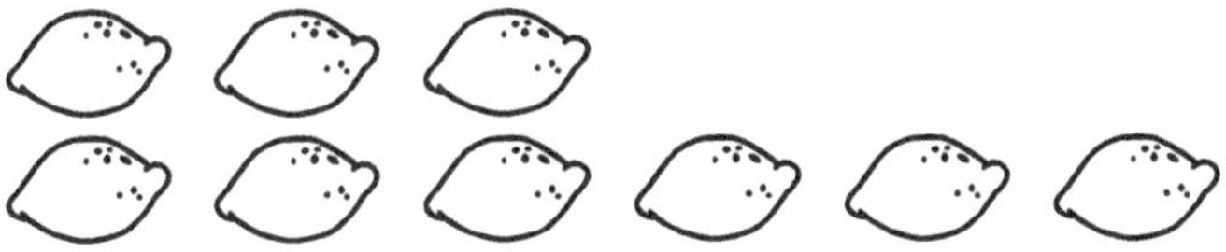 • | • 8

 • | • 9

12.

 • | • 6

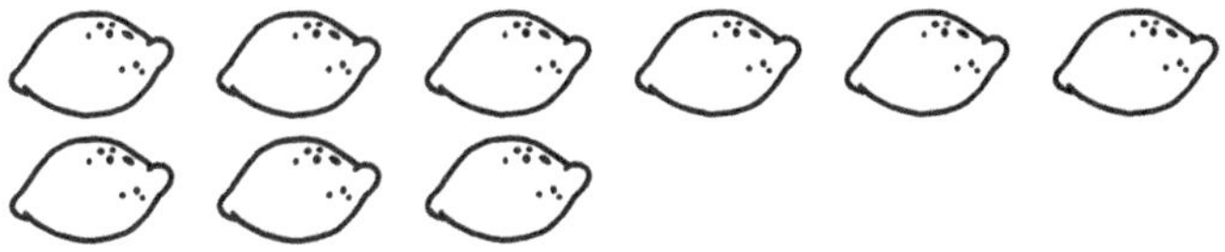 • | • 9

CCK-31 Writing 8 and 9

☐ Trace.

1.

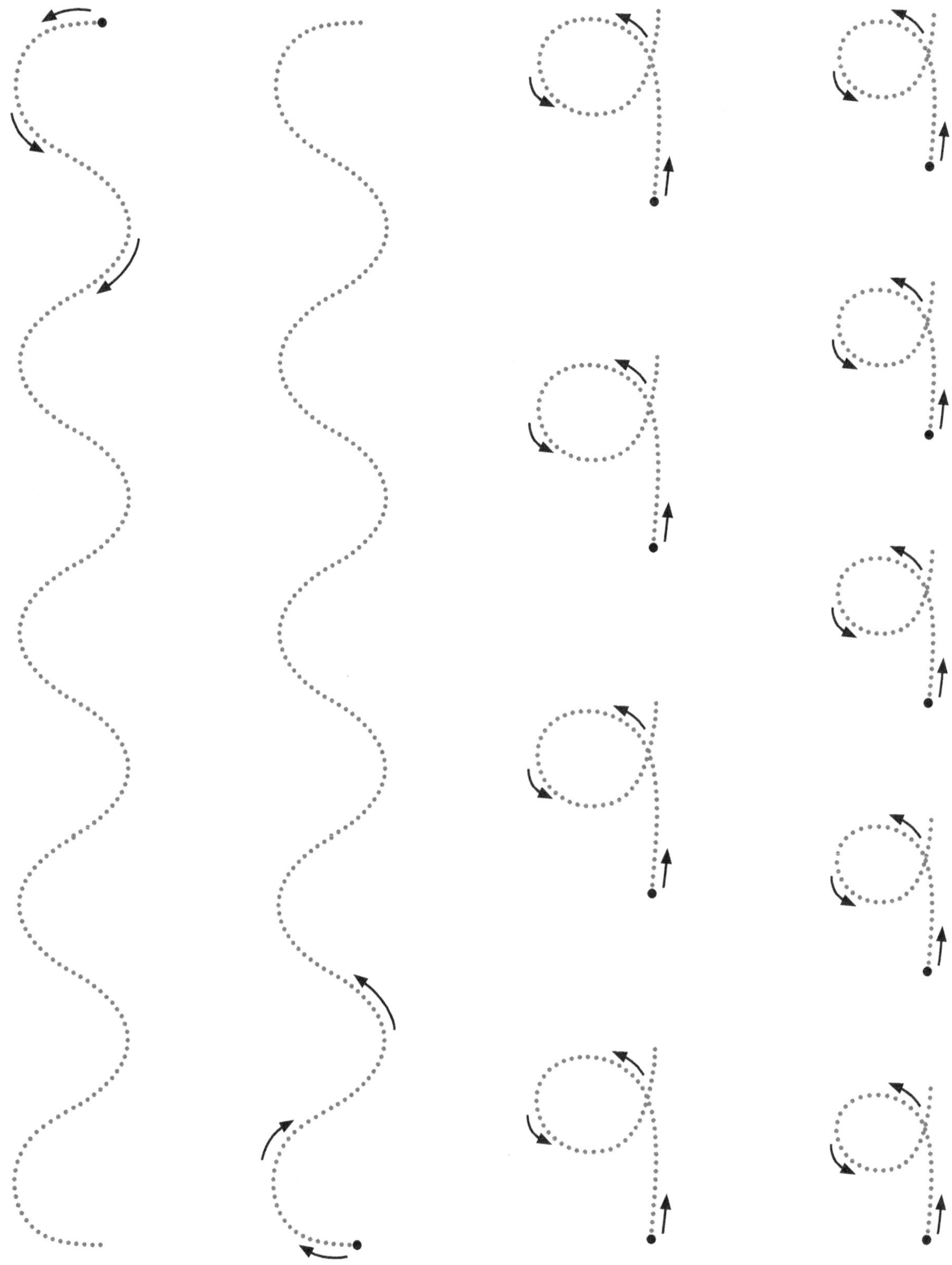

☐ Trace.

2.

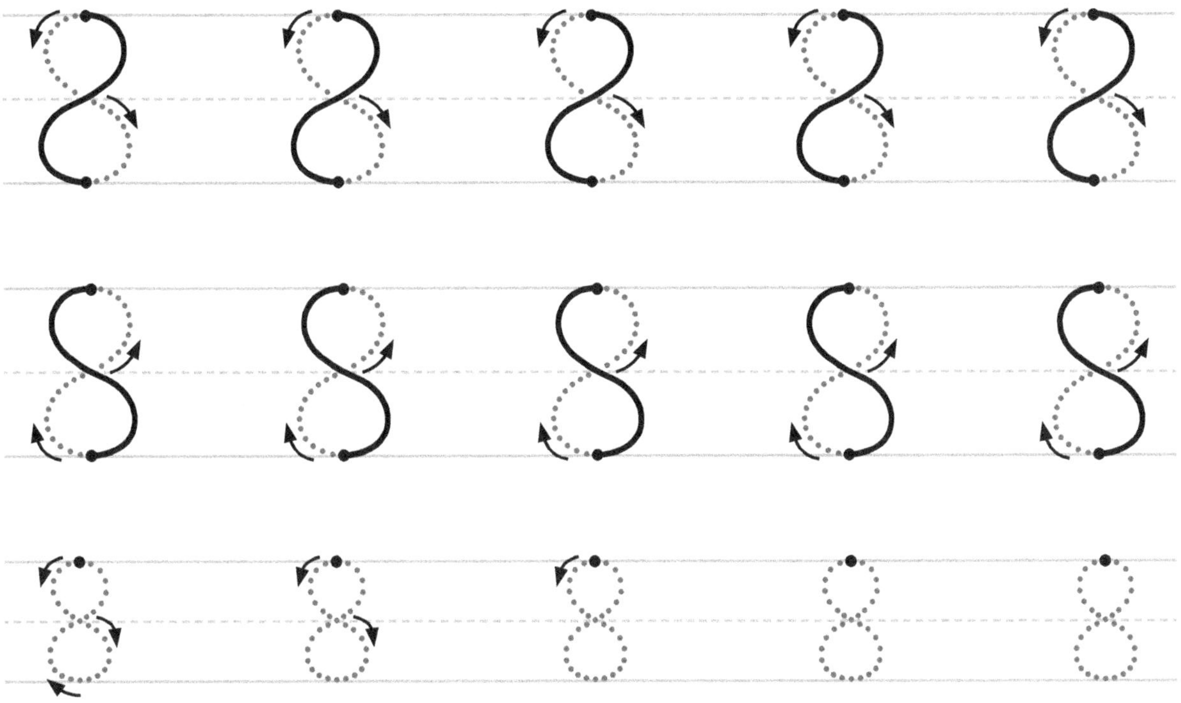

3.

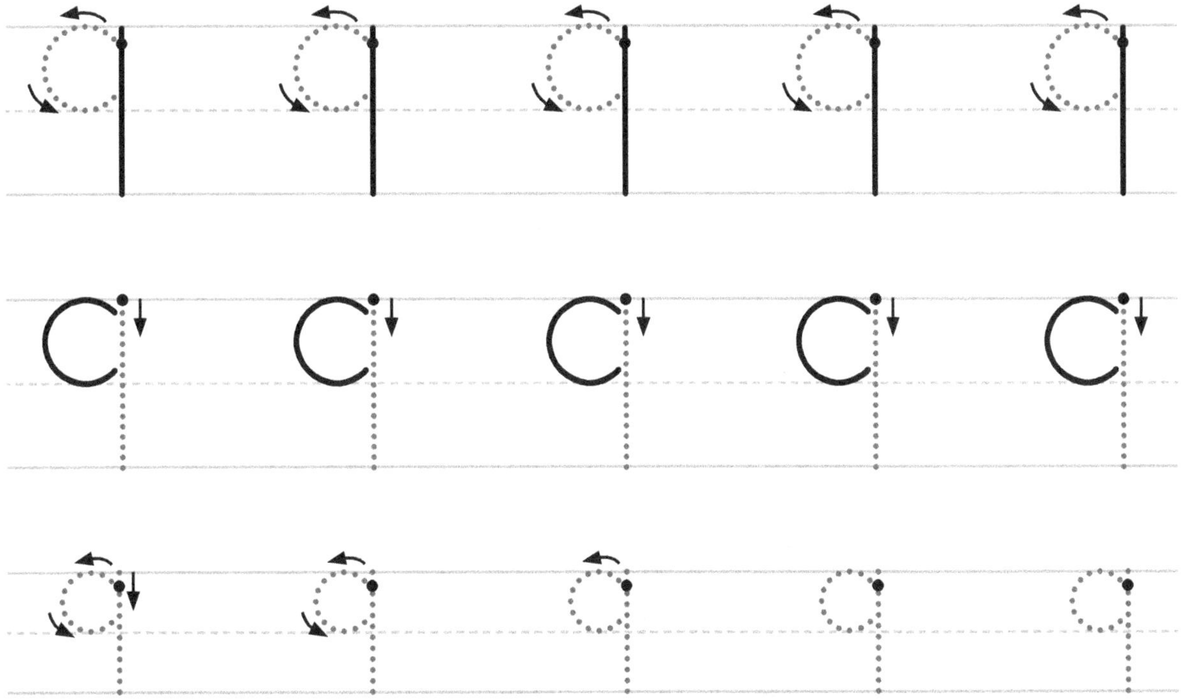

CCK-32 Counting 10

How many?

☐ Count. Circle the number.

1.

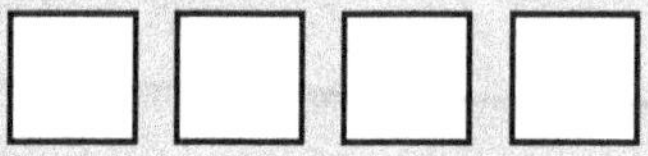

1 2 3 4 5 6 7 8 9 10

2.

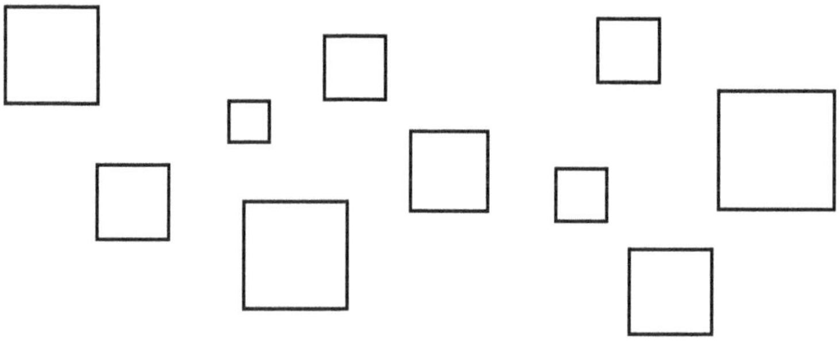

1 2 3 4 5 6 7 8 9 10

3.

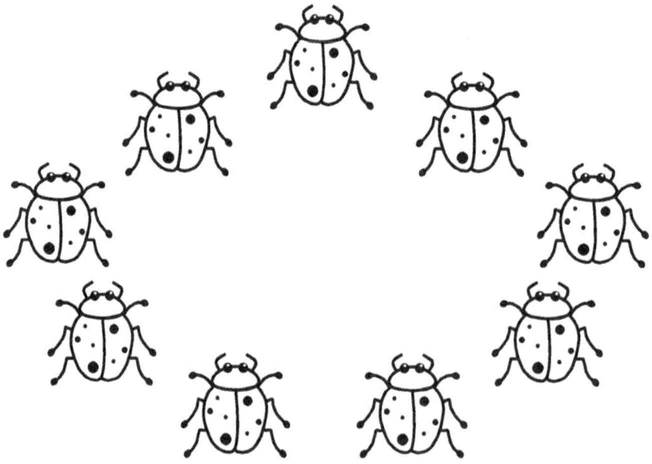

1 2 3 4 5 6 7 8 9 10

How many?

☐ Count. Circle the number.

4.

1 2 3 4 5 6 7 8 9 10

5.

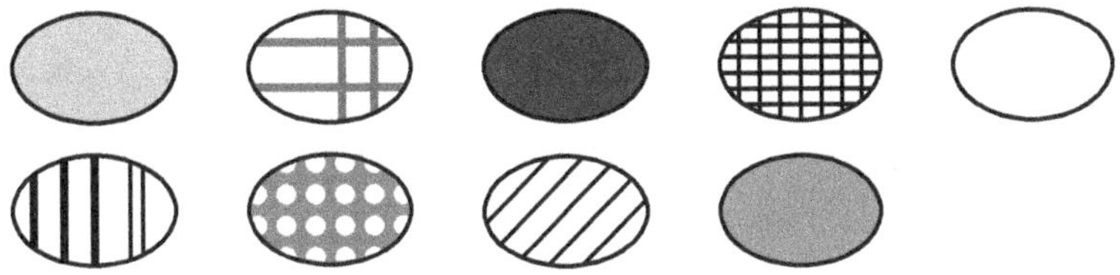

1 2 3 4 5 6 7 8 9 10

6.

1 2 3 4 5 6 7 8 9 10

☐ Show counting out.

7.

5

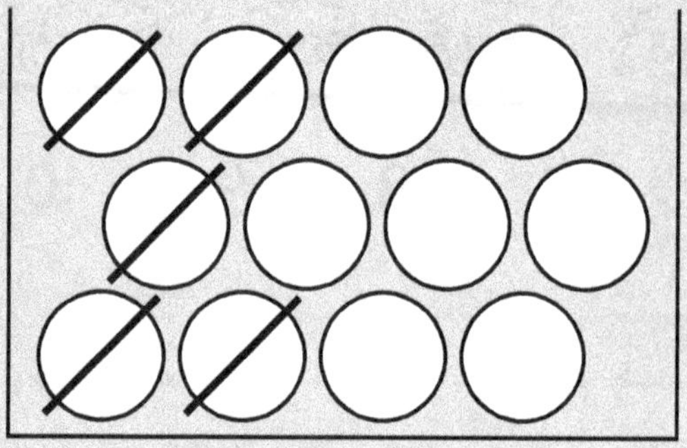

8.

8

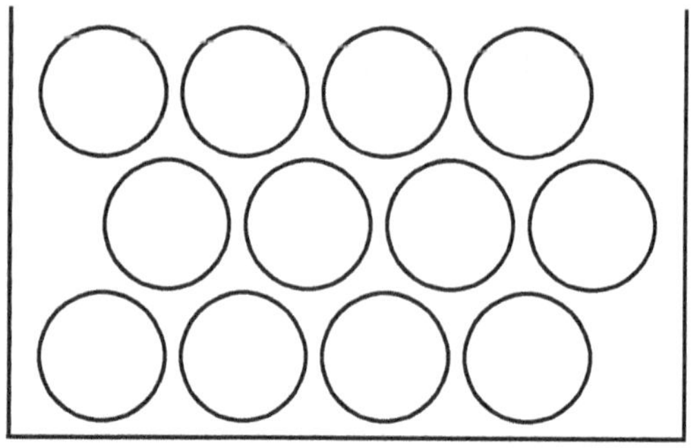

9.

7

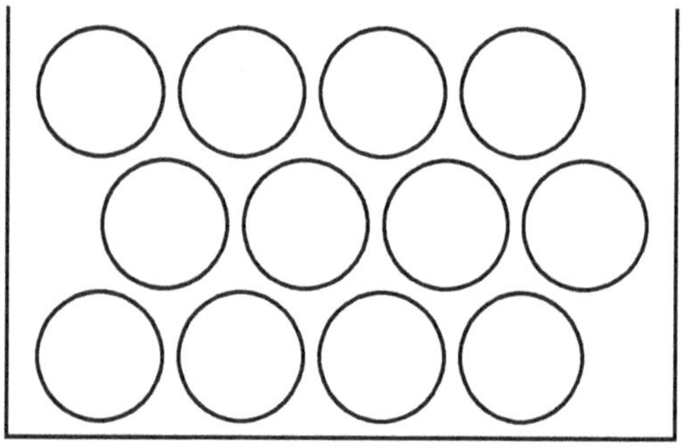

10.

9

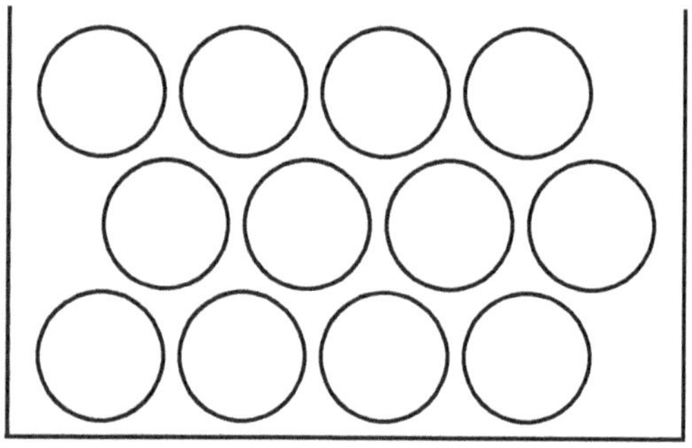

11.

10

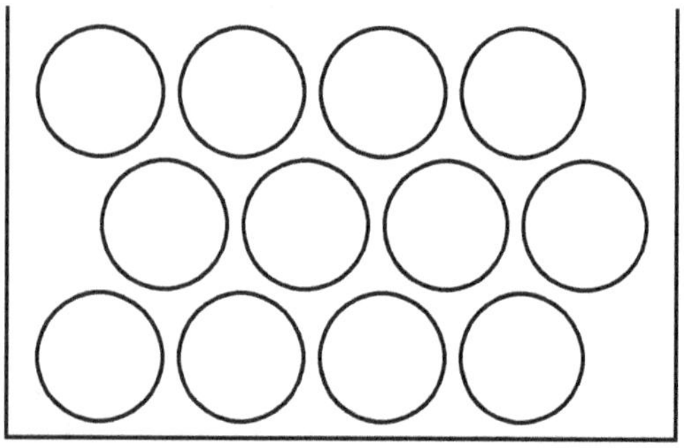

12.

6

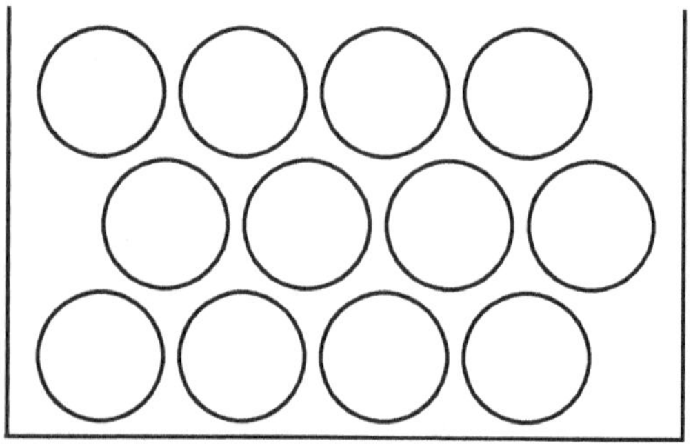

CCK-33 The Number 10

☐ Match by drawing lines.

1.

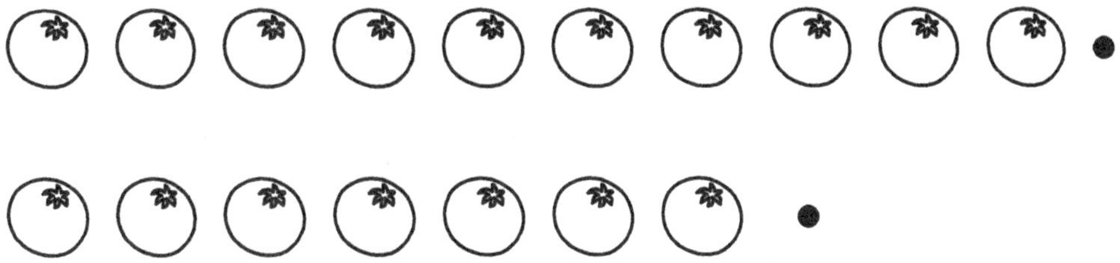

• 7

• 10

2.

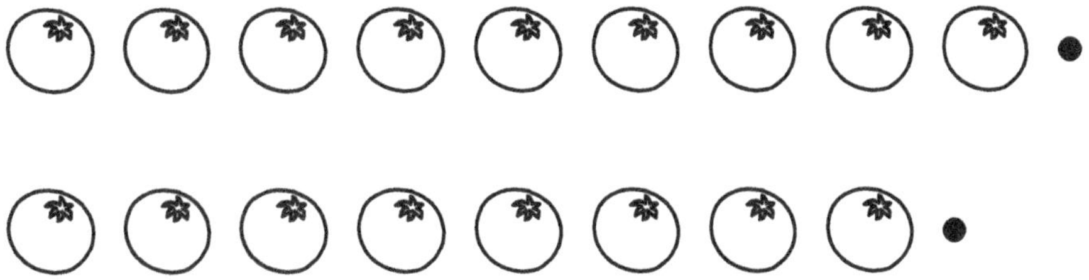

• 8

• 9

3.

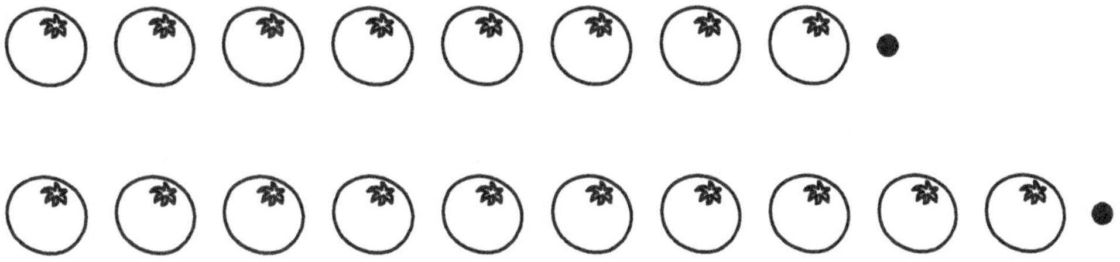

• 10

• 8

4.

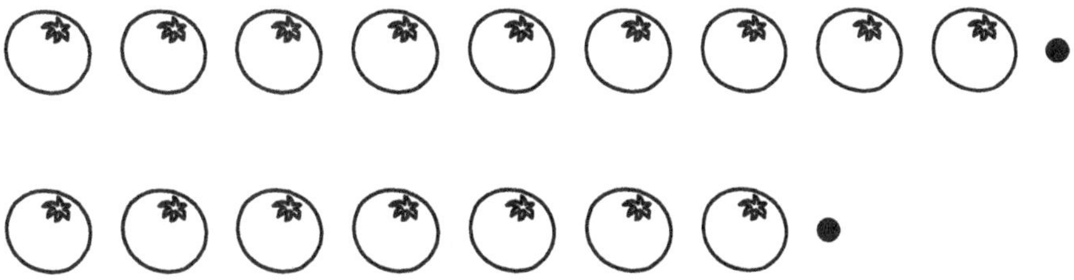

• 9

• 7

Match by drawing lines.

5.

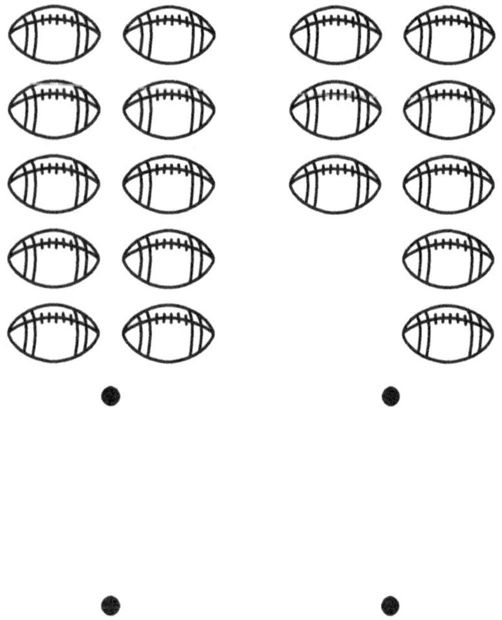

8 10

6.

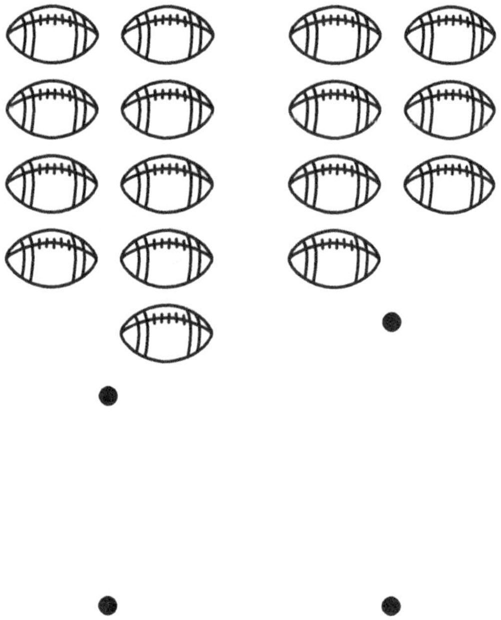

9 7

7.

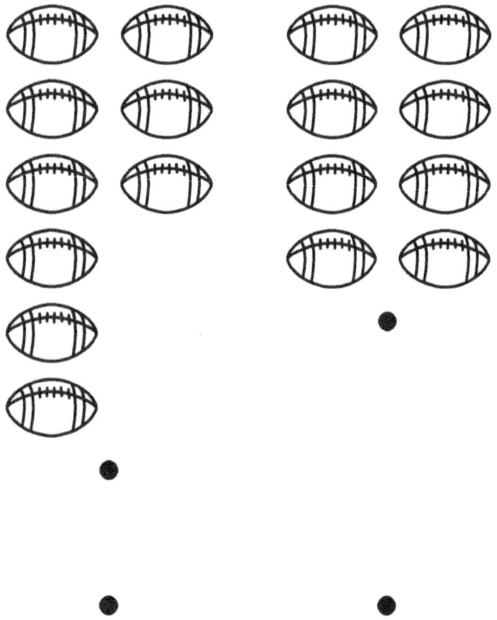

9 8

8.

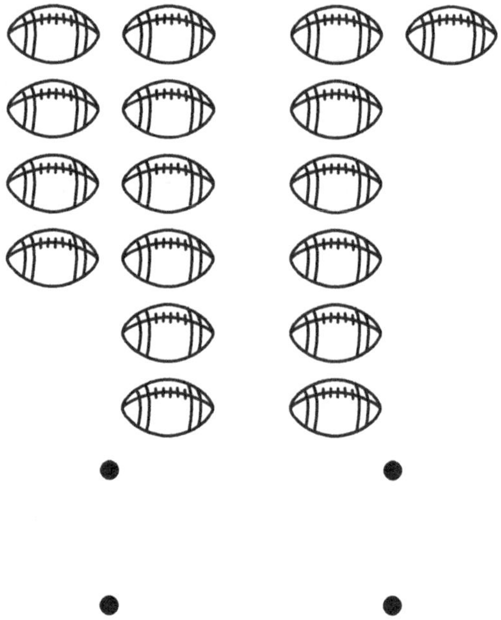

7 10

CCK-34 Writing 10

☐ Trace.

1.

2.

☐ Write 10.

3.

☐ Trace.

4.

1 2 3 4 5

6 7 8 9 10

1 2 3 4 5 6 7 8 9 10

5.

1 2 3 4 5

6 7 8 9 10

1 2 3 4 5 6 7 8 9 10

CCK-35 Review of 0 to 10

☐ Trace.

☐ Color the number of squares.

1.

3

2.

8

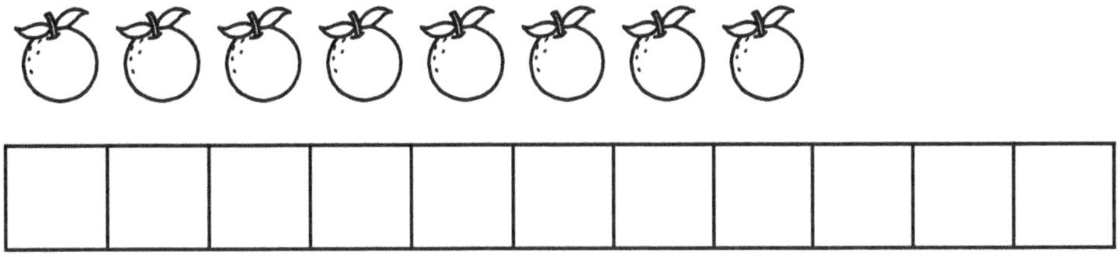

3.

6

4.

10

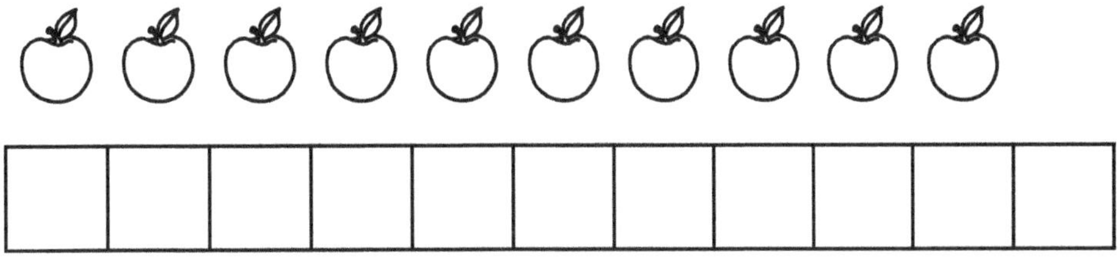

CCK-36 Counting to 50

☐ Trace.

1.

40 41 42
43 44 45
46 47 48
49 50

2.

4 4 4 4 4 4 4

☐ Write 4.

3.

CCK-37 Equal To

- [ ] Match by drawing lines.
- [ ] Color ☺ for equal. Color ☹ for not equal.

1.

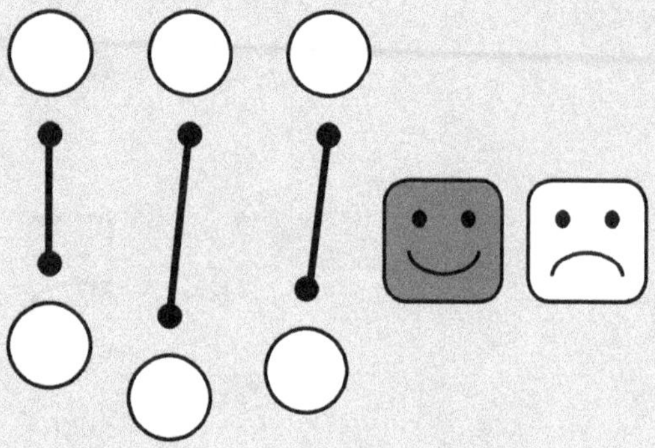

2.

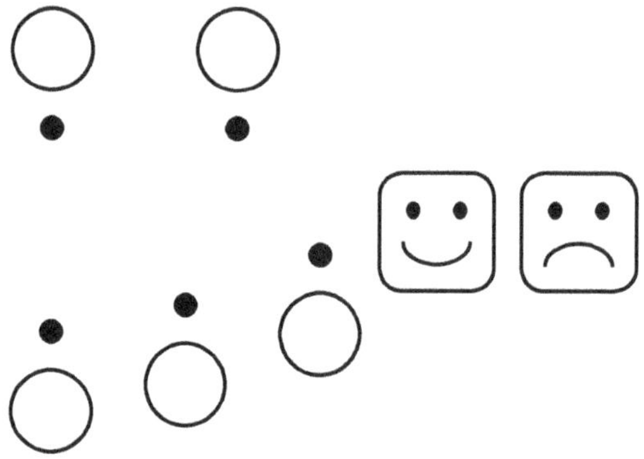

3.

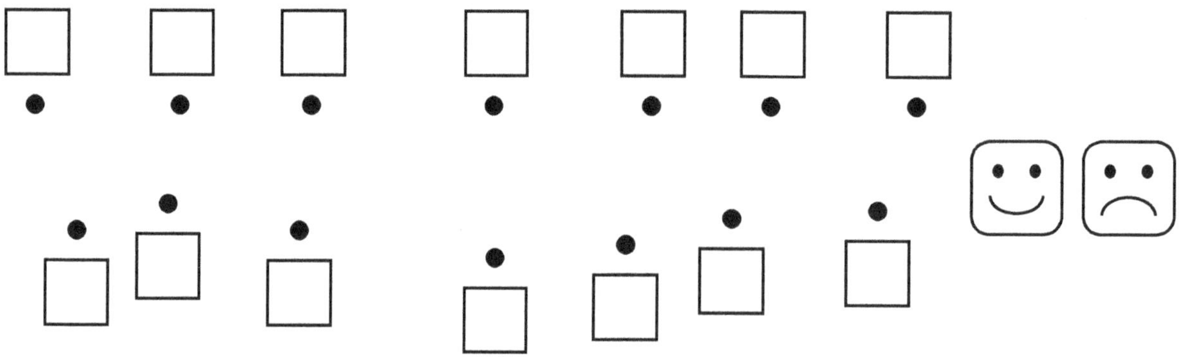

4.

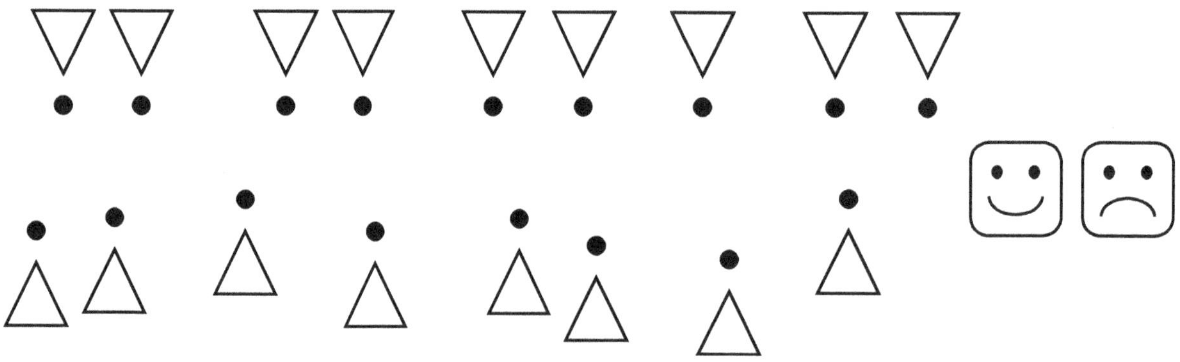

☐ Match by drawing lines.

☐ Color ☺ for equal. Color ☹ for not equal.

5.

6.

7.

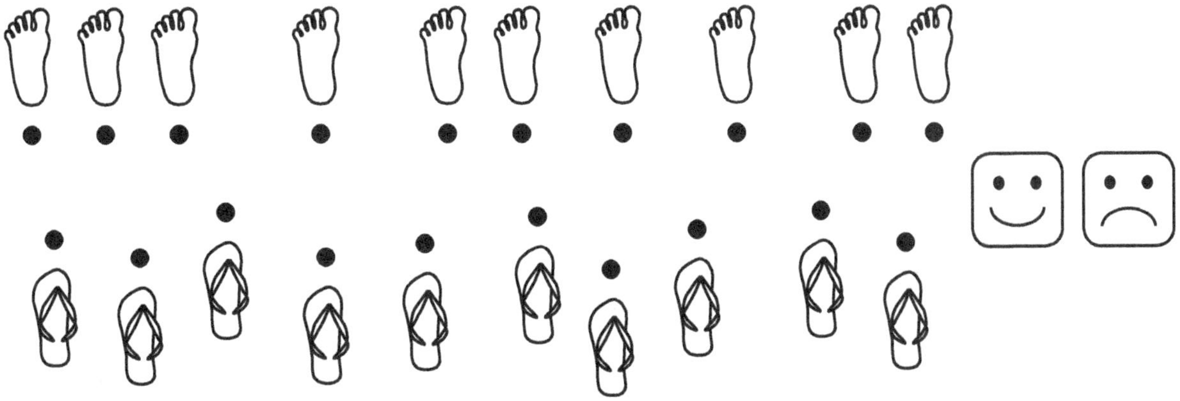

☐ Count. Circle the number.

☐ Color ☺ for equal. Color ☹ for not equal.

8.

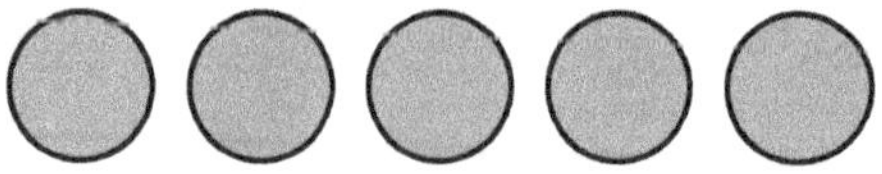

1 2 3 4 5 6 7 8 9 10

1 2 3 4 5 6 7 8 9 10

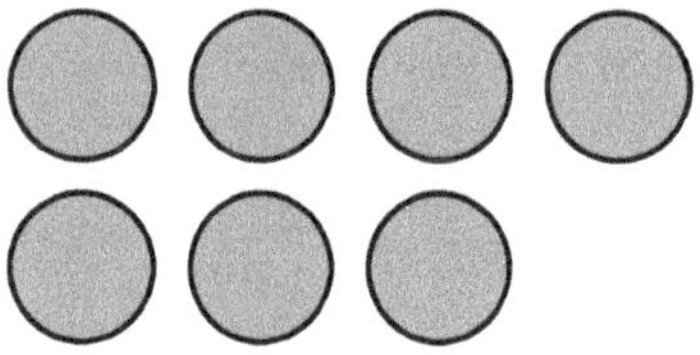

9.

1 2 3 4 5 6 7 8 9 10

1 2 3 4 5 6 7 8 9 10

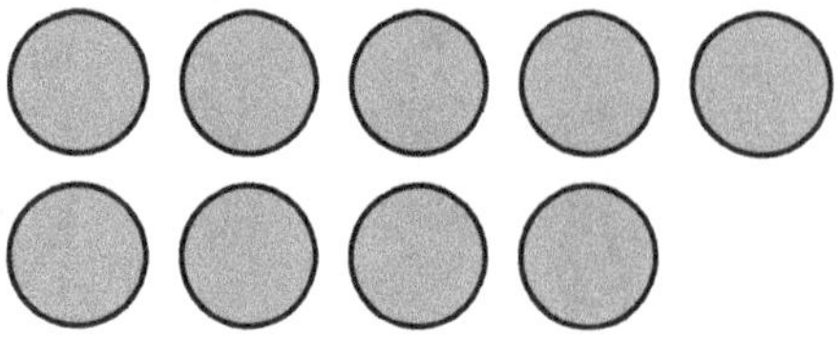

☐ Count. Circle the number.

☐ Color ☺ for equal. Color ☹ for not equal.

10.

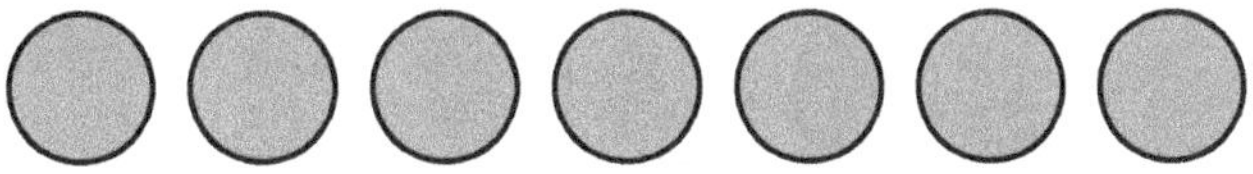

1 2 3 4 5 6 7 8 9 10

1 2 3 4 5 6 7 8 9 10

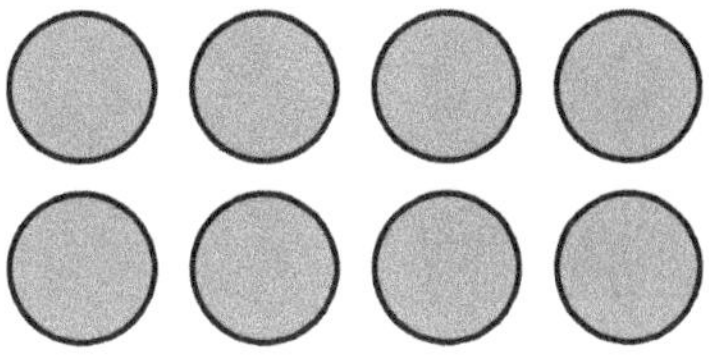

11.

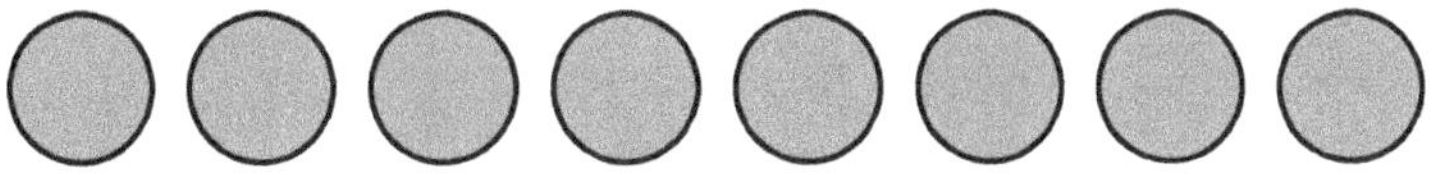

1 2 3 4 5 6 7 8 9 10

1 2 3 4 5 6 7 8 9 10

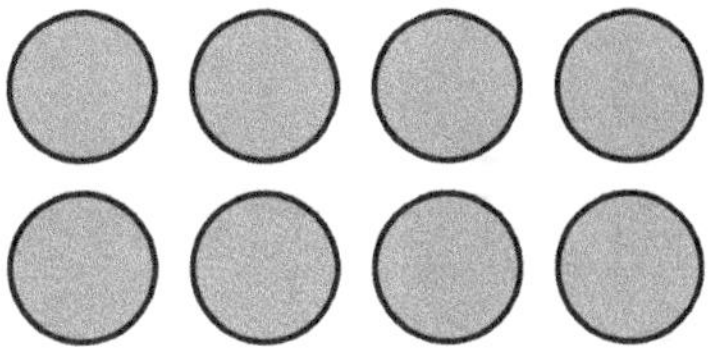

☐ Count. Circle the number.

☐ Color ☺ for equal. Color ☹ for not equal.

12.

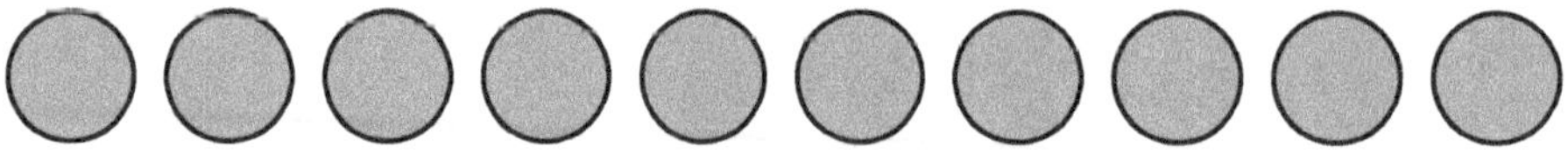

1 2 3 4 5 6 7 8 9 10

1 2 3 4 5 6 7 8 9 10

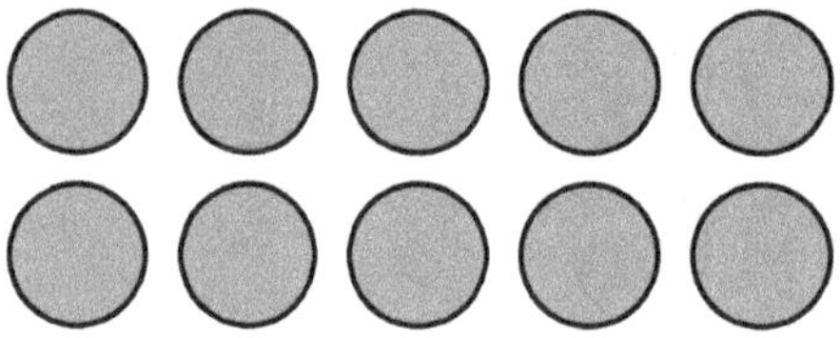

13.

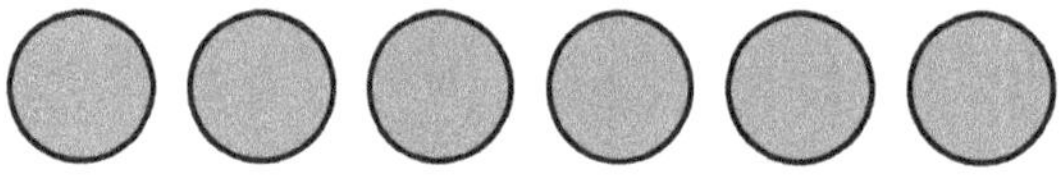

1 2 3 4 5 6 7 8 9 10

1 2 3 4 5 6 7 8 9 10

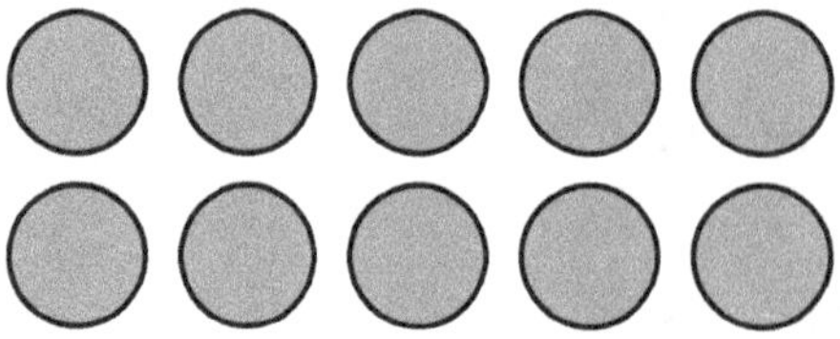

☐ Count. Circle the number.

☐ Color  for equal. Color  for not equal.

14.

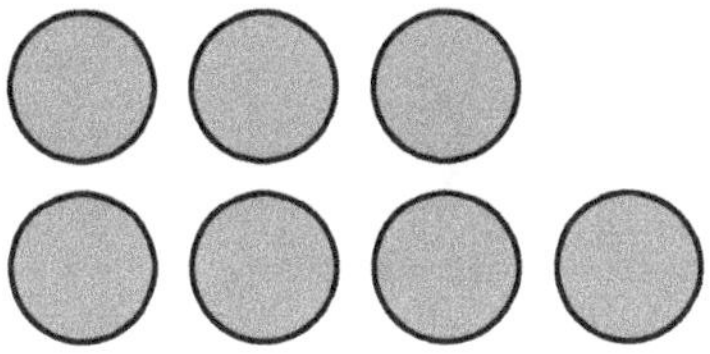

1 2 3 4 5 6 7 8 9 10

1 2 3 4 5 6 7 8 9 10

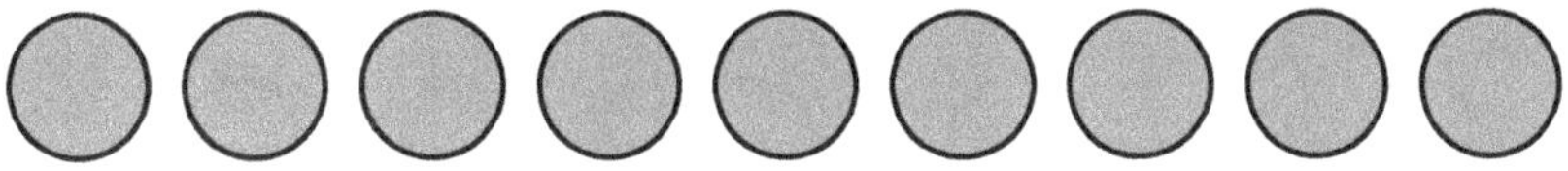

15. BONUS

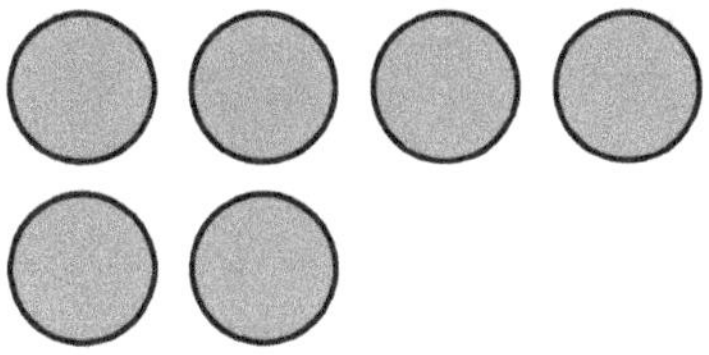

1 2 3 4 5 6 7 8 9 10

1 2 3 4 5 6 7 8 9 10

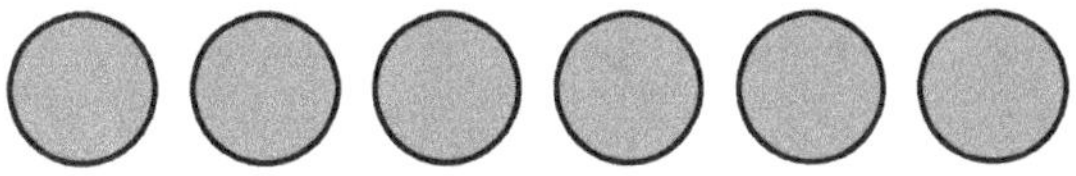

CCK-38 Greater Than

☐ Match by drawing lines.

☐ Color the ☼ for the group that has more.

1.

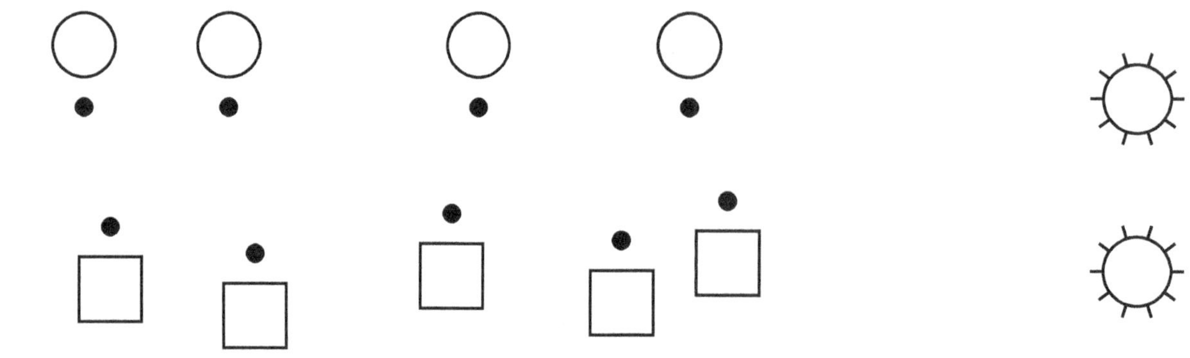

2.

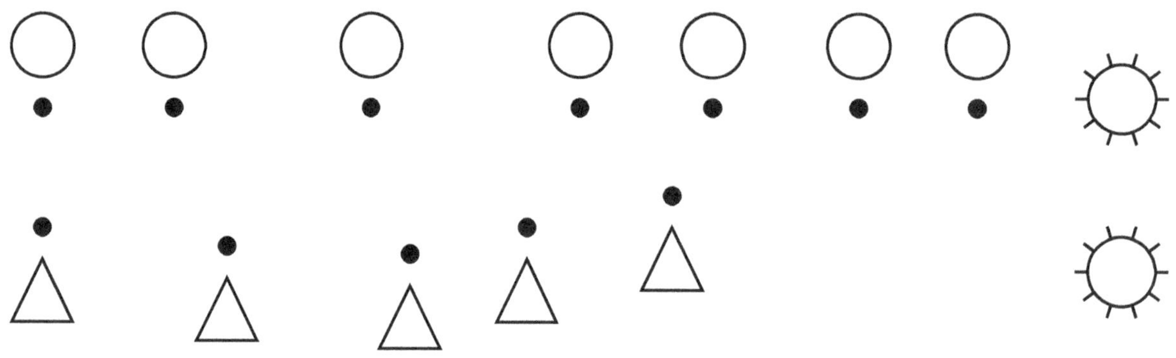

3.

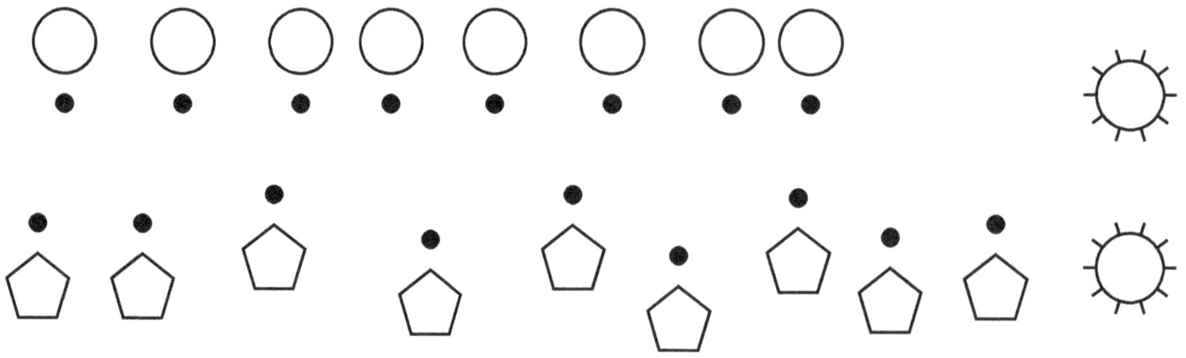

☐ Match by drawing lines.

☐ Color the ☼ for the group that has more.

4.

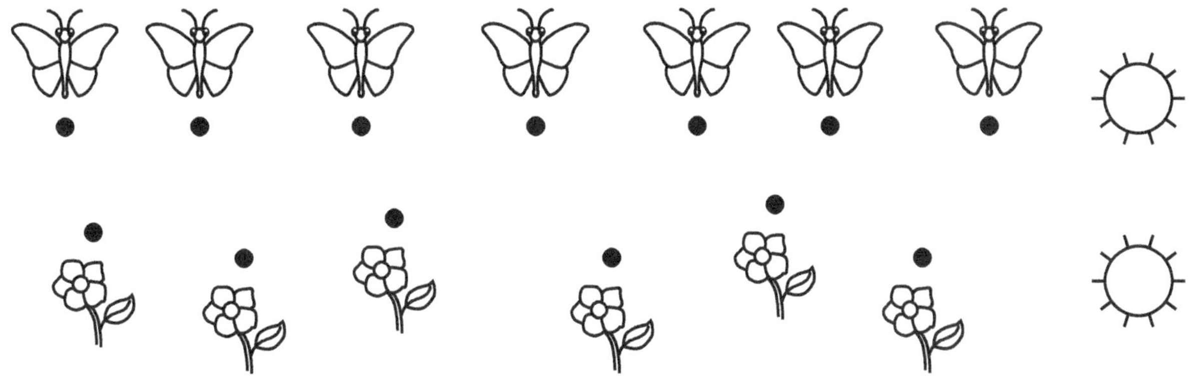

5.

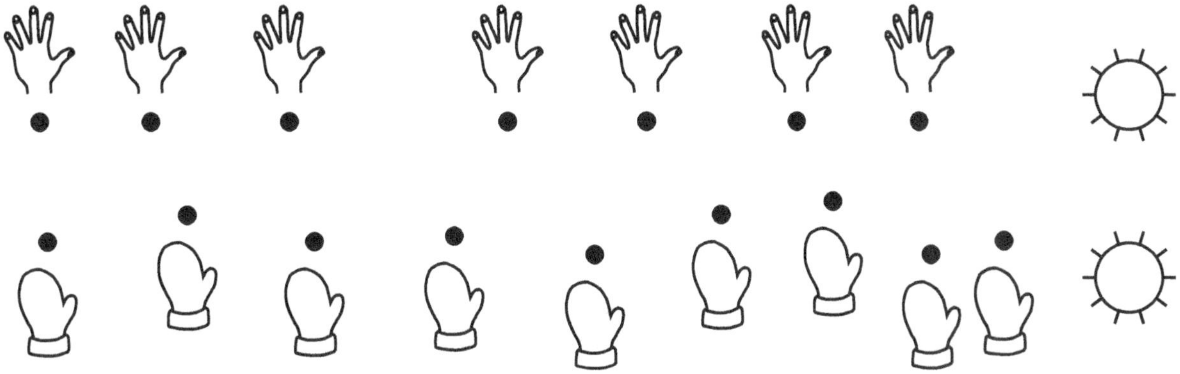

6.

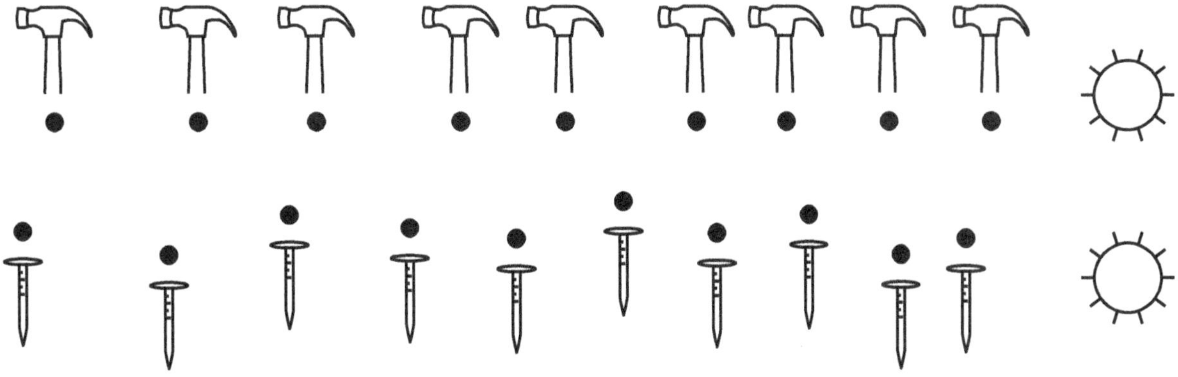

☐ Count. Circle the number.

☐ Color the ☼ for the greater number.

7.

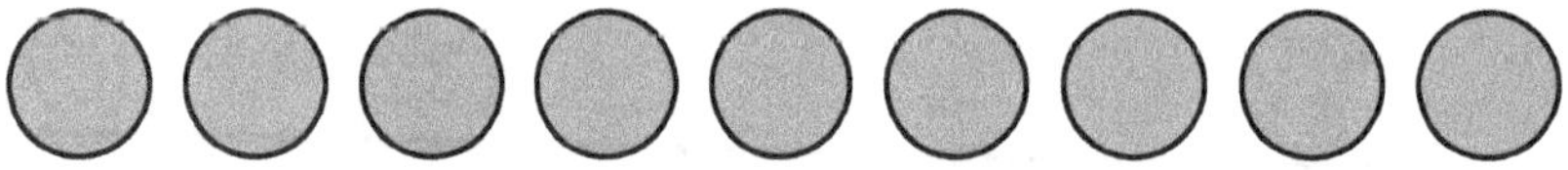

1 2 3 4 5 6 7 8 9 10 ☼

1 2 3 4 5 6 7 8 9 10 ☼

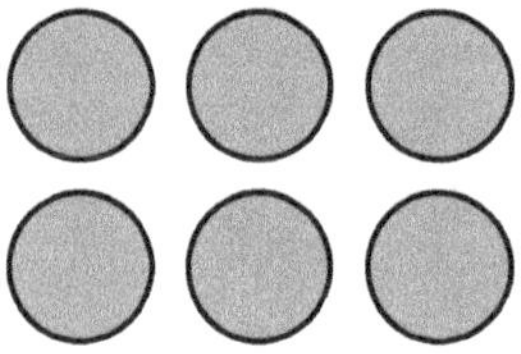

8.

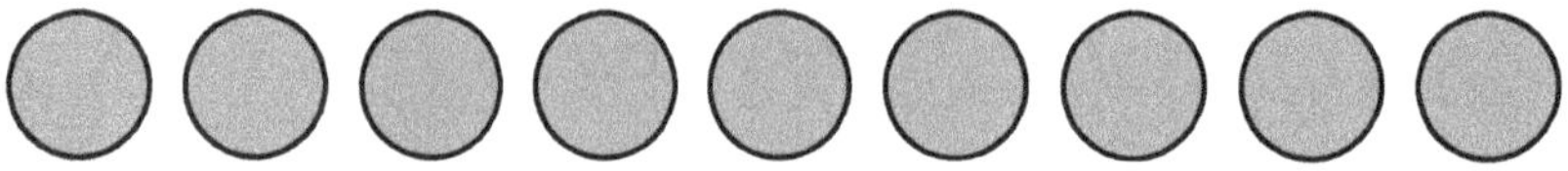

1 2 3 4 5 6 7 8 9 10 ☼

1 2 3 4 5 6 7 8 9 10 ☼

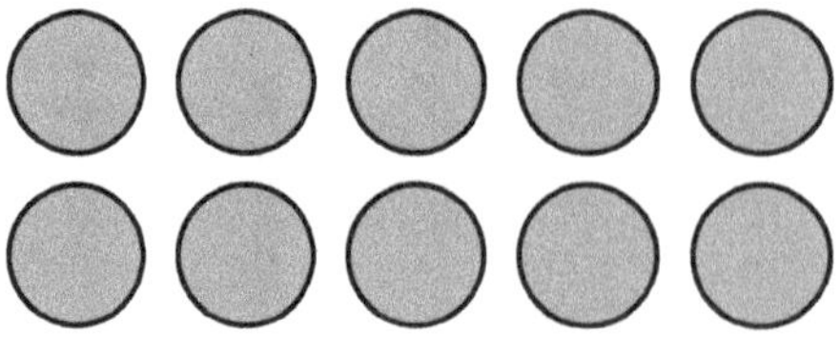

☐ Count. Circle the number.

☐ Color the ☼ for the greater number.

9.

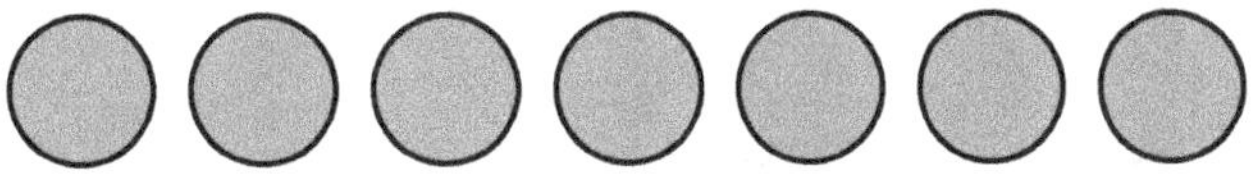

1 2 3 4 5 6 7 8 9 10 ☼

1 2 3 4 5 6 7 8 9 10 ☼

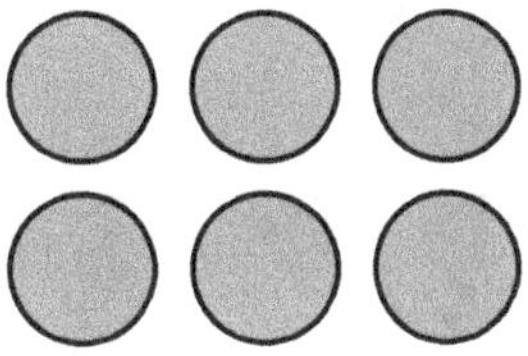

10.

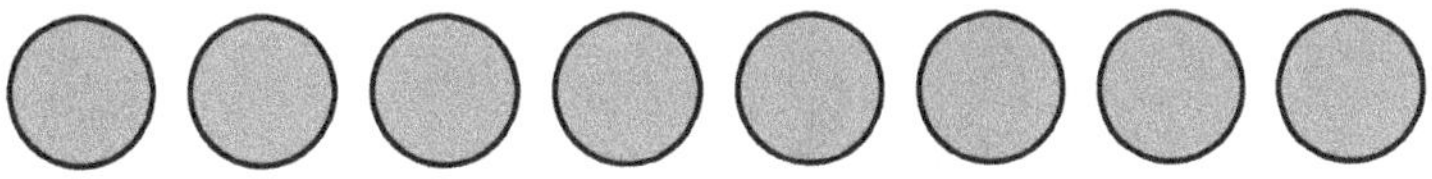

1 2 3 4 5 6 7 8 9 10 ☼

1 2 3 4 5 6 7 8 9 10 ☼

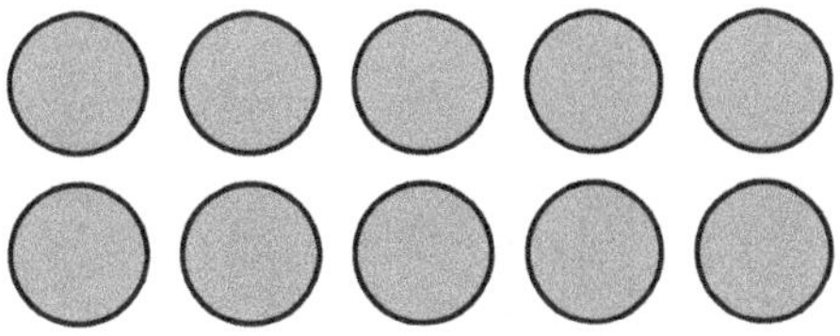

☐ Count. Circle the number.

☐ Color the ☼ for the greater number.

11.

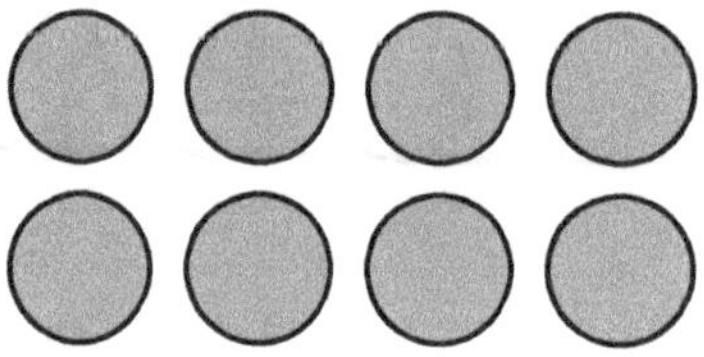

1 2 3 4 5 6 7 8 9 10 ☼

1 2 3 4 5 6 7 8 9 10 ☼

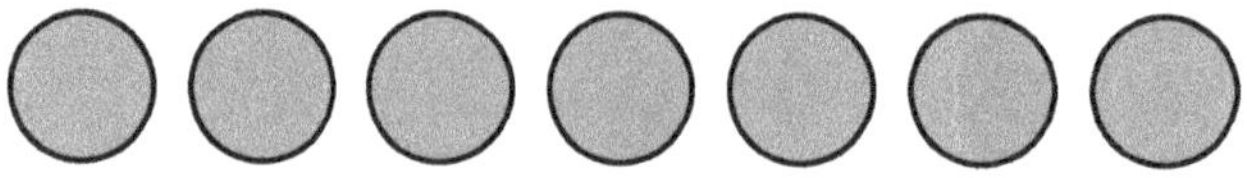

12.

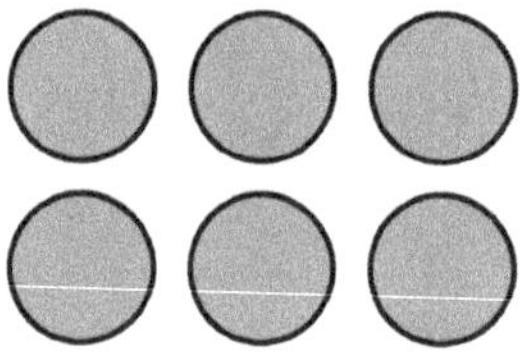

1 2 3 4 5 6 7 8 9 10 ☼

1 2 3 4 5 6 7 8 9 10 ☼

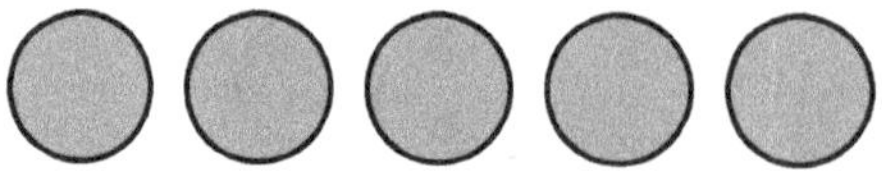

☐ Count. Circle the number.

☐ Color the ☼ for the greater number.

13. BONUS

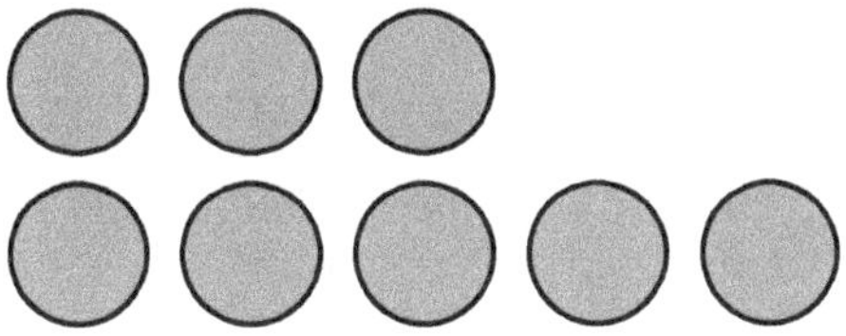

1 2 3 4 5 6 7 8 9 10 ☼

1 2 3 4 5 6 7 8 9 10 ☼

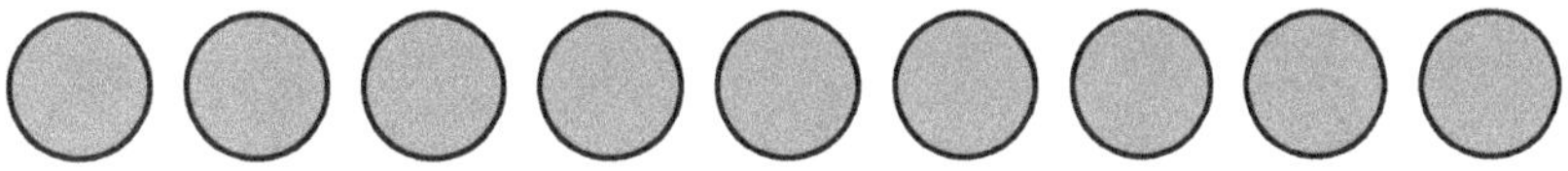

14. BONUS

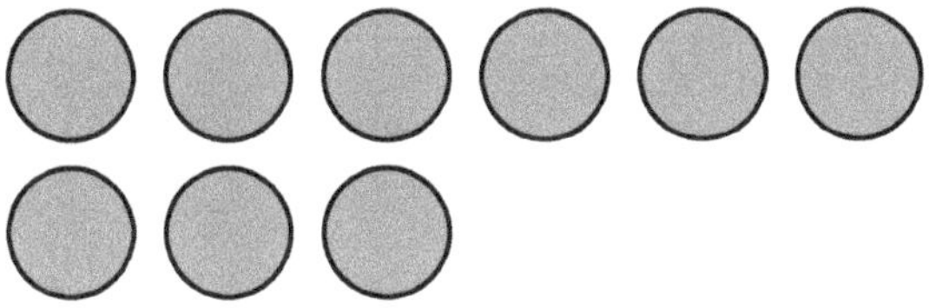

1 2 3 4 5 6 7 8 9 10 ☼

1 2 3 4 5 6 7 8 9 10 ☼

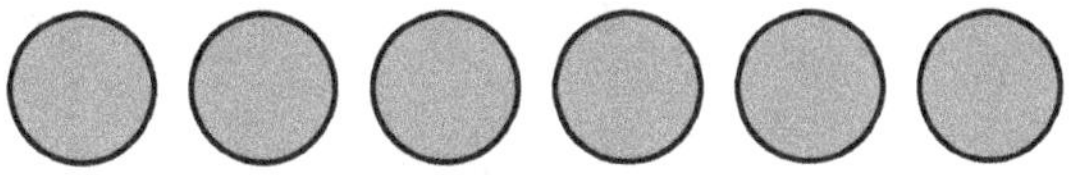

Less Than

☐ Match by drawing lines.

☐ Color the ☼ for the group that has fewer.

1.

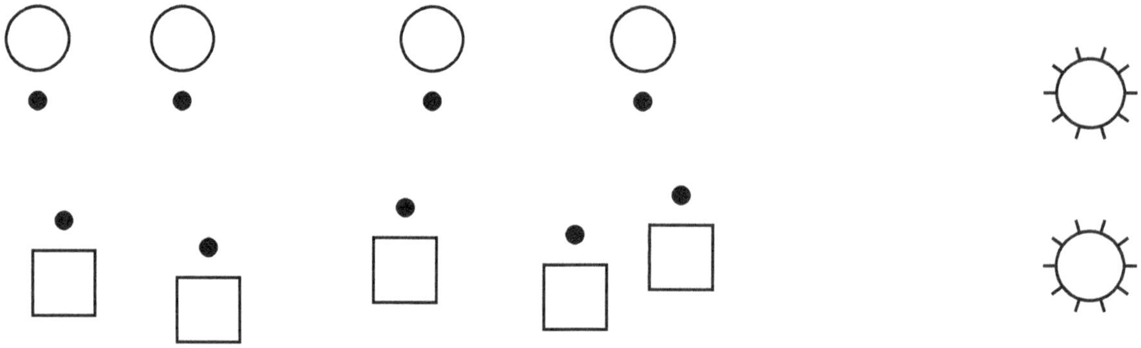

2.

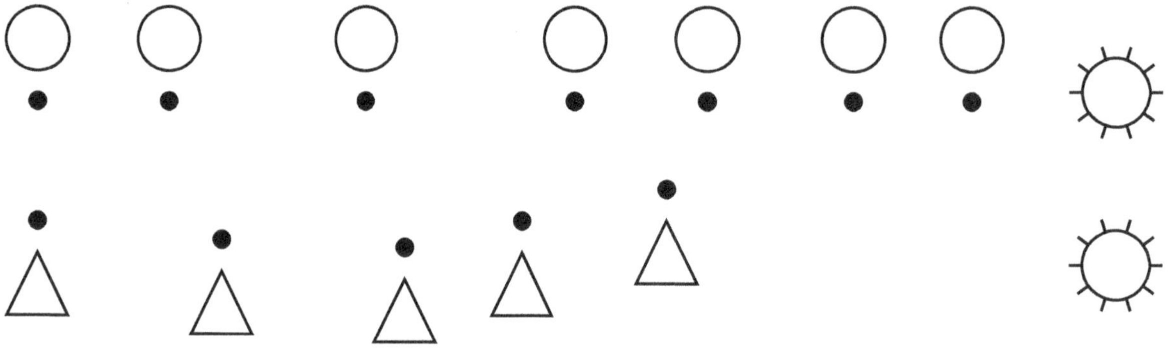

3.

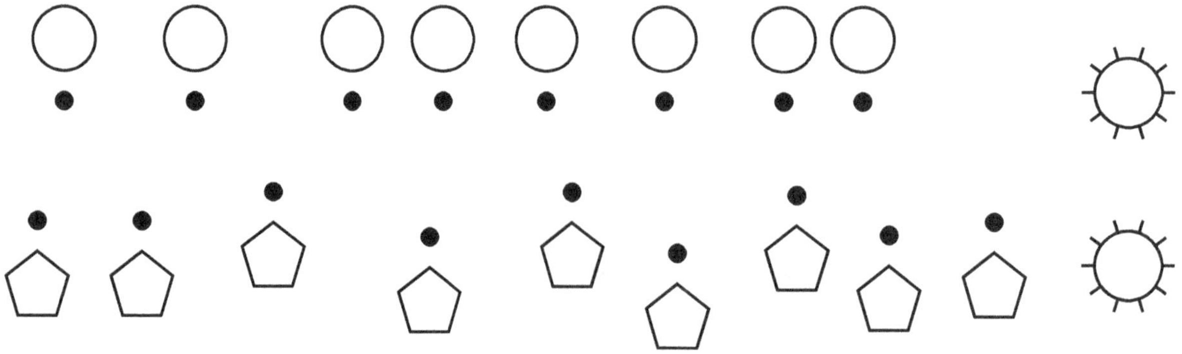

☐ Match by drawing lines.

☐ Color the ☼ for the group that has fewer.

4.

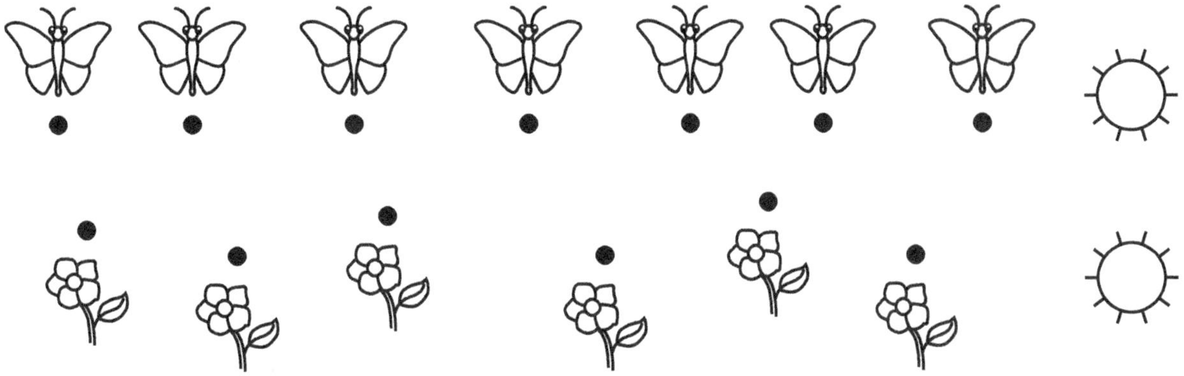

5.

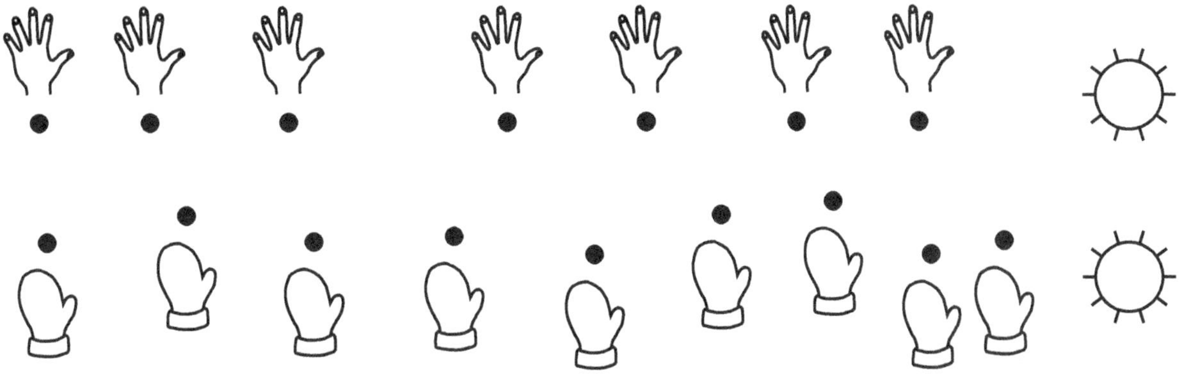

6.

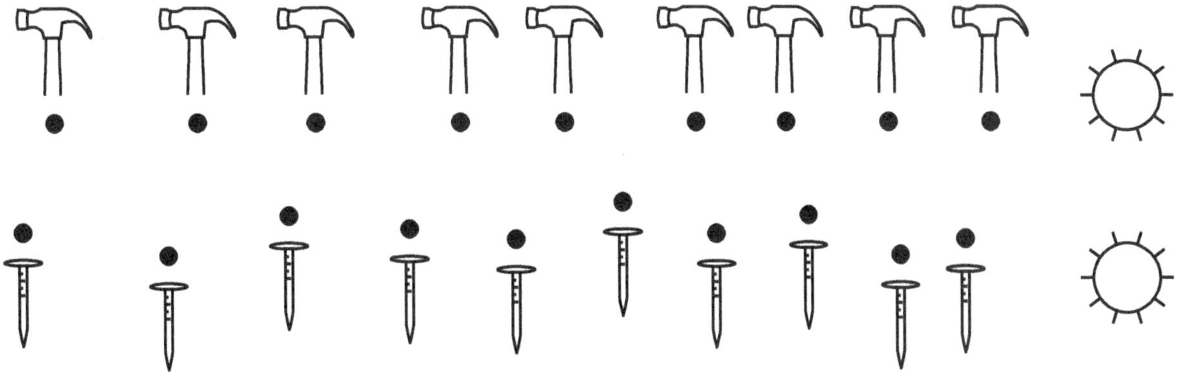

☐ Count. Circle the number.

☐ Color the ☼ for the number that is less.

7.

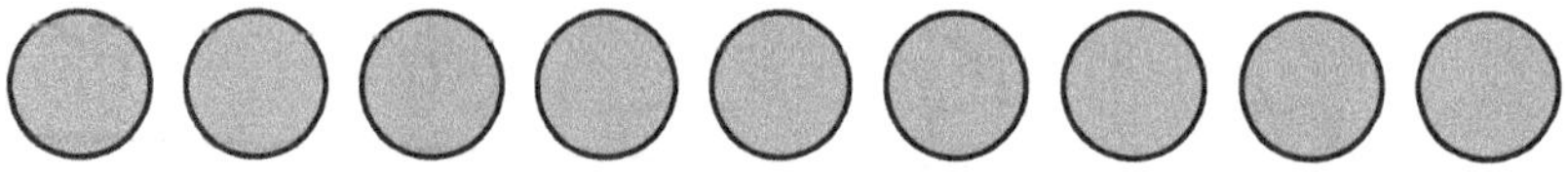

1 2 3 4 5 6 7 8 9 10 ☼

1 2 3 4 5 6 7 8 9 10 ☼

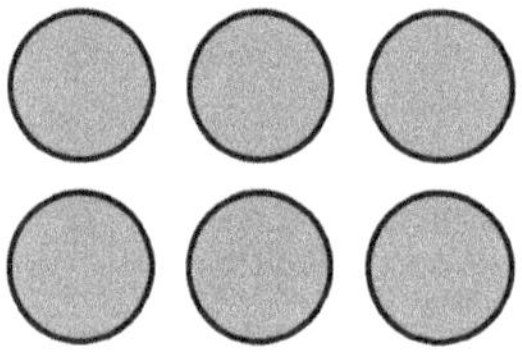

8.

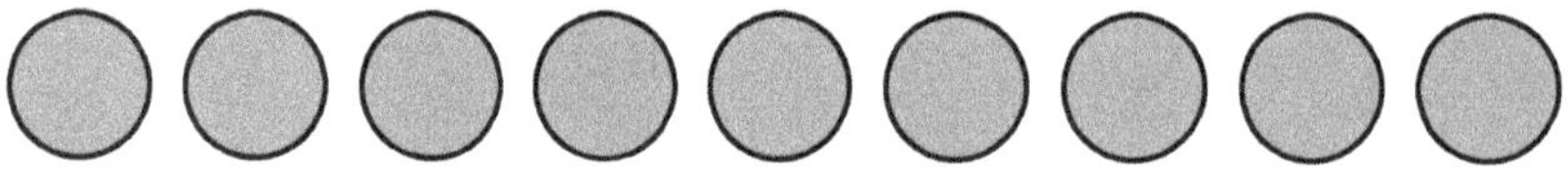

1 2 3 4 5 6 7 8 9 10 ☼

1 2 3 4 5 6 7 8 9 10 ☼

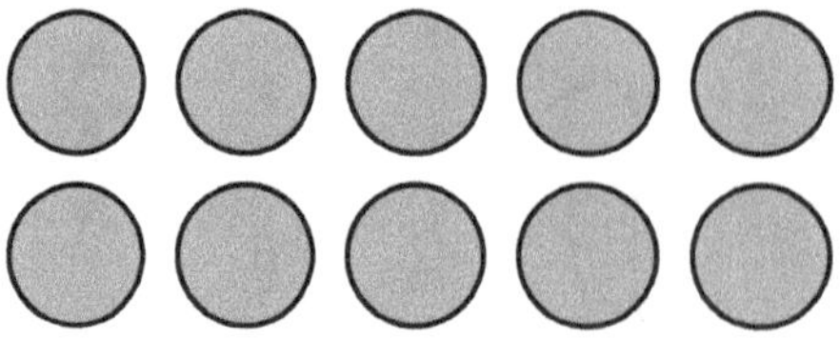

☐ Count. Circle the number.

☐ Color the ☼ for the number that is less.

9.

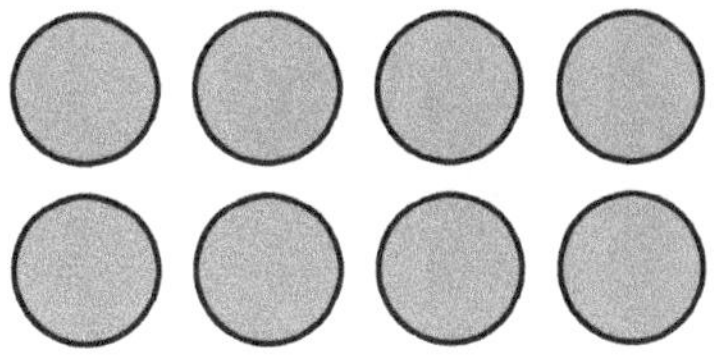

1 2 3 4 5 6 7 8 9 10 ☼

1 2 3 4 5 6 7 8 9 10 ☼

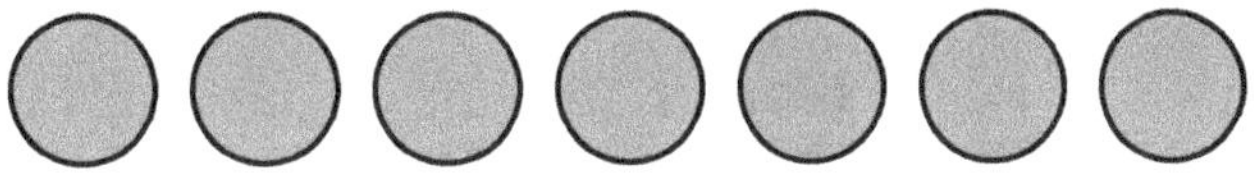

10.

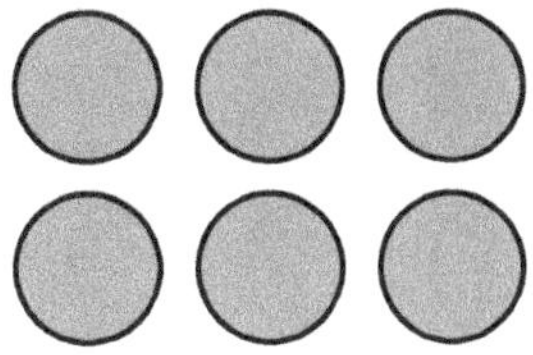

1 2 3 4 5 6 7 8 9 10 ☼

1 2 3 4 5 6 7 8 9 10 ☼

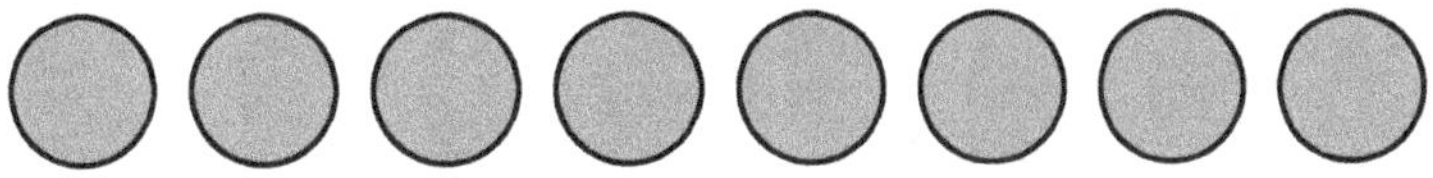

☐ Count. Circle the number.

☐ Color the ☼ for the number that is less.

11.

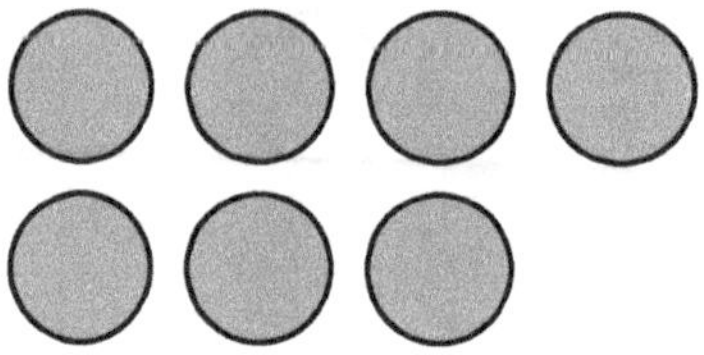

1 2 3 4 5 6 7 8 9 10 ☼

1 2 3 4 5 6 7 8 9 10 ☼

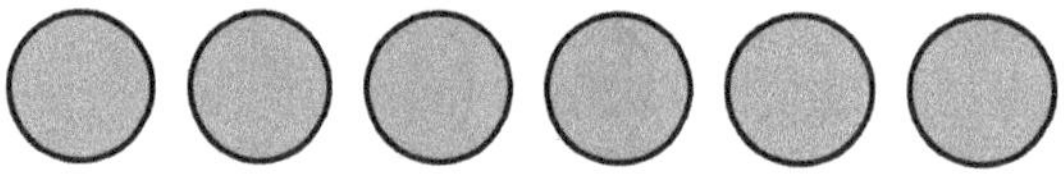

12.

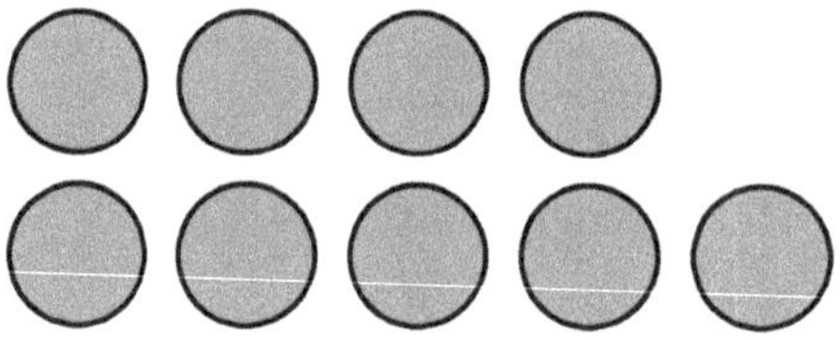

1 2 3 4 5 6 7 8 9 10 ☼

1 2 3 4 5 6 7 8 9 10 ☼

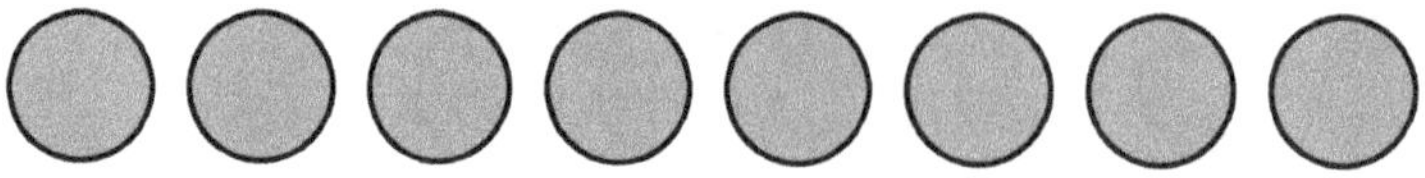

☐ Count. Circle the number.

☐ Color the ☼ for the number that is less.

13. BONUS

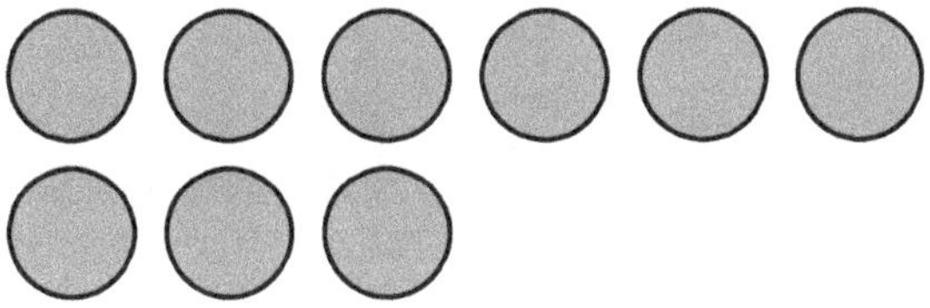

1 2 3 4 5 6 7 8 9 10 ☼

1 2 3 4 5 6 7 8 9 10 ☼

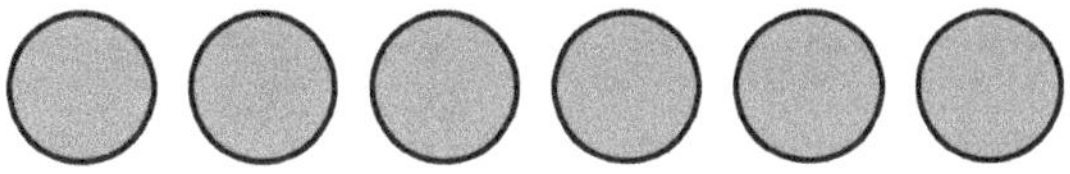

14. BONUS

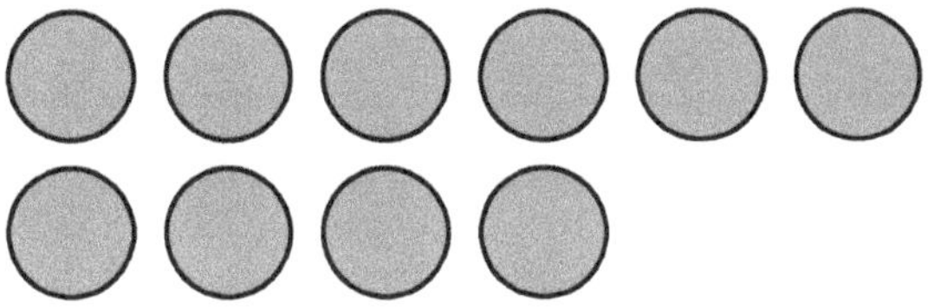

1 2 3 4 5 6 7 8 9 10 ☼

1 2 3 4 5 6 7 8 9 10 ☼

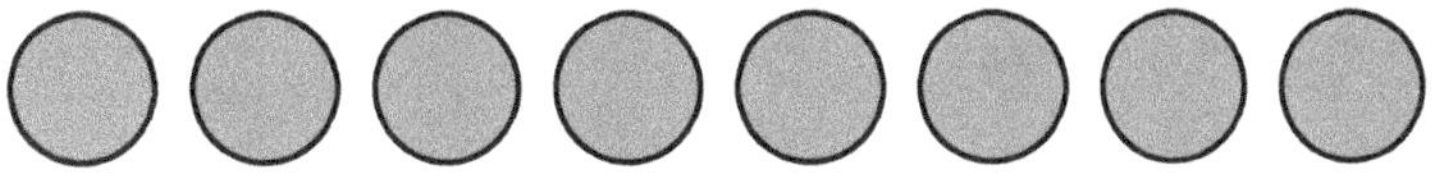

CCK-40 One More Than

☐ Draw a line below the number.

☐ Circle the next number.

1.

4	1	2	3	<u>4</u>	(5)	6	7	8	9	10

2.

9	1	2	3	4	5	6	7	8	9	10

3.

5	1	2	3	4	5	6	7	8	9	10

4.

2	1	2	3	4	5	6	7	8	9	10

5.

8	1	2	3	4	5	6	7	8	9	10

☐ Match by drawing lines.

☐ Circle the extra ●.

☐ Write how many extra.

6.

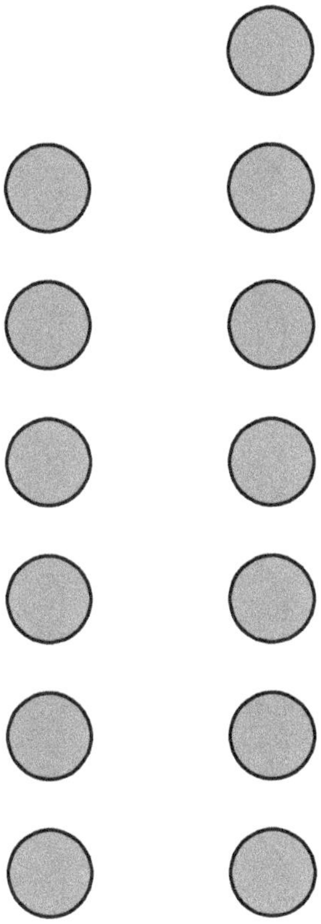

6 7

______

7.

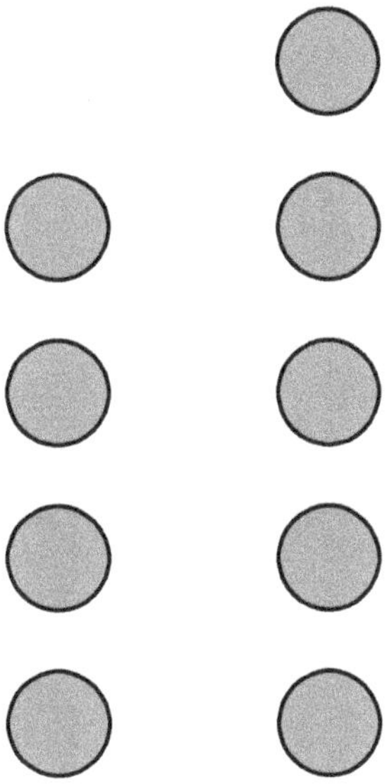

4 5

______

8.

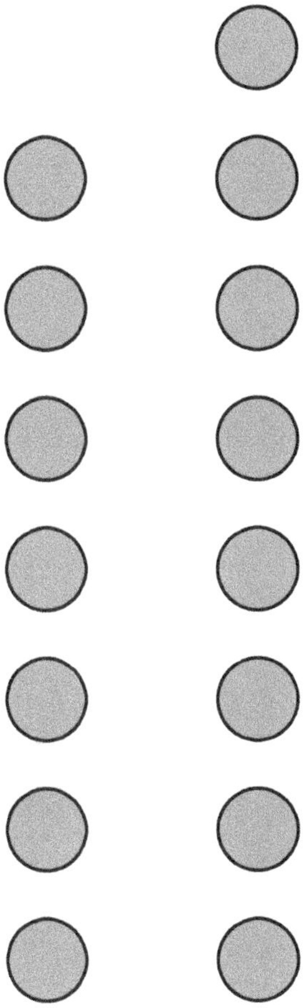

7 8

______

☐ Write the next number.

☐ Color to show the next number.

9.

4 ______

10.

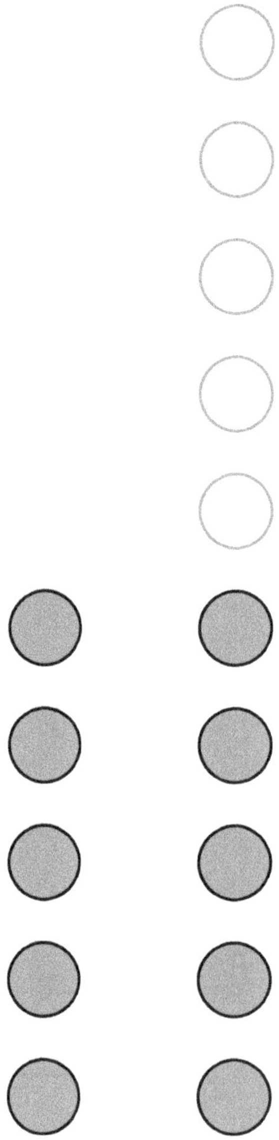

5 ______

11.

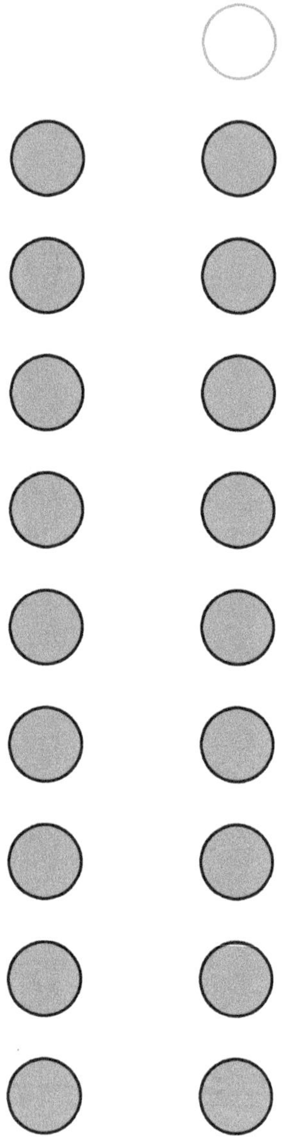

9 ______

☐ Write the next number.

☐ Color to show the next number.

12.

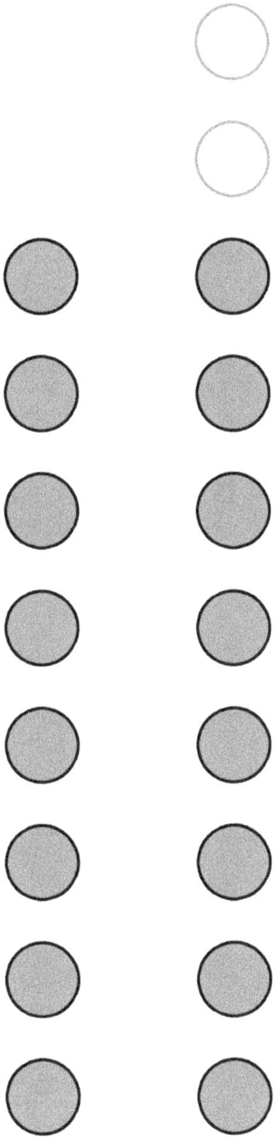

8 ______

13.

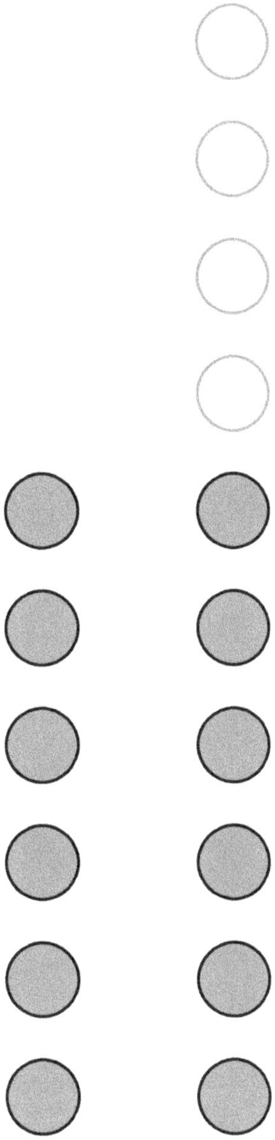

6 ______

14.

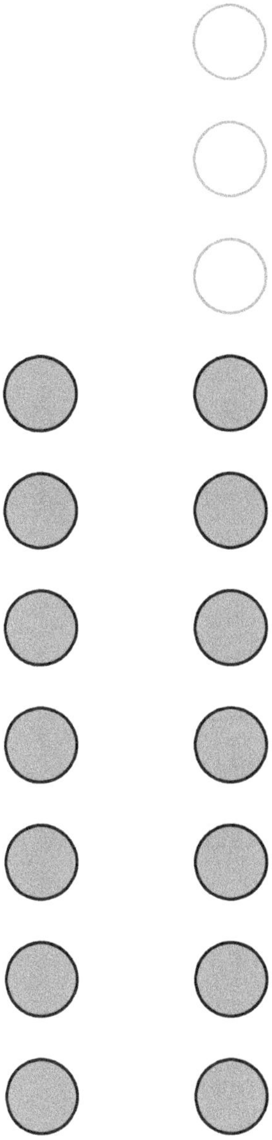

7 ______

CCK-41 Comparing Numbers

- [ ] Circle the numbers.
- [ ] Color the ☼ for the greater number.

1.

7 ☼

2 ☼

1 2 3 4 5 6 7 8 9 10

2.

3 ☼

9 ☼

1 2 3 4 5 6 7 8 9 10

3.

10 ☼

1 ☼

1 2 3 4 5 6 7 8 9 10

4.

4 ☼

6 ☼

1 2 3 4 5 6 7 8 9 10

☐ Color to show the numbers. Match.

☐ Circle the number that is less.

5. 1 4

6. 4 2

7. 3 5

8. 6 2

9. 3 6

10. 1 5

☐ Color to show the numbers. Match.

☐ Circle the greater number.

11.

9 5

12.

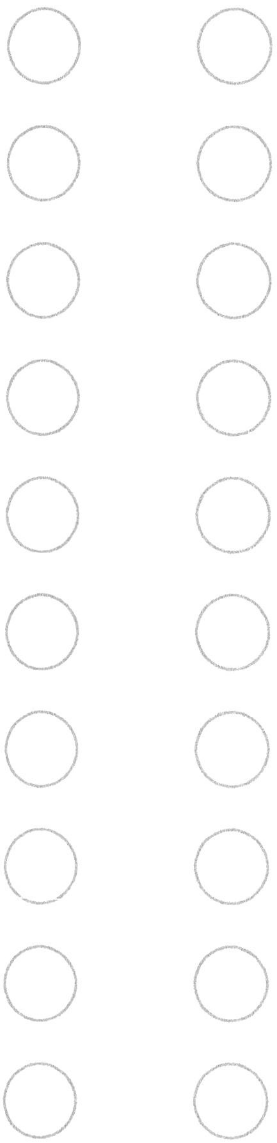

8 3

13.

6 10

MDK-1 Counting to 60

☐ Trace.

1.

50 51 52

53 54 55

56 57 58

59 60

2.

5 5 5 5 5 5 5

☐ Write 5.

3.

Sorting into Two Groups

Where does each shape belong?

☐ Draw a line.

1.

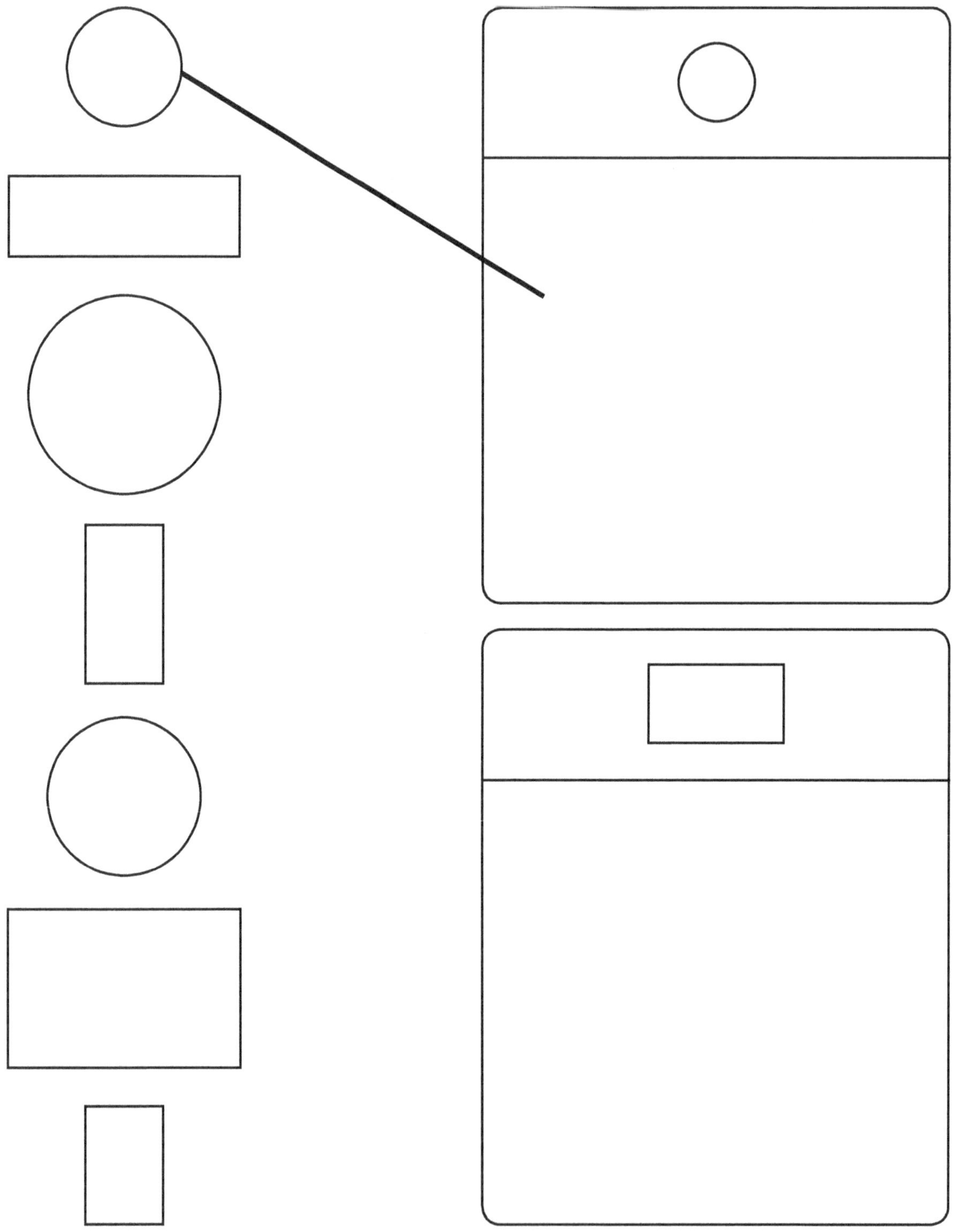

Where does each shape belong?

▢ Draw a line.

2.

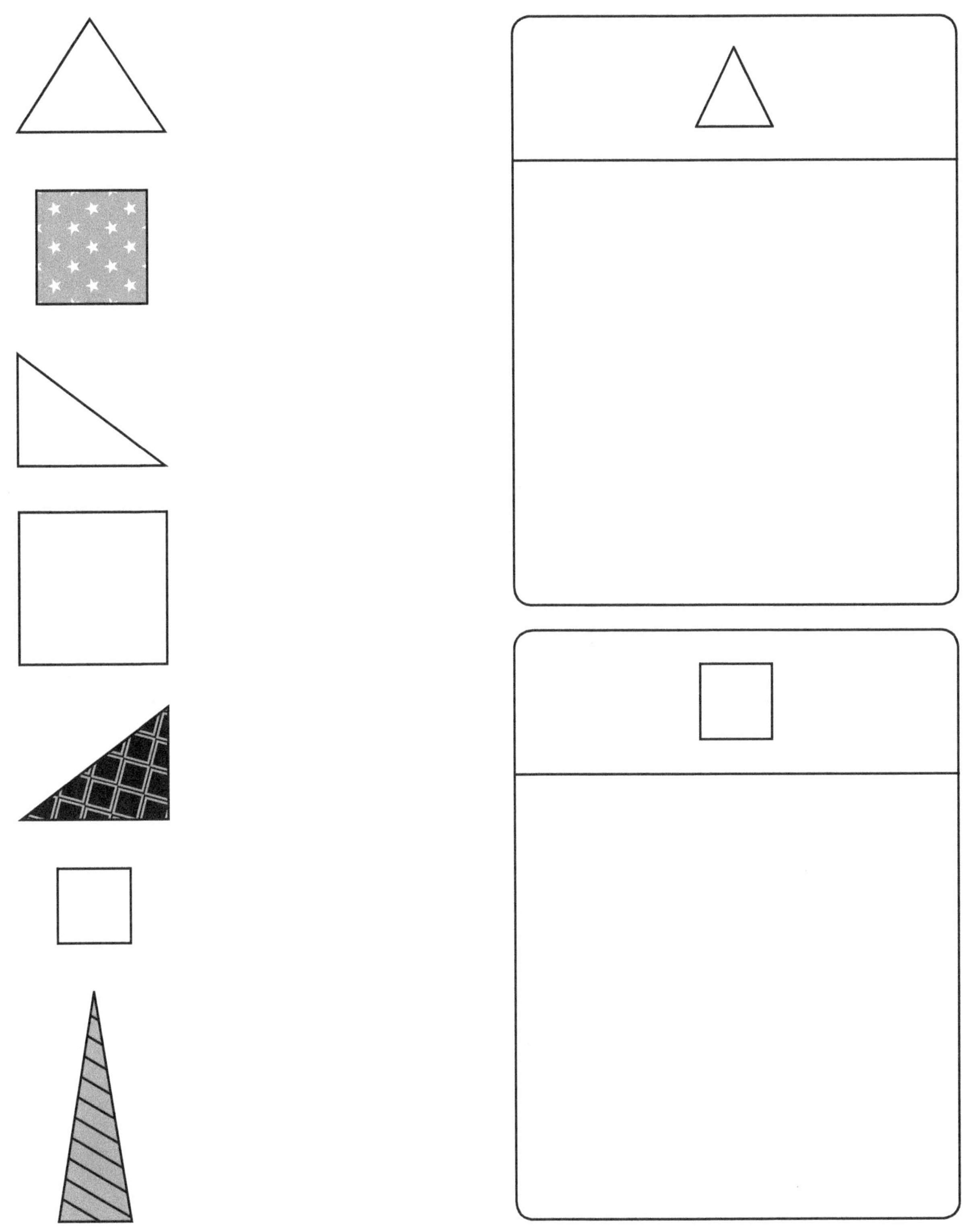

☐ Write how many △.

☐ Write how many □.

3.

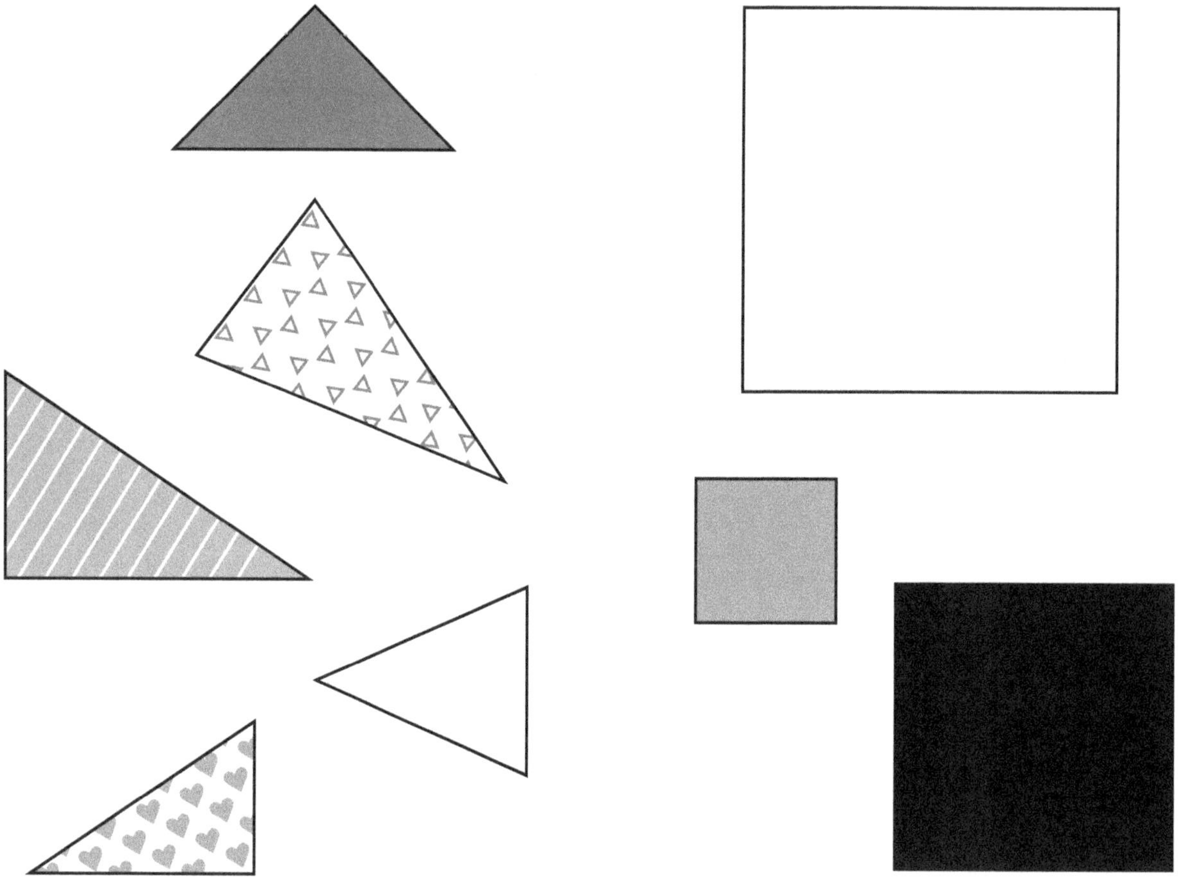

Are there more △ or □?

☐ Circle the answer.

4.

△ □

☐ Write how many △.

☐ Write how many ▭.

5.

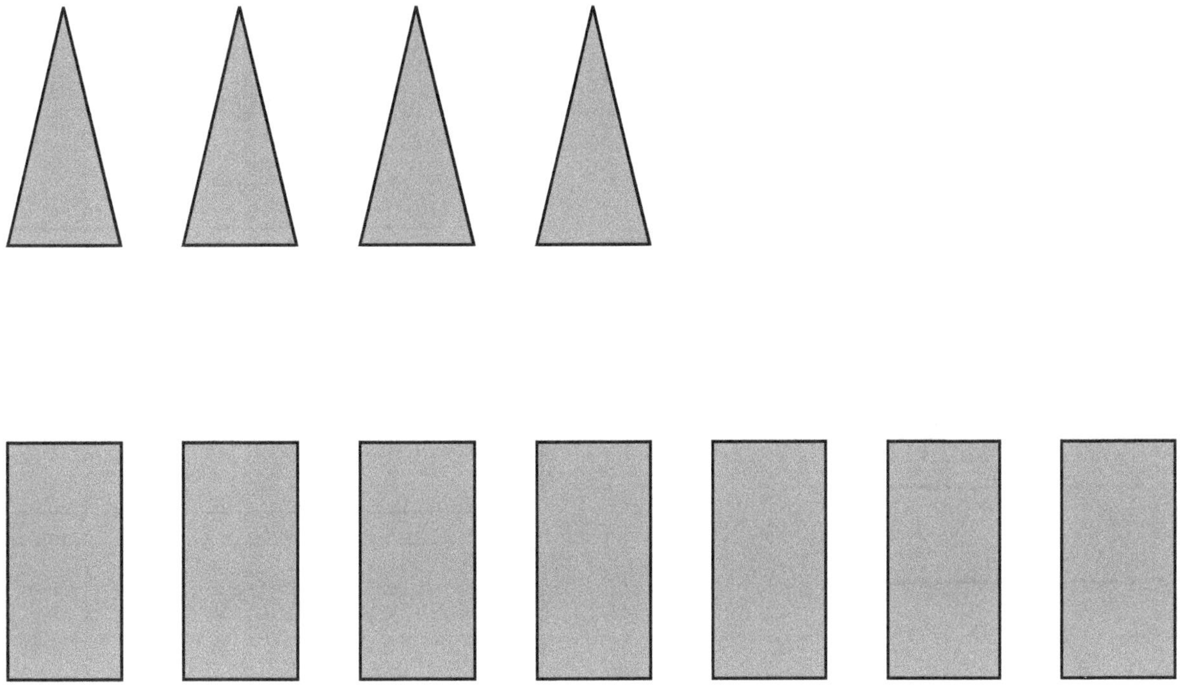

△ ______ ▭ ______

Are there more △ or ▭?

☐ Circle the answer.

6.

△ ▭

MDK-3 Sorting into Three Groups

Where does each shape belong?

☐ Draw a line.

1.

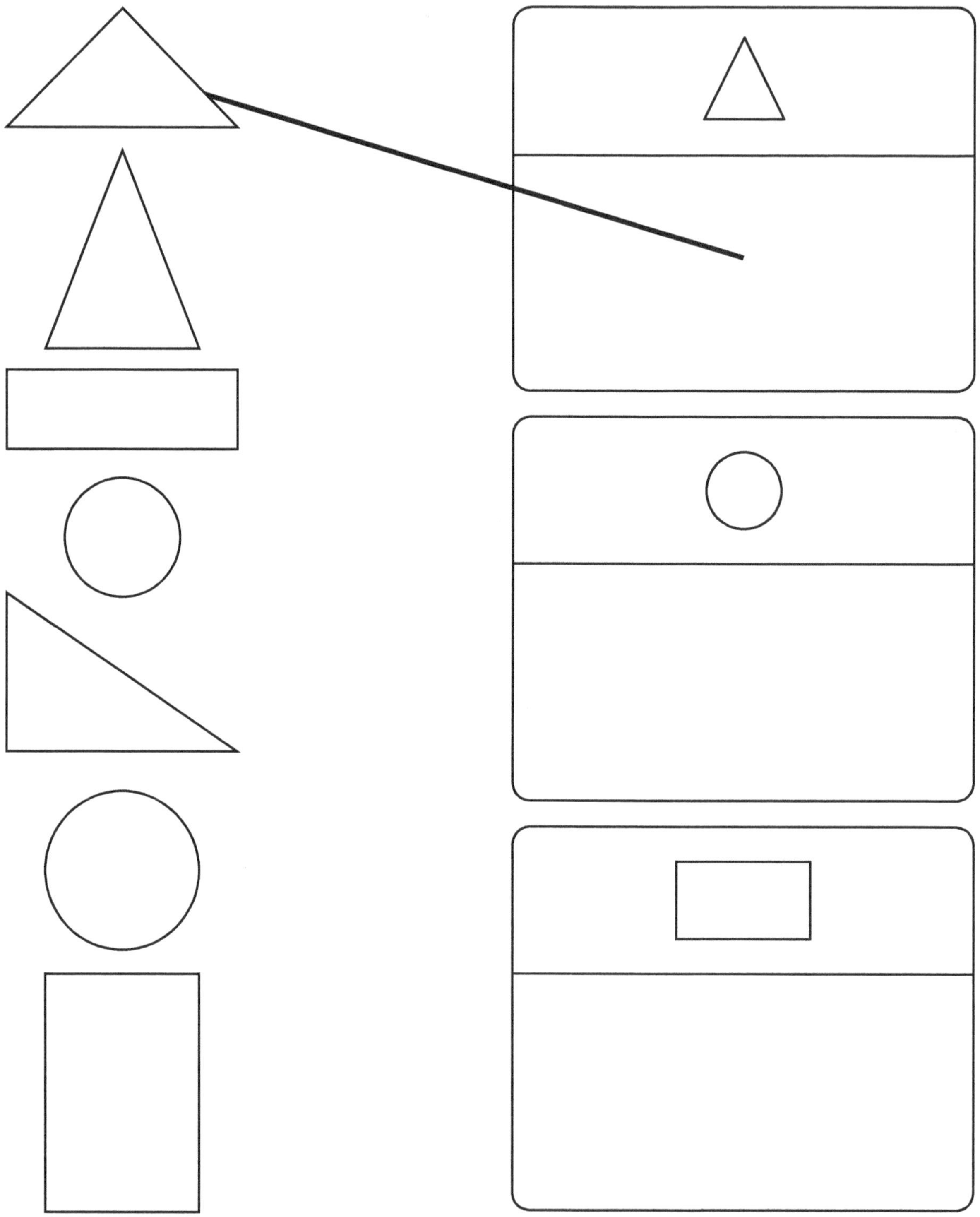

Where does each shape belong?

☐ Draw a line.

2.

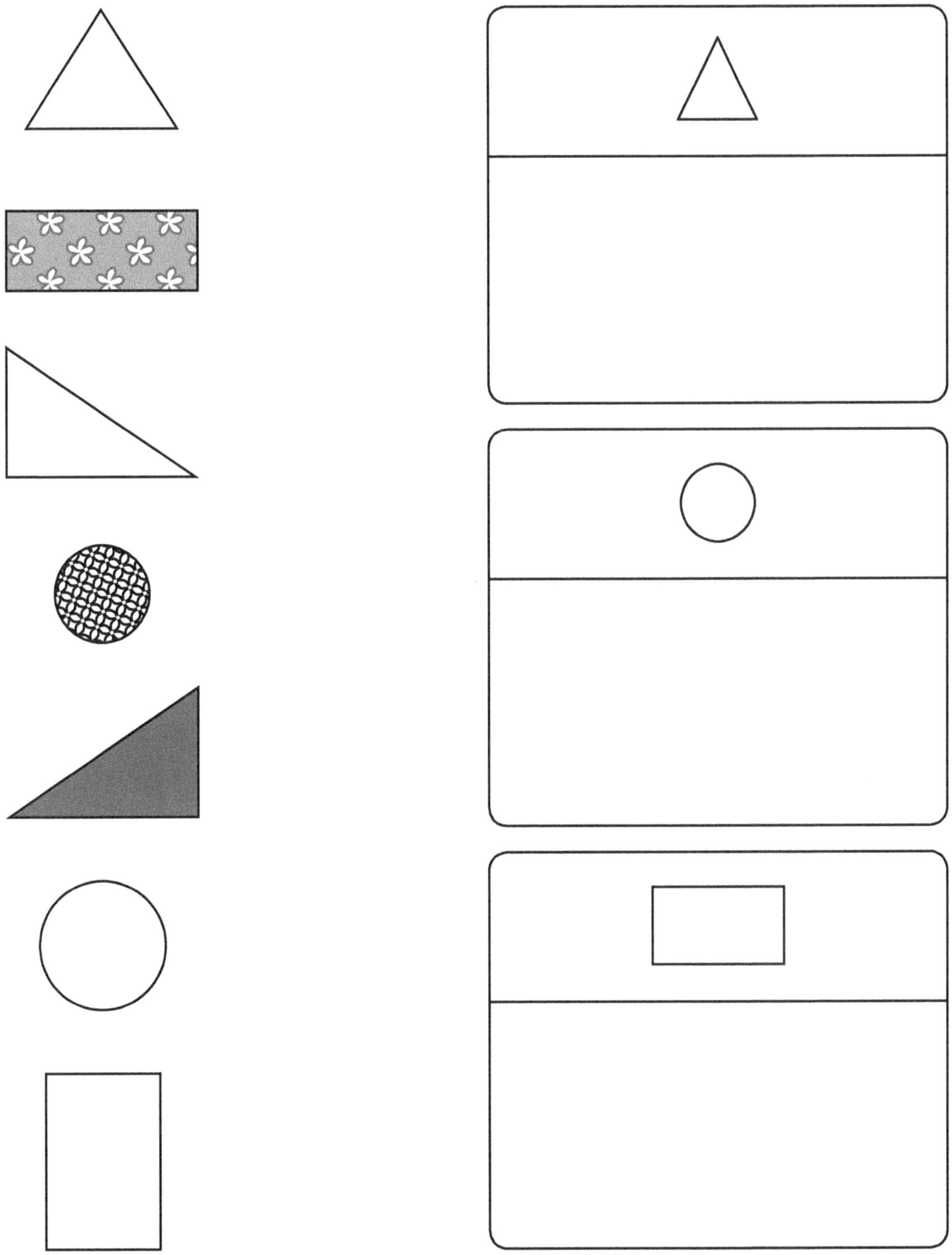

☐ Write how many of each shape.

3.

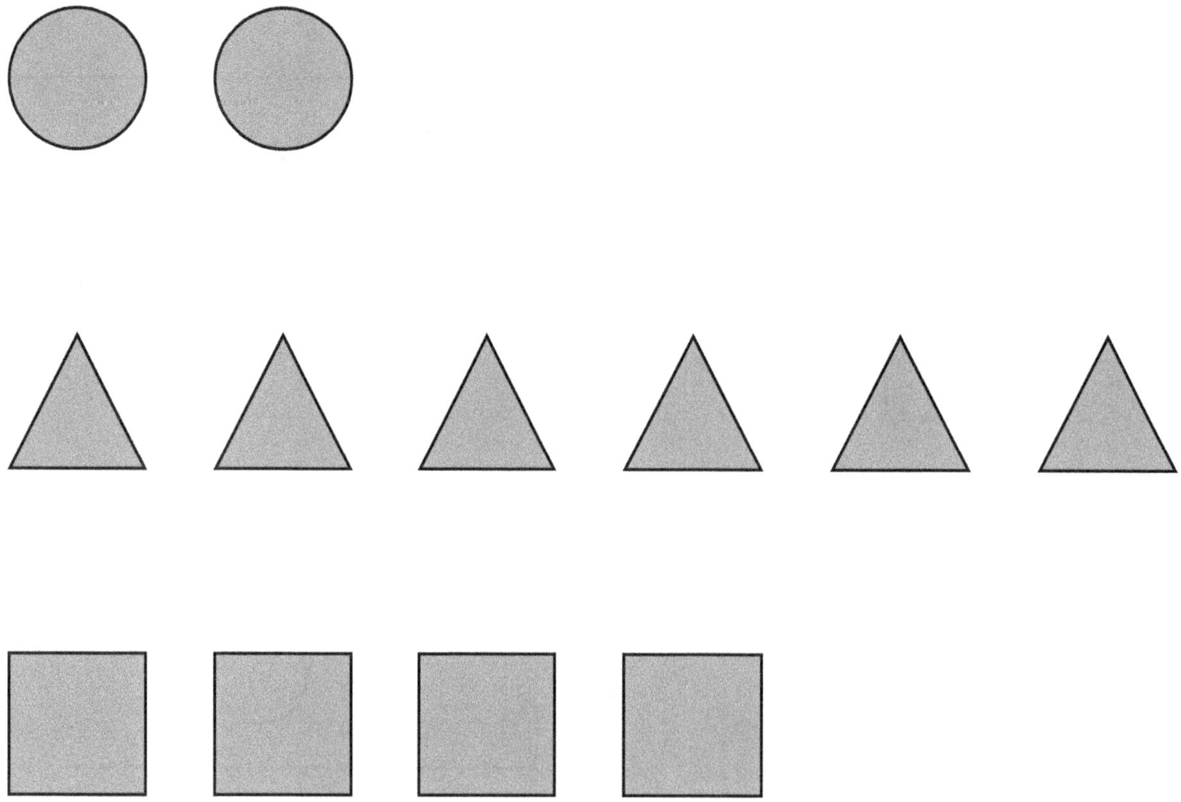

Are there more △ or □?

☐ Circle the answer.

4.

How many of each fruit?

☐ Draw a line.

5.

  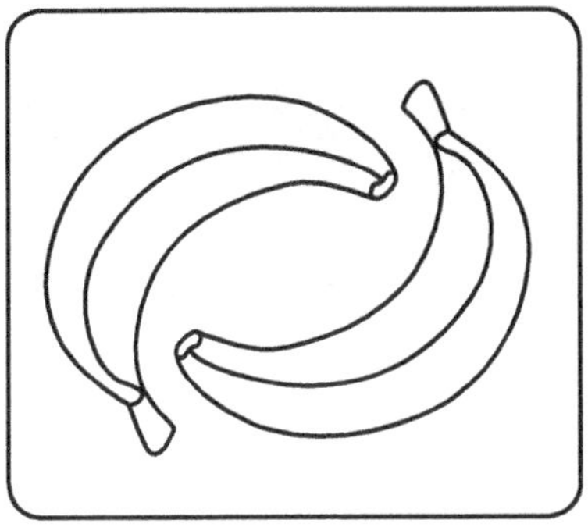

1	2	3	4	5

6.

1	2	3	4	5

MDK-4 Many Ways to Sort

☐ Draw lines to sort by color.

☐ Draw lines to sort by shape.

1.

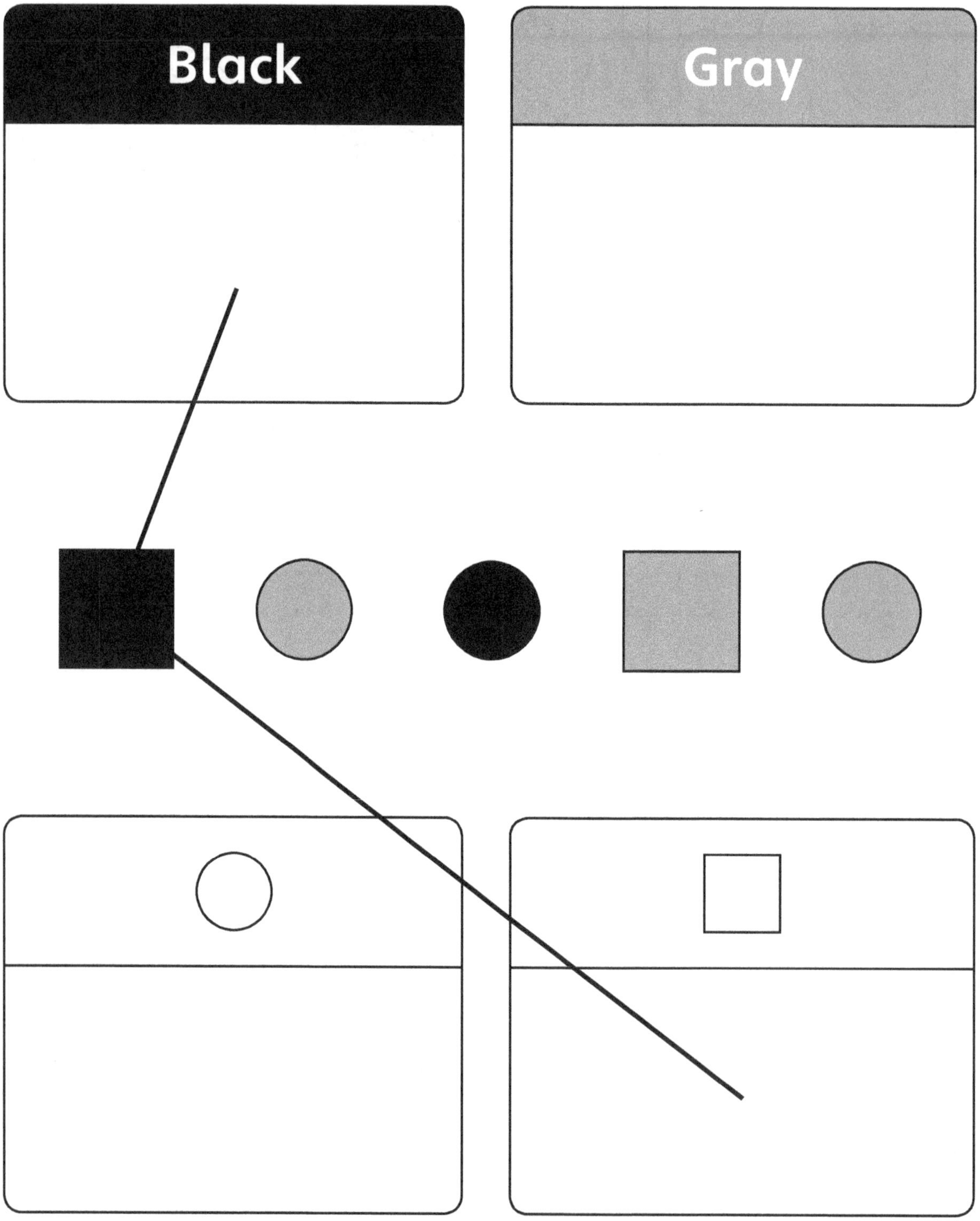

☐ Draw lines to sort by color.

☐ Draw lines to sort by shape.

2.

MDK-5 Sorting by Numbers of Corners and Sides

How many corners?

☐ Draw a line.

1.

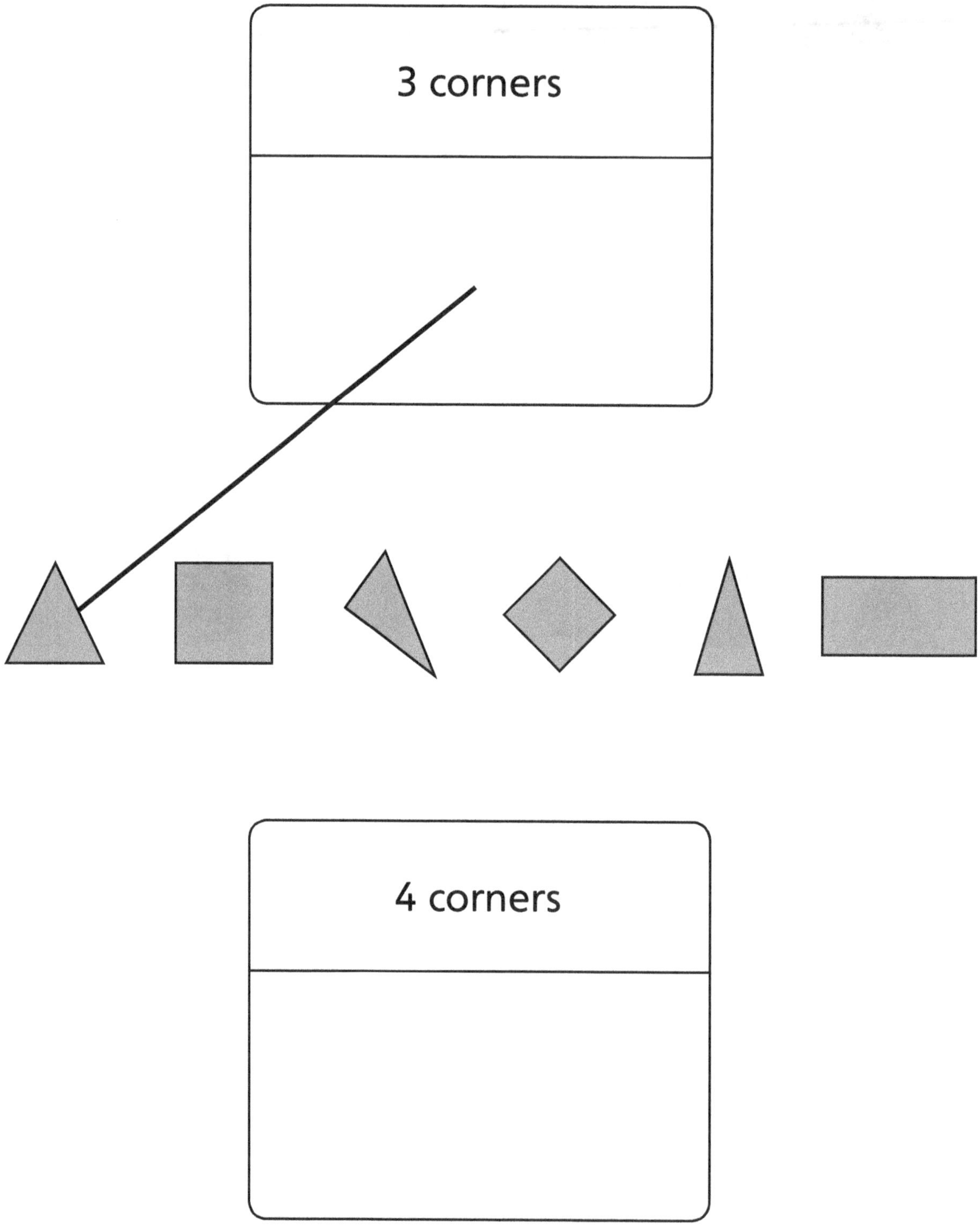

How many sides?

☐ Draw a line.

2.

3 sides

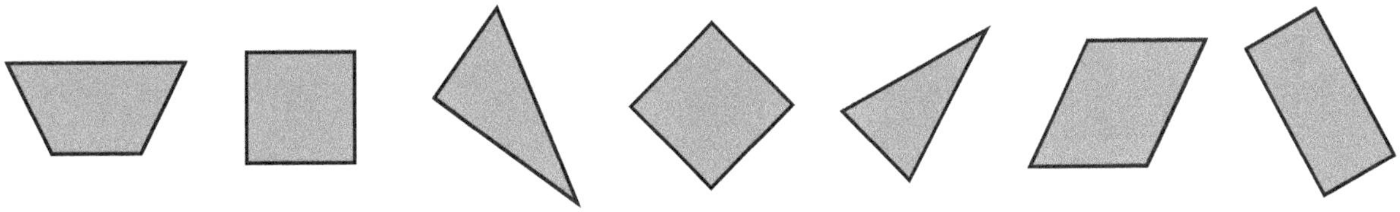

4 sides